CASTAWAY
RESOLUTION

To purchase any of these titles in e-book form, please go to www.baen.com.

CASTAWAY RESOLUTION

ERIC FLINT
RYK E. SPOOR

CASTAWAY RESOLUTION

A Baen Books Original

Baen Publishing Enterprises
P.O. Box 1403
Riverdale, NY 10471
www.baen.com

ISBN: 978-1-9821-2441-0

Cover art by Sam Kennedy

First printing, March 2020

Distributed by Simon & Schuster
1230 Avenue of the Americas
New York, NY 10020

Library of Congress Cataloging-in-Publication Data

Names: Flint, Eric, author. | Spoor, Ryk E., author.
Title: Castaway resolution / Eric Flint, Ryk E. Spoor.
Description: Riverdale, NY : Baen Books, [2020] | Series: Boundary
Identifiers: LCCN 2019053848 | ISBN 9781982124410 (hardcover)
Subjects: GSAFD: Science fiction.
Classification: LCC PS3556.L548 C373 2020 | DDC 813/.54—dc23
LC record available at https://lccn.loc.gov/2019053848

Pages by Joy Freeman (www.pagesbyjoy.com)
Printed in the United States of America
10 9 8 7 6 5 4 3 2 1

ACKNOWLEDGMENTS

No SF novel is written in a vacuum, and the following people helped fill my vacuum with better prose:

My Beta-Reading group, who vigilantly pounced on any errors or questions and forced me to back up and reconsider when I went haring off in the wrong direction. And while everyone contributed, I want to specifically thank Charles Crapuchettes and Kengr for their attention to my physics. Any errors are due to me, not them.

Stephanie Osborn also provided insight into key events toward the end of the novel.

And as always, my wife Kathleen, for giving me the time amidst an always-hectic household!

c~a~

DEDICATION

This book is dedicated to my
daughters Victoria and Domenica,
who inspired the characters of
the four Kimei daughters.
Love to you both!
—R.S.

I'm not sure if this is an acknowledgment or a
dedication or just a tip of the hat, but I need to
express my gratitude to many horrible, slavering
monsters who have eased my way and lightened
my task over the past many years and volumes,
starting with the great river kraken slain by Guo in
my first novel *Mother of Demons*. I'd bestow upon
each and every one of them the Vulcan blessing
May you live long and prosper except for the
awkwardness that I'm even now plotting to bring
down the next one. That aside, many thanks!
—E.F.

CASTAWAY RESOLUTION

PART 1

DISASTER

Chapter 1

Sue Fisher tried to force herself to stay awake. *Three more hours of this. If only something would* happen!

But nothing ever happened in Orado Port Control. Once in a great while a starship would arrive—an event scheduled usually *years* in advance—or somewhat more frequently, one of the intersystem shuttles or the few private vessels would want to dock. Mostly, though, it was just the automated manufacturing pods, bringing raw materials from the asteroid mining operations to be sent down the beanstalk to the ground, or collecting manufactured cargo or key materials from the ground and distributing them around the system.

If I actually had to do *anything, that would make it less boring.* But all of that was automated. The only reason she was there—the only reason *anyone* would be here on the Port Control Deck—was that regulations stated that a qualified human observer would be present at all times in case of emergency. AIs could handle virtually any situation a human could—usually better. It would take something extraordinary to make the AI even consider cutting a human into the loop, or for Sue to decide to override the machine herself.

And the last time there had been an emergency in Orado system had been—

ERRRRT! ERRRRT! ERRRRT! ERRRRT!

Sue snapped out of her half-daze, adrenalin washing through her in a cold tingle that drove subtle spikes into her gut as she focused, triggering a situational download to her retinals.

The first thought she had was: *a starship? There isn't one due for at least six months, the* Explorer's Compass *out of Vellamo.*

But the second thought was spoken, as enhanced imagery from the distributed telescopic array materialized. "Oh my *God*."

It was one of the *Initiative* line of colony vessels, immense transports three kilometers long and over a kilometer wide that carried colonists and cargo to and from the now dozens of colonial worlds spread out as much as a hundred light-years from old Sol. Sue had seen *Initiative*-class ships twice before, beautiful graceful spindles with a perfect, sparkling circle of a habitat ring standing out from the central body.

Except that this one was anything but perfect. Chunks were *gone* from the hab ring, cut in what seemed impossibly smooth arcs, as though some titanic spacegoing shark had taken a series of bites out of that circle of carbonan, titanium, and steel.

She couldn't believe what she was seeing. *What in the name of God happened to her? You can't attack a ship in Trapdoor, and even if you could, how could you find a ship between the stars? But if it wasn't an attack, what was it?*

Even as she was taking in that horrific sight and trying to grasp what it meant, she saw that there was an incoming transmission.

"Mayday, Mayday, Mayday. Orado Port, this is *Outward Initiative*, out of Earth," it began. But not in the calm, measured voice of a ship's AI, which nearly *always* controlled communications, but the exhausted, worn, yet triumphant tones of a human being. "Request assistance *immediately*. We have suffered severe damage on multiple ship systems, we have multiple severely injured people on board who require medical assistance, and our remaining ship systems are unreliable. Mayday, Mayday, Mayday. Orado Port, this is *Outward Initiative*, out of Earth..."

She sent a query to the station, and once again found herself stunned. *According to the schedules received eight months ago,* Outward Initiative *should still be* en route *to Tantalus! Her closest approach shouldn't have brought her closer than ten light-years from Orado!*

Focus! Her brain had finally caught up to the situation. She restrained the impulse to try to respond directly by radio; *Outward Initiative* had arrived about one point two billion kilometers outsystem from Orado Port, meaning that the mayday itself had taken over an hour to get there. Unfortunately, that part of the Orado system currently had almost *nothing* there. Odds were that she really was the first person to hear that terrible message, and if she tried to respond by radio, it would take hours just to ascertain the ship's condition and decide what kind of help was needed and could be sent.

But there was an alternative. "Orado Port," she said aloud.

"Yes, Sue?" answered the Port's AI instantly.

"Relay that alert to the Portmaster immediately, even if you have to wake her up from a dead sleep. Alert the *Alabastra* and *Vilayet* that we will probably need towing duty and they should prepare to intercept *Outward Initiative* and help bring her home, and they'll need to have medical personnel aboard. This is a rescue operation; I don't see a Nebula Drive deployment yet, and with that much damage they *certainly* won't be able to do short-range Trapdoor hops, so I don't think they can come in by themselves. Also, make sure that President Jami is briefed. Whatever happened here...I don't think anyone's ever seen it before."

"No reasonably parallel situation is found in my databanks," Orado Port said. "That is why you were immediately given full authority. What are your intentions?"

She was already pulling on her EVA suit, settling her helmet over short-cropped blonde hair. "I'm taking *Raijin*."

Chapter 2

Raijin lay before her, a perfect sphere of polished silver and glass cradled in a setting like an egg cup, every feature of airlock, impulse jets, Trapdoor coils, and all others meticulously set as flush with the surface of the sphere as possible. At her approach, the circular airlock door swung open, and she could feel her omni establishing full link connections, readying the little ship for launch. *I wonder if—*

"I'm here, I'm here!" came a somewhat breathless voice behind Sue.

The sight of the cheerful face under too-curly-to-restrain hair made Sue smile with relief. "So you *were* here. Thanks, Orado!"

"It was the obvious next step," the station replied.

Sue extended her hand; the other took it. "Dr. Pearce, I'm glad you were able to make it. Orado's briefed you?"

"Well, *summarized*, yes," Dr. Carolyn Pearce said. "I can't really believe it myself. Do we have any idea what *happened* to—"

"None. That's why we're heading out." She noted the black case—a far more advanced version of the legendary "black bag" of traveling physicians—and nodded. "That's all you need?"

"Without holding us up much, yes." Dr. Pearce clambered into *Raijin* with practiced ease; she'd been one of the physicians of Orado Station for twelve years, much longer than Sue had been here. Sue could hear the harness snapping shut around the doctor even as Sue got into the pilot's seat. "*Raijin*, prepare for launch immediately."

The spherical perfection of *Raijin* was the key to its unique performance. It, and all the other "Lightning" rescue and courier

7

vehicles were designed to allow the most carefully controlled Trapdoor jumps possible. A normal Trapdoor vessel had to take roughly thirty seconds for a minimum jump, and had what amounted to a startup and cooldown time that was short but variable. However, "variable" when dealing with something moving at roughly seventy times the speed of light meant that you might end up ten million kilometers to either side of your ostensible target with only a total startup/cooldown variation of one second.

But *Raijin* could boast a maximum variation in endpoint location of less than one hundred thousand kilometers, a hundred times better than standard commercial drives and ten times better than even tuned Trapdoor drives on more standard craft. Moreover, its minimum jump time had been reduced to about one second, meaning that it could manage jumps of twenty million kilometers with good accuracy. The perfect sphere simplified the field interactions immensely, making it possible to approach the theoretical minimum response times of the Trapdoor Drive.

With three separate propulsion systems—a fusion reactor to drive a nuclear rocket, the Trapdoor Drive, or an extremely large-volume Nebula Drive—*Raijin* and its siblings could carry messages from point to point, or more importantly rescue people, at speeds far in excess of any conventional drive ship, if the job could be done by no more than three people.

"Orado Station, this is *Raijin*. We are prepared for launch. Check our flight path."

"Flight path is clear. Launching now."

The bottom literally dropped out of the "egg-cup" in which *Raijin* sat, and the spherical ship shot outward. The launch bay was located on the edge of the rotating ring of Orado Station, and thus the centripetal force which had kept her sitting solidly on that surface was gone, releasing *Raijin* to follow the commands of Newton for a few minutes before she would end up sneering at him and Einstein both.

"Wheee!" she heard from Dr. Pearce's seat, and despite the gravity of the situation Sue chuckled. It *was* a rather fun way to launch.

"Glad you like it, Doc. Some of my passengers have been less than thrilled with that process."

"I'll bet they hate roller-coasters, too. How long to *Outward Initiative*?"

"Depends on how good I am today."

According to the data, *Outward Initiative* had been at one billion, two hundred and fifty-three million, five hundred thousand kilometers from Orado Station at time...*mark*. Fortunately, the huge ship hadn't entered "hot"—going at high relative speed—or it would have taken a long time to adjust her speed to match. The relative speed was about five kilometers a second, well within *Raijin*'s twenty kps delta-vee from its nuclear jet. That also wasn't fast enough to matter much at Trapdoor speeds, so she discounted it for the most part.

That's just *under a one-minute jump.*

The key to *real* performance here, however, depended on the pilot. Even the best AIs yet made could not match human gut instinct on the final instantaneous adjustments to the field just before jump. Some liked to claim this was proof of some ineffable human superiority, a sense beyond the material; Sue thought it simply showed that current AIs didn't quite know how to integrate everything from the tactile feedback on the controls, the sound and vibrations transmitted through the ship, the miniscule variations in the system readouts, and simultaneously apply it to the external conditions that were fed to a modern pilot through their retinals and haptic simulation links that could make the pilot very nearly *be* a part of the ship.

"Well, here goes. Orado Station, *Raijin* preparing for in-system Trapdoor jump, estimated time fifty-nine point seven seconds."

"Confirmed, *Raijin*. Jump when ready."

She grasped the controls, both physically and mentally, concentrated on the *feel* of the ship. *Nice balance. Resonance sounds almost perfect.* Very *slight beat coming from coil seven...about five point seven hertz.*

She nudged the jump parameters just a *hair*...and activated.

A faint green sparkle shimmered and Orado Station—and the stars themselves—disappeared. *Raijin* was now hurtling through a lightless void, the Trapdoor Space. The only light that existed there was from *Raijin* itself, but its perfectly spherical exterior had no angle or vantage to project light upon itself, nor to provide a view, so the screens were darker than the waters of distant Europa's oceans, a perfect blackness that made ebony and pitch seem bright.

"You said fifty-nine seconds?"

"Turned out to be fifty-nine point six nine seven seconds by the jump command. The exact *full* time of transition varies slightly."

"You changed it?"

"A bit. Felt right. If my instincts are still good; been a long time since I had to try this." She felt the usual tension rising. "We're about to find out. Here it comes. Jump completion in three, two, one—"

The stars sprang into existence again—and in the first screen, to the lower left, something that was not a star, something large enough to show signs of structure.

Sue let out a completely unprofessional whoop of triumph. *I can see it without magnification! We've got to be less than six thousand kilometers away!*

"*Outward Initiative*," she said into the radio, "This is Lieutenant Susan Fisher, pilot of *Raijin*, S&R out of Orado Station."

"From *Orado*?" came the same voice that had given the Mayday. "Thank God! *Raijin*, do you have any medical personnel on board?"

"*Outward Initiative*, this is Dr. Carolyn Pearce," her passenger said. "I am a fully qualified physician, frontier, traditional, and nanomedical."

The relief in the voice was palpable. "Wonderful. This is Masashi Toriyama, acting captain of *Outward Initiative*."

"We're on our way, Captain," Sue said, checking vectors and activating *Raijin*'s nuclear rocket. Acceleration shoved them both back in their seats. "We'll be matching with you within an hour.

"Now that we're close enough to talk—can you tell us what happened?"

"Something I've never seen before—nor heard of. We were cruising along on Trapdoor just as smooth as you like, and suddenly the field stability alert starts screaming. We followed the book, authorized an emergency stop, but the field oscillations were so out of control that it took us thirty seconds just to damp them enough to do the shutdown."

"Jesus," Sue heard herself say. "Oscillations? You're saying that the *Trapdoor Field* is what did that to you?"

"Oscillation depths were increasing so fast that if we'd been a second or two slower in reacting it might have bit straight through into the main hull," Toriyama said. "As it was...well, you saw.

Took five chunks out of the hab ring, compromised the integrity of the ring itself—part of what took us so long to get here was that we had to repair the ring well enough to keep it rotating."

The hab ring—as its name implied—was where most people lived; it rotated, providing effective gravity for the crew and passengers. But that meant..."How many people..."

"...did we lose?" Captain Toriyama's voice was grim. "Fewer than we might have, I suppose. We happened to be in an emergency drill at the time, so everyone except a skeleton crew was in the lifeboats already. No one was killed in the living quarters, but we lost six lifeboats out of the hundred twenty on board. Wasn't the worst of it, though, the bad luck was just starting. We lost *all three* of our ships' doctors—two were on the lifeboats and the third... well, she was too close because she'd gotten a call that someone was sick on one of the boats and the captain gave her permission to go tend to them."

"That was a violation of—"

"Lieutenant, I'm fully aware of that. So was he. But routine... routine kills, whenever routine stops. You know that. We'd had twenty-odd of these drills and everything had gone just fine."

Sue shook her head, but she couldn't argue with Toriyama, either. There wasn't an organization in the world that didn't start to relax when nothing broke the routine and everything kept working fine. It was the price you paid for working with humans. "Never mind, Captain. Go on." *Raijin* vibrated to minor thrusts, as the automatic systems adjusted their vector to match more closely with *Outward Initiative*.

"Well, like I said, we lost six lifeboats and all three doctors. Total of sixty-two people, mostly colonists." Sue's omni informed her that this was out of a complement—passengers and crew—of one thousand, one hundred, and fifty-seven. "That was bad enough, especially since it included Chief Master Sergeant Campbell, our head of security *and* navigation and piloting backup. But it wasn't long after we got shut down and started trying to fix the vital damage, that people started getting sick."

"Sick?" Sue repeated. *A disease at the same time?*

"Good *God*," Dr. Pearce said. "Trapdoor intersection radiation pulse, yes?"

"I'm *impressed*," Captain Toriyama said. "Took us a while to figure that one out."

"I was present at the cleanup for an accidental ground activation of a drive."

The thought of even a small Trapdoor drive being activated at ground level made Sue shudder. "So where the field was cutting off those chunks, it was also causing big radiation bursts."

"Exactly."

"Were the lifeboats taken intact or . . . not?" asked Dr. Pearce.

"Thinking of survivors? Let me check." There was a pause. "It looks like *LS-88*, *LS-5*, and *LS-42* disappeared in a single piece. The others were . . . cut apart, one way or another. I don't know if they actually stayed intact when they . . . fell across the field."

"You have recordings?"

"Some, but they'll need some cleanup, at the least. The Trapdoor radiation pulses damaged things severely. The lifeboats themselves are heavily shielded, but the hab ring is light and relies on ship systems to keep it protected from radiation when we're traveling in interplanetary mode; of course, there's normally *no* radiation in Trapdoor space except what we bring with us."

"How many people were affected by the radiation sickness?",

"Two hundred thirteen—most of the skeleton crew, unfortunately, plus a lot of passengers whose shuttles were near the intersections; despite the shuttle shielding, a lot of people got hit hard. We lost fourteen—one of them the captain, which is why I'm acting captain now. About half of the others recovered fairly well, but we've had to improvise nanostasis for the rest; I'm hoping Dr. Pearce can help out there."

"I am sure I can. If you've kept them alive this long, they'll make it. Anyone else?"

"Unfortunately, yes. We had to repair and rebalance the hab ring so we could rotate and give most people some gravity again, and *then* we had to replace Trapdoor coils and balance the field . . . well, there were injuries, both among the remaining crew and the passengers." His voice dropped to a confidential tone. "We've also got several Bemmies on board, and that hasn't helped matters."

Sue let out a long breath. The genetically engineered amphibious version of the aliens discovered on Europa were viewed by many with a combination of suspicion, concern, and sympathy. There had been several very well-publicized breakdowns of the early generations, and many people didn't like being around them—with "didn't like" ranging from mild discomfort to raging anti-alien sentiment or plain old-fashioned phobia, since—by human standards—they could be pretty scary, like a combination of a vampire squid and a slug weighing up to three hundred kilograms.

Add that kind of xenophobia to the panic on board a vessel limping into port after an inexplicable accident... "Have there been any... incidents?"

"None *yet*, but I'm real glad we're here now. The Bemmies' pod didn't get away unhurt, though; one of their younger children was on board one of the lost lifeboats."

"What? Why weren't they all on the same boat?"

"Harratrer followed procedure; he went to the nearest lifeboat, as the emergency rules dictate, rather than making his way four lifeboats farther down."

So in addition to all this, there's a bereaved family of Bemmies. Never dealt with that before.

Outward Initiative now loomed up hugely, the great ring arching above and below as they approached almost perfectly aligned with the immense ship's main spindle-shaped body. "All right, Captain, I'm going to have to pause and pay attention as we dock. We've got towing vessels *en route*, and Dr. Pearce will tend to your injured. Once I'm on board, my job—*our* job—will be to figure out what happened." She grasped the controls and looked somberly at the shredded remains of the hab ring. *Because if this can happen once... it could happen again.*

Chapter 3

"Welcome aboard, Lieutenant Fisher, Dr. Pearce," Captain Tori-yama said. Sue was slightly surprised to see that while many of his features were as Japanese as his name, his skin was the color of coffee without much cream; he was also tall and not bad looking at all, and would probably be even better looking without the circles under his eyes and the worry lines engraved on his face. Next to him was a woman who looked to be about forty-five, some gray in her brown hair, tanned, narrow-faced with keen brown eyes.

"Thank you, Captain." Despite all the efforts of modern nano-filters, she could still catch a faint whiff of burned electronics. *The air must have been* foul *for a while after the disaster.* "Two tow vehicles, *Alabastra* and *Vilayet*, will be arriving here in a few days. Have you prepared a room for us to work in?"

"The day briefing room is where we did most of our deci-sionmaking after the disaster. We could use that, as long as you don't mind microgravity; it's in the center of the main hull." He looked to Dr. Pearce and gestured to the woman next to him. "Doctor, this is Janice White; she's an RN and the closest thing to a doctor left on the ship."

Pearce and White shook hands. "You have a medical facility intact?"

"Mostly intact. You'll see when we get down there, Doctor. Follow me."

As the other two departed to address the pressing medical issues, Sue recalled herself to her own mission. "Microgravity isn't a problem for me," she said. "That will do just fine. Lead on."

As Toriyama led her down a corridor and then to one of the spoke elevators which connected the hab ring with the main body, she noticed something strange. "My omni's not connecting with your shipboard network, Captain, just some local comm nets."

"That's because the shipboard network is still mostly down, Lieutenant. All the major AIs were taken out by the radiation pulses, and we really haven't had the luxury or, really, resources to devote to trying to fix or replace them. Assuming that the replacements work. No, don't ask me how the radiation got to the central core; we've got a lot of guesses but no proof."

The elevator doors slid open; Sue jumped slightly at the sight of a horse-sized creature with three hook-clawed, multibranched arms or tentacles.

"My apologies," the creature said in a deep, slightly buzzing voice, "I should not have been waiting so near the doors."

"No, it's not your fault at all. I knew there were Europans on board. I'm Lieutenant Fisher."

"My formal name is Kryndomerr, but please call me Numbers."

Toriyama was noticeably relieved by her reaction. "You've worked with Bemmies before?"

"During my undergrad work on Luna, yes. Call me Sue, then, Numbers. I would guess you're a mathematician?"

"That is my profession. Analysis of datasets for anomalies is one of my specialties, which would seem a useful talent for this investigation, yes?"

"Yes indeed. Glad to have you aboard, Numbers." Now that they were in the central body, there was virtually no sensation of gravity—the radius of the main hull was less than a tenth of that of the hab ring—so she followed the big Bemmie by extremely long, flat jumps. "You've assembled all the data on the event?"

"As much as we could without the automatics, and the damage that we have sustained," Numbers said. "That is not quite as complete as we would like."

They reached what was obviously the briefing room, with microgravity chairs, presentation projectors, and other accoutrements of such locations, including a zero-g coffeepot. Sue turned to Captain Toriyama. "Captain, prior to the disaster, what was your position on *Outward Initiative*?"

"I was second in command with a primary responsibility for the engineering department."

About what I thought. "Then, Captain, I must request that you leave and not involve yourself in the investigation further. A board of inquiry will have to be convened into this event, and you will be directly involved. If I find evidence of negligence or other irregularities, this may reflect poorly upon you; at the same time, if I find no such evidence, that work must be clearly done separate from your involvement."

Some of the worry lines deepened; he had clearly understood from the beginning that he might be held *responsible* for the disaster. "Yes, Lieutenant. That's why Numbers here is available. He was a colonial, not one of the crew. I have had a list of other colonials you may be able to consult, for information separate from that of the crew."

Well done. "Good work, Captain. I appreciate your cooperation."

Captain Toriyama saluted and then turned, departing the briefing room without a backward glance.

She looked over at Numbers, who was arranging a number of articles in careful order. "Colonists? I didn't know that they were yet allowing you—"

"We are the first," Numbers said; the pride in his voice was unmistakable. "Our pod petitioned extensively for the opportunity, from the oldest to the youngest. It was the proudest day of our lives when we were notified that we had been selected for this opportunity." The vibrant shifting patterns on Numbers' skin— generated by bioluminescent chromatophores similar to those seen on Earthly squid—suddenly grew muted and dim. "Little Harratrer was especially happy to go, because it meant he could stay with his best friend."

"Harratrer is the one of your people who was lost?"

The Bemmie expanded and then contracted, causing his body to bob up and down—the closest equivalent to a nod that they could manage. "He was called 'Whips' and was my second son. Studying to be an engineer, and was near the top in his class."

And his best friend was obviously a human, since this is the only Bemmie family aboard. Interesting. "My sympathies, Numbers."

"Appreciated, Sue." He completed his placing of objects (with appropriate adhesion clips to keep them from moving) on the table. "Might I ask about your profession? You piloted *Raijin* to us with frightening precision, but you are now an investigator?"

Sue laughed. "My official title is *Emergency Watch Officer,* which basically means 'person that you hope doesn't have much to do.' My job's to respond to emergencies the automatics don't know how to handle. Piloting's my avocation, investigation and handling of emergency procedure's my responsibility, and engineering analysis is my main professional training."

"I see. You have the skillset to get to an emergency quickly, the training and authority to run an investigation, and the professional knowledge to understand how the emergency happened."

"Basically. There aren't many of us in any given solar system, which is good ... because it means that there aren't enough emergencies like this to require more. Modern safety systems are extremely good."

She floated to the table. "Records of the event from all systems ... testimony from witnesses ... video recordings ... prior maintenance data ... you've done a good job pulling this together."

A ripple of light and color showed Numbers appreciated the compliment. "I simply thought about what *I* would need to fully understand the event."

"Well, you seem to have thought it out well." She strapped into one of the seats; floating at random was a pain. "Let's get started, then."

Chapter 4

Sue shoved her hair back and forced it back under the restraining clip. "Well, *now* I'm even more mystified than I was before." She drifted over to the coffee dispenser, filled the transparent carbonan cup again.

Numbers floated nearby, chaotic patterns flickering over his hide. "Yes."

"I'd *expected* to find a flaw somewhere—neglected maintenance, a mistuned coil, a one-in-a-million abrupt coil failure, *something*. The symptoms sure *looked* to me like some kind of beat between coils that turned out to have a positive feedback resonance. But..." Sue shook her head.

"Agreed. Instead, we have found nothing but exemplary records of service, coil condition monitoring records showing microtuning being regularly performed to maintain an overall synchronization less than one microHertz, absolutely *nothing* to show a fault anywhere in either maintenance or design. No apparent manufacturing or component flaws, either."

"No. Those would almost all show themselves immediately in the synchronization data, if nowhere else." She looked across to the Bemmie's two visible eyes and grinned. "Good news for Captain Toriyama and his crew, anyway."

"Yes. There will still be a Board of Inquiry but this part will be mostly formality."

Her smile faded as she looked down. "But knowing what it *isn't* doesn't help so much. We need to have an answer for what it *was*, or at least whether it's something that could happen again."

"I have acquired data on all known lost ships," Numbers said. "I assumed that if anything like this had occurred before, we would already know about it. Therefore, if this phenomenon had been encountered by anyone else—"

"—the ship would have been completely destroyed. That fits with the recordings; Captain Toriyama was right in guessing that his ship would have been completely destroyed if they had been a second or two slower to respond. Good thinking."

Sue checked status first. In the last few days, the tow ships had arrived, docked and deployed their oversized Nebula Drives. *Outward Initiative* was finally underway to Orado; it would of course take a few months to actually reach Orado from this far out. Sue was tempted to go back to Orado Station using *Raijin*, but she really did have everything she needed to carry out the investigation here.

She took a sip of coffee, resettled herself in the seat. "All right, let's see if we can get anything from that data."

Her omni displayed the data as a multidimensional plot of glittering stars, showing time and date of loss, type of ship, location of loss, ship size, and many other factors. The first thing that struck her was that there was too much data from the past. "I think we should filter to, um, nothing older than about fifty years."

"Why fifty years?"

"Because that was about the time that they deployed the current Trapdoor Coil design and basic operation guidance. Ships before then would have had some of the flaws the redesign was intended to eliminate."

Numbers buzzed pensively. "That will heavily reduce our numbers."

"I know, but it doesn't do any good to look at data that's on ships not built like this one."

"True. It's just that with delays on the order of a year between scattered systems, and months even on closer systems, propagation of records and data can take years. We'll be missing a lot of the most recent info."

"Let's try it anyway."

The plot darkened, then reappeared, this time with far fewer dots—but still quite a few. *Across human-settled space, we're using a lot of FTL vessels.*

There didn't seem to be a clear pattern here. "Do you see anything?"

"No, I..." Numbers' multibranched arms slowed, froze. "Wait. Let me try something."

The display darkened again, and then suddenly rematerialized. The scattering of dots representing lost ships had returned, but now they were mostly grouped into two separate populations, one low down and spread out along the x-axis which seemed to account for about seventy percent, one higher and focused far down the x-axis, though with still considerable spread, that comprised twenty-five percent of the total; the remaining five percent were scattered separate points.

Sue sat forward abruptly, knocking the sealed coffee cup away; she ignored it for now, as it was practically indestructible and not large enough to hurt anyone. "Well, *that* is interesting. What are our axes?"

"Estimated travel distance at loss for the x-axis, versus maintenance score history on the y-axis."

Sue stared. "That means that most losses in the last fifty years fall into two separate categories—one group is what you'd expect, ships that weren't maintained too well. But the *other*..."

"...is ships with *extremely* high maintenance scores—usually new ships, or commercial vessels like this which try to keep all the drive systems in tip-top shape for efficiency and economy of operation! Yes, yes!" Numbers quivered and patterns like strobing squares and triangles circled across his body. "How fascinating! Not at *all* what I would have expected."

"I certainly wouldn't have." Sue's brain raced, trying to make sense of this. It was an assumption in essentially any engineering discipline: keep your machine in top condition, and it was less likely to suffer failure. But this graph seemed to say that you were actually safest if you kept it in 'pretty good' condition—not neglected and mistuned, but not perfectly tuned and polished either, and that made *no* sense.

Except, of course, it *had* to make sense. The division was too clear to ignore. "What's the p-value on this division?"

"Extremely low—about 0.00004."

"So essentially *no* chance that this just a random artifact in the data." She rubbed her chin. "Freaky, as a friend of mine might say. Why hasn't anyone else noticed this?"

"Well, I can't say that *no one* has, but it's only been relatively recently we've been accumulating enough data to make this pattern obvious. For all I know, of course, there could be a paper on it already published and on its way from Earth."

The coffee container gave a rippling chime as it struck the table; she caught it and put it back where it belonged. "You know what this means?"

"Probably not in the sense you intend. What?"

"There's some kind of flaw in the *current* design. A subtle one, but just the kind of thing that doesn't show itself for years until enough people are using it, or when you extend the design to some new regime. Can you sort this by size of ship?"

"Certainly."

The new plot showed what she suspected. "Looks like this disproportionately affects larger ships, don't you think?"

"Yes; p of less than 0.009. What sort of phenomenon are you talking about?"

"Well..." she searched her memory for a good example. "Oh, here's one engineering students have looked at for years—the Tacoma Narrows Bridge on Earth, back in the 20th century. They built this really long, very narrow and shallow bridge high up over an area that had regular high winds. The design might have been fine somewhere else, under other conditions, but where it was it got exposed to winds of the right magnitude to induce really severe aeroelastic flutter that ended up tearing the bridge to pieces. After the fact they figured out what was going on, but no one really thought much about it beforehand, and it was really some minor design changes that led to the disaster."

"Oh. I think I remember that, but my instructors called it an example of runaway forced resonances."

"Argh," Sue said, rolling her eyes. "It's been mistaught like that for centuries, I suppose it always will be. It *looks* like a resonance effect, I'll admit. But it's not, really. Resonance comes from a natural frequency of the structure, like my coffee container here"—she bounced it on the table, causing a ringing chime before she caught it—"being stimulated by some external force. If the stimulation's in-phase with the natural frequency or frequencies of the object, the resonance can build."

"But this isn't a resonance effect."

She shook her head. "No. The coils were all pretty much

perfectly in tune. No sign of beats or resonances between them. The field was about as perfect as a crystal..." she trailed off as a sudden idea struck her.

"What is it, Sue?"

She picked up the coffee container, stared at its shining crystal perfection. "Perfection...that might be it!"

The big Bemmie gave a momentary flicker of reddish annoyance. "Might be *what?*"

Lieutenant Sue Fisher sat forward eagerly. "Come on, Numbers— I've got some simulations for you!"

Chapter 5

Portmaster Michael Ventrella—newly inducted a month and a half before—gestured for everyone to sit as he entered. "We're not a huge organization, let's not get too formal," he said. "I hereby convene this official Review and Inquiry Report for Incident OR-7-FTL, the event which resulted in crippling damage to colony vessel *Outward Initiative*. Are representatives of all interested parties here?"

Captain Toriyama stood. "I am Acting Captain Musashi Toriyama. I represent both the crew of *Outward Initiative* and the Colonial Initiative Corporation, as there is no ranking official of the corporation present in Orado system."

Sue saw the portmaster raise an eyebrow. "That puts this doubly on your head, sir. You understand that you may be in the position of having to remove *yourself* from command, or worse, if you or those under your command are found culpable?"

"I do, sir. But as the current commanding officer of *Outward Initiative*, the corporate directives are clear as to the fact that I also represent the company, and there are hardly any representatives of CIC here at the moment; I understand a new office is under construction and will be occupied in four to six months—"

"Never mind, then, Captain. As long as you understand your position, we can proceed." Toriyama seated himself.

The androgynous person who rose next was someone Sue already recognized. "Len Bowie, Ambassador for the System," they said. "We will represent the interests of the citizens of the System who were aboard *Outward Initiative* and, if it is acceptable to you, those of the few citizens of other colonies who do not have representatives present."

"The System," in Bowie's context, meant "the original solar system." Earth's system was fairly well united, unlike most of the scattered colonies, and its massive population and industrial base still dominated humanity's policies.

"That is acceptable. Lieutenant Fisher, you represent Orado Port and the investigative team?"

"Yes, sir."

"Good enough. Let's get this underway, then. I'm not much for formality, so we'll just move forward as makes sense. Lieutenant, you want to start?"

Sue stood up. "Thank you, Portmaster. Just to review, a quick summary of the events: *Outward Initiative* was slightly more than halfway through its journey to Tantalus, a new colony a bit over a hundred light-years from Earth. There had been no incidents of note during the journey, and all systems were operating at nominal.

"At 17:35 local ship time, during a routine emergency drill, a fluctuation developed in the Trapdoor field. This fluctuation grew at a tremendous rate, completely overwhelming automated attempts to damp it down by stabilizing the field generators further. An alert was immediately sounded and the crew attempted to counter the fluctuations sufficiently to shut down the Trapdoor drive safely. They did in fact achieve this by attempting a synchronized unbalancing of the drive coils—a risky approach, but probably the only one that would have worked, given later data. However, this was not achieved in time to prevent severe damage to the hab ring and the loss of six lifeboats and, at the time, sixty-two people. Radiation pulses also caused a cascading shutdown of multiple systems, including all shipboard AIs."

She played an excerpt of the logs she'd been able to recover—the sudden eerie half-appearance of a starfield, the green blazing fire of a Trapdoor field shearing through metal and composite, the shocking destruction of the proud colony vessel in a matter of seconds.

"With the Trapdoor Drive finally shut down, the *Outward Initiative* was in normal space, severely damaged. It required two and a half weeks to use onboard resources to sufficiently repair and reinforce the vessel and allow it to rotate again; during that time, the extent of radiation sickness became obvious, affecting over two hundred crew and passengers, of which nearly half had to be kept in nanostasis. Those lost from the immediate and sub-sequent events included all three medical doctors and the ship's commanding officer, as well as others.

"Nonetheless, basic repairs were completed, the Trapdoor coils rebalanced sufficiently to fit the changed profile of the *Outward Initiative* after the damage, and the ship made a relatively uneventful emergency trip here to Orado, the closest colony to their path at the point of failure, a trip of slightly less than two months."

"A question, if I may?"

She looked over at the Earth system representative. "Yes, Ambassador Bowie?"

"You mention that six lifeboats were lost. Were any sufficiently intact to function?"

"We believe three of them were physically intact. Whether any of their shipboard systems still *functioned* remains in question."

"Have any search and rescue ships been dispatched to search for survivors?"

She glanced at Ventrella, who rolled his eyes but nodded. "No, Ambassador, there have not."

Bowie's blue eyes narrowed. "Then may I inquire as to *why* not?"

"The short answer is that it would be a waste of time and energy. Do you wish a longer answer?"

The eyes met hers. "Yes. One with sufficient detail to satisfy me, unless the answers are inherently unsatisfying."

Sue chuckled. "All right, Ambassador. In a way, they *are* inherently unsatisfying. The best answer is that, as the old book says, 'space is BIG.' Even with the recordings of the event that we've been able to recover from *Outward Initiative*, we can at best determine when *by shipboard time* the lifeboats were severed from the ring. But they, and the final shutdown of the *Outward Initiative*, were separated by up to thirty seconds, and thus by millions of kilometers. If *Outward Initiative* had been able to do the search itself, right then, the lifeboats could probably have been recovered. But the starship's sensing suites were badly damaged, those of the lifeboats undoubtedly were *worse* off, and *Outward Initiative* was in no shape to search.

"But we can't actually tell exactly where that accident *happened*. There are a few flashes of a starfield in the moments during the oscillation, and of course clear images after the ship stopped, but that is not in any way good enough to locate the accident to within better than, say, a volume the size of the entire Earth System, with nothing to serve as a marker. The lifeboats measure perhaps thirty meters long; finding a thirty-meter object in a volume billions of kilometers in radius is a very nontrivial task.

"We'd also expect, if anyone was on them, they would attempt to make it to the nearest colony—here. There are Trapdoor drives on those lifeboats, although they have to run periodically rather than constantly; so we actually haven't quite reached the point at which we would expect to see them arrive; it took more than two months for *Outward Initiative* to make it here and at best the lifeboats would take nearly three times that long—almost six months—to make the trip. There is, unfortunately, effectively *no* way to detect them underway."

"I see. But from your tone I presume you do not expect them to arrive?"

"Well...*LS-42* and *LS-88* had more than enough rations to survive that long. *LS-5*...well, maybe, but they had a Bemmie on board who would have needed a lot more food, plus the dry environment on the shuttle would not have worked well for his survival. More importantly, though, simulations based on the damage suffered by *Outward Initiative* indicate that many shipboard systems would have failed. *LS-88* might have had the right combination of personnel on board to survive—if they weren't irradiated to death—but the others..."

Bowie nodded. "Understood. My apologies for the diversion."

"Not at all. It was an important question." She took a breath. "Returning to the main point of this meeting...First, let me address what is undoubtedly the most pressing question.

"It is our considered finding, backed by physical evidence as well as modeling and deduction, that the crew of *Outward Initiative* were in no way responsible for what happened to their vessel. Indeed, the record shows that they had taken exemplary care of their ship throughout its lifetime, maintaining it to the highest standard of civilian or, truth be told, military organizations. This was a ship, and a crew, that others would use as an example. In addition, their swift and efficient actions on the day the disaster happened were in fact responsible for saving the lives of most of those aboard; a delay of another second or two could easily have led to the destruction of the entire vessel."

She could *see* Toriyama's shoulders sag in relief; he closed his eyes, then opened them, smiling brilliantly. "Thank you, Lieutenant!"

"I thought you'd like to find out your fate right away," she said. "Good work, Captain."

"Then," said Bowie, "what was the cause of the disaster? An unexpected component failure?"

Sue grinned. "Oh, no, Ambassador, something *much* more interesting." The grin faded. "And something that has apparently destroyed thirty-seven vessels in the last fifty years."

She projected an image with her omni so the others could see it—a stylized representation of a Trapdoor vessel like *Outward Initiative*, with the Trapdoor field shimmering around it, a long ovoid shape some distance from the vessel's hull. "Most of you are aware that a Trapdoor field is generated by precisely spaced coils of a particular design, which must be properly in phase to generate an effective Trapdoor field. Biases of the coils allow effective navigation, directing the ship, although most navigation consists of pointing the ship in the desired direction in normal space, then activating the drive.

"In most cases, the drive envelope fluctuates slightly; this is partly due to variations in the...well, spacetime characteristics, I guess would be the best way to put it, of Trapdoor space. In essence, Trapdoor space isn't completely featureless. The other fluctuations, much more noticeable, are from slight mismatches between Trapdoor coils, and at a 'beat' rate between 5 and 500 Hertz, or cycles per second, most commonly at particular peak frequencies which have to be damped out because they are resonance frequencies between the field coils—they could cause the fluctuations to go out of control. And in fact, that was what I initially thought had happened."

The simulated field showed oscillations of the field swiftly progressing to a destructive level.

"However, once we started looking at the data, that just didn't fit. First of all, as you can see from the simulation there, such an oscillation tends to actually cause the field to 'pucker' inward at the ends, trying to turn the field into a sort of donut shape; this would usually result in damaging the main ship body at its fore and aft ends. You *can* get radial spiking, but it's rare.

"More importantly, the data showed that the coils weren't

just acceptably balanced, they were *exceptionally* well-balanced. This was one of the best maintained ships I have ever had the privilege to examine."

"Well?" the Portmaster said after she paused. "Don't keep us in suspense, Lieutenant. It wasn't sabotage, was it?"

"No. In all honesty, in a way, the crew of *Outward Initiative* caused the accident—just not in any manner they could *possibly* have predicted."

"What? *How?*" demanded Captain Toriyama.

"By doing your maintenance *too* well," she said.

There was silence, then Bowie laughed. "All right, Lieutenant. Answer us the riddle."

"Resonance was the key," she said. "Both Kryndomerr—the Bemmie mathematician—and I looked at the phenomenon and thought *resonance*, just from the way it all happened, but that seemed impossible. But then we happened to think about what it is that makes a really *good* resonance work.

"Think about the classic trick of breaking a wineglass by singing or playing a note. There are *two* key requirements. The first is that there be a known resonant frequency; the second is that the energy input—the sound—be of a sufficient volume to keep the vibration increasing; that volume is determined by the quality of the glass, as a lower-quality glass will dissipate far more energy and require more input to achieve destructive resonance."

The others nodded.

"Well, Trapdoor space, as I mentioned, isn't completely uniform. And as it is the Trapdoor field that is an interface between the ship and Trapdoor space, any nonuniformity acts directly on the field, causing the variations I mentioned earlier. So—"

"My *God*." Toriyama had clearly seen it. "There's some kind of underlying pattern—a field structure—in Trapdoor space. And if you have a well-enough maintained field..."

"...and you travel long enough, not adjusting your course, leaving your field effectively 'rigid,' so to speak, and your field just *happens* to have the right size to vibrate at the right wavelength...yes. The intersection between the field and the space itself creates a positive feedback resonance that swiftly builds up out of control." Sue showed them the graph that Numbers had created. "This was the real clue; Kryndomerr first saw this and pulled it out of the data. An entire population of well-maintained and mostly very large vessels going missing on long-run missions, whose fields—partly due to the development of standards in design, operation, and maintenance—have similar effective surface areas with respect to Trapdoor space."

The Portmaster was frowning. "Are you certain of this?"

Sue considered. "As sure as I can be without running actual experiments. Kryndomerr and I came up with models showing how it worked, and demonstrating that the resonance was very likely to proceed along the radial dimension as experienced by *Outward Initiative*. In addition, the simulations and accident statistics indicated that this phenomenon may be a greater danger along particular routes and directions, meaning that the 'structure' of Trapdoor space has a systematic variation that may give us more clues as to the actual nature of the Trapdoor space."

Ventrella nodded. "Then you *must* summarize this report and have it transmitted to as many locations as we can reach. We don't have many ships available to go long distances, but we'll have to figure something out. This is *vital* information and we must get it to all the large colony and transport ships as soon as possible."

"Yes, sir."

Ventrella looked at the others. "Given this, I think this meeting is complete. Do any of you have any remaining questions?"

After a pause, he stood. "Good. Inquiry complete; this was, effectively, an Act of God; no one could have predicted it given the known information at the time, and the crew did everything they could to minimize the damage to both ship and personnel. I will so state in the record."

She waited for the others to leave, shaking Bowie's hand and—after a hesitation—giving the relieved captain a hug as well as a handshake.

Once the room was otherwise clear, she turned. "Portmaster?"

"What's on your mind, Lieutenant?"

"In the report—I want to include a full research writeup, for publication in *the Journal of Interstellar Spaceflight*."

He looked at her quizzically. "Well, of course. That's good research there, and worth probably more than *one* paper. Not bad for someone normally doing disaster inspection. What's the problem?"

"There's one thing I need to make sure of..."

Chapter 6

Numbers stared at her with all three eyes, one of them flicking back and forth to look at the display near him. "The 'Kryndo-merr Resonance'?"

"You and I did the work together, but you were the one who first found the pattern that showed something was causing well-maintained ships to disappear, and then did the hard work of deriving the function and building the models that showed that it actually worked the way we thought."

The Bemmie's hide showed a doubtful blue-and-pink pattern. "*You* were the one who came up with the basic idea, though." She saw, past the big alien, his pod or family, waiting at the nearby shuttle.

"Resonance? Come on. We both thought 'resonance' at the beginning, we just couldn't figure out how there could be a resonance once we saw the maintenance records," Sue said. "Yes, I did come up with the idea that a near-perfect field might resonate, but you were the one that came up with the model that showed that it could actually *happen*. Numbers, thousands of people thought it should be possible for people to fly through the air, the idea was ancient, but only the Wrights, Langley, Whitehead, and a few other pioneers made it *real*."

Two eyes closed, the other narrowed, as different colors and patterns chased across Numbers' body. "Is that the *only* reason you put my name on the effect, and my name first on the paper that *you* actually wrote? I'm terrible at writing."

She laughed. "All right, no, it's not. You guys have enough roadblocks in your way getting ahead in our society. It costs me

33

nothing but a little credit to put your name first, and this is a big, splashy, important event in the history of space travel. If you get a lot of the credit, it will show a lot more people how much you have to contribute, not just by diving and swimming and so on, but in *thinking* fields, just as much as us. And you *did* do a lot of the work, so it's not in any way a lie."

The big Bemmie rubbed his arm-tendrils uncertainly for a moment, then relaxed. "Then...thank you, thank you *very* much, Sue. I'll make sure to always mention *you* if anyone asks."

She gave the alien a friendly slap on the back. "I'd expect no less, given how I'll be talking you up." She looked at her omni display. "Your family's continuing on? You're sure?"

"Yes," he said emphatically. "Whips...Whips would not want his loss to stop us. We were honored beyond all other pods in being chosen; we cannot give up now, or it is possible that it will be a long time before any of our people is given the chance again." His colors muted again for a moment. "And it has now been nine months. More than enough time for any survivors to have made it here...and longer than any of them could have survived."

She held back a reflexive, well-meaning offer of hope. Kryndomerr was right; there weren't enough supplies on any of the lifeboats to allow them to survive to this point, and even fewer supplies had been on *LS-5*, the boat that Numbers' son had been aboard. "My sympathies again. But I'm sure you're right." She gripped the bases of two of his arms with her hands, the equivalent of a warm handshake. "Good luck on Tantalus. And maybe I'll find a way to come out that way and visit."

"Please do. My pod...my family would be honored to have you as a guest."

She stood and watched as Numbers and his family—Windharvest, Dragline, and Pageturner—boarded the shuttle to the finally repaired *Outward Initiative*. All four of them stopped just before boarding and gave her a wave-and-flattened-bow that was the deepest sign of respect, echoed by the solemn color pattern on each. She waved and bowed back; a few moments later, the landing shuttle launched and was gone.

Sue stood there a moment, just letting the quiet efficiency of Orado Station soak into her. She thought back to the time just before *Outward Initiative*'s arrival, and felt a pang of guilt. *I was wishing something would happen then. I should always remind myself what* "*something happening*" *means in space.* This "something" had cost over two hundred people their lives. Some might have died long after the others, drifting in space in nonfunctioning shuttles; they obviously had not survived.

From now on, she promised herself, *I will be happy to have nothing to do.*

She smiled, and headed towards Port Control. *Back to what I devoutly hope will be many years of boring duty!*

PART 2

SETTLERS

Chapter 7

"All right, everyone," Laura Kimei said, "settle down."

Sakura knew this was mostly directed at Francisco and Hitomi; the two youngest members of their unplanned colony were running around, chasing a virtual animal projected on their retinals by Hitomi's omni, which was running some kind of game for them. Looking around the big table in the center of the clearing, she could see most of the others were already seated and paying attention.

Laura, Sakura's mother, sat at one end of the long, oval-shaped wooden table. Akira, her husband and Sakura's dad, was on her right, and on her left was Caroline, Sakura's big sister. Laura had dark brown wavy hair and sharp brown eyes, and was the tallest of Sakura's family at a hundred eighty-three centimeters, though Sakura thought she might pass Mom sometime soon. Akira Kimei's hair was long, ebony black, and ruler-straight, and his eyes were the same color; he was about ten centimeters shorter than his wife, which made him slightly shorter than Sakura but still quite a bit taller than Caroline, whose hair was as straight as Dad's but as brown as Mom's; Sakura's hair reversed that, being wavy but black as space.

Hitomi, crowned with golden hair that had no precedent at all in their family, was just clambering into her high seat next to Dad. She hadn't grown noticeably in the year since they arrived so she was still barely a hundred centimeters tall. Francisco Coronel was next to her, but though he wasn't that much older than Hitomi his surprisingly red hair topped her blonde mop by thirty-five centimeters—and he was still the second-shortest of

39

the group of castaways at that. His red-brown skin contrasted sharply with Hitomi's light tan.

Melody Kimei sat next to Caroline, her black eyes distant as she looked at something—probably a book or some set of plans—projected in front of her. Melody was the genius of the family, but somewhat less insufferable about it than she had been before the disaster.

Between Melody and Sakura was a platform where other places had chairs; that was necessary, because next to Sakura was her best friend Whips, the only non-human member of their group, a *Bemmius Novus Sapiens* massing well over two hundred kilograms and almost two and a half meters long from his tripartite beak to the base of his tail tentacles. Built long and low, Whips needed a platform a good part of a meter high to allow him to see above the edge of the table, though he could raise himself up considerably on any two of his three multipronged tentacle-arms.

Across from Sakura was the squat, powerful form of Tavana Arronax. Tavana's cocoa-colored skin and black, fluffy hair, like his first name, came from his Polynesian ancestry, while his sharp gray eyes were a legacy of some unknown French colonial back in Tahiti's history.

On Sakura's other side was Maddox Bird, about her own height even though he was a year younger, his hazel eyes glancing swiftly around the table from beneath his somewhat ragged light-brown bangs. Next to him was his older brother, Xander Bird, Tavana's complete opposite as he was extremely tall—a hundred ninety centimeters—and topped with a profusion of curly blond hair above eyes as blue as Hitomi's.

At the far end of the table was Sergeant Samuel Morgan Campbell, topping even Xander by eight centimeters and probably another twenty kilograms of pure muscle. The grizzled, close-cropped graying hair contrasted with the dark-coffee complexion and eyes, and even more with the flamingly red hair, brilliant green eyes, and utterly diminutive stature of the woman on his other side, Lieutenant Pearce Greene Haley.

"It's been a few days since we got our new friends settled in their temporary home," Laura gestured to the large emergency shelter on the farther side of the clearing, "and we've all been talking about how the arrival of *Emerald Maui* changes things, and where we go from here, and Pearce suggested that we should go over everything we know now."

Even Hitomi had stopped fidgeting. *She's changed. I guess we all have. She knows when we're going to talk about important things and she really does want to know what's going on.*

"That's right," Pearce said. "First, I thought you'd all appreciate a summary of what we've got on *Emerald Maui*, and so Caroline and I worked with Tavana and Maddox to get it all figured out. Caroline?"

"Thanks, Pearce. Well, first, of course, we have the *Emerald Maui* itself. She can't *fly* any more, and maybe won't ever, but she's still a watertight, very tough craft that could easily carry all of us if she had to. Not that we'd want to go looking for another place to build on, but it's nice to know we could."

The whole group of colonists nodded. *We're living on a giant floating continent,* Sakura thought. *And we know from what happened to the sergeant's group that even these things can break apart. So yeah, that's a relief.*

"More importantly, *Emerald Maui* gives us access to a powerful reactor and generator. How long will it work, Sergeant?"

"Well, that depends a lot on how much we work it, Caroline," Campbell said easily. "But given the amount of boron-11 we have on hand...I'd say at least twenty years. The reactor itself is fully colony rated, which means as a system it's good for at least seventy-five years. So if we could use the stuff we have to somehow refine more boron-11 out, the reactor could last us for many decades."

Decades. Electric power for decades. Sakura saw her own grin echoed around the table. She was proud of all the things her family and Whips had come up with in the year and more they'd been marooned—candles and torches, hand-powered cranks to move things, ceramics and even, now, iron—but the thought of being able to get back some of the luxuries they'd lost...

"Onboard, *Emerald Maui*—which was *LS-88*—was carrying a *lot* of stuff we will be incredibly happy to have. First off—Mom, they had a bunch of medical supplies that were part of your shipment."

"*My* shipment?" Laura leaned forward. "Which ones?"

"We haven't uncrated it to make sure, but according to the manifest it contains one of the nanoprogramming stations, a transportable field surgery, and one of the instrument and drug packages."

Relief spread visibly over her mother's features. "Oh, thank God. I've been doing everything with improvised measures. Having even *some* of those supplies will make such a huge difference. Go on."

"Enough clothing for everyone to have two or three changes of clothes, if we don't mind all wearing the same stuff."

"You mean *real* clothes, not the stuff we've been trying to put together ourselves?" Melody said eagerly. "I don't *care* what it looks like, I'll wear it!"

"We already knew about the hundred emergency medical kits," Caroline went on. "And about the three JD-CAT excavators. There's a bunch of field rations left which would support us for a while if we needed it—we'll save those for emergencies, along with the remaining Joe Dinners. The really *important* stuff, after the medical equipment, is that there's a whole bunch of colonial hunting and survival gear, assorted hand tools, and a bunch of spare power packs in the five most common sizes."

"Hunting? Are we talking firearms?" Akira Kimei asked.

"There are a fair number of firearms available," confirmed the sergeant. "About twenty sidearms and thirty rifles, mostly for hunting, though there's two military full-auto rifles in there—probably for the local militia. Plus there's six hunting bows and quite a few arrows."

"Ammunition?"

"Because these are for colonies, most of 'em work along the lines of your SurvivalShot there, but using larger power packs. So basically if you maintain your weapon well and keep your power pack charged, you should be good to go for a long time. The military weapons have a few cases of ammo each."

"Good to know," Laura said. "I suppose we'll have to teach everyone how to properly use them, then. It will make hunting easier, I'd think."

"Than using handmade, hand-powered weapons? Damn straight it will," Campbell said with a grin. "Not to knock what you people have accomplished here, you've done wonders, but you won't have to do so much of the Stone Age reborn tricks from now on."

"Speaking of which," Xander said, reaching under the table,

"we've got a present for all of you." He pulled out a package and slid it down the table to Laura.

Sakura grinned, because she could see it had been wrapped in packing polymer, like using discarded wrapping paper for a new present. Her mother quickly opened the improvised package, and suddenly looked up with a broad smile. "Oh, *thank* you, all of you!"

"What is it, what is it, come *on* Mommy, let me *see!*" Hitomi said, bouncing in her seat.

Laura reached in and began sliding hand-sized metallic objects to each one of them. Sakura caught hers and stared. "Oh my *God.* A *TechTool!* Whips, *look!*"

"I know!" Whips said, brandishing his own. "*Vents,* this would have made *so* many things easier!"

That was an understatement. The TechTools were larger, more sophisticated versions of the Shapetools several of the Kimeis had had when they were marooned. If one thought of a Shapetool as the modern equivalent of a Swiss Army Knife, a TechTool was a medium-sized toolbox that included not only an array of knives, screwdrivers, wrenches, levers, and so on but instrumentation to evaluate everything from voltage to vibration. They also could interface with most omnis to allow accurate work guidance and active shifting of the tool to whatever was needed at a given point in a task.

"Well, we're glad you like 'em. It was sure a pleasant surprise for us when we found a small crate of them in the survival supplies," Campbell said. "So that's the basic summary of what we've got, with a few odds and ends. We'll finish uncrating everything in the next couple weeks and get a detailed list then. Next up is figuring out what we'll be doing for the next, oh, year."

Sakura winced. It was wonderful to have all this new stuff to work with, but inside, part of her had been trying to pretend that this somehow meant they might be going home soon. "So there's no way for us to get *Emerald Maui* to fly us home?" she asked.

"There *might* be," Xander Bird said, surprising her. "But there's a lot of big *ifs* involved."

"Are you saying the Trapdoor Drive might still operate?" Akira's voice held the same tension that gripped Sakura.

"*Oui,*" Tavana said promptly. "The Drive, it is not perfect, but we are not pressured by time here as our crew was when we were marooned in space. If we take time and use all the resources we now have...I think we can make much better coils, and if we use much of the cargo space not for big machinery but for supplies, *Emerald Maui* can carry us a long ways indeed."

"But the wing and the drives on that side?"

"That's a problem," admitted Xander. His eyes surveyed the group—skipping quickly past Whips. "but maybe not an impossible one. A lot of the basic systems are still intact. If we can manage to launch at all, I think we can figure out a way to fly her. The question is if we can fix her up to launch. But there's another alternative."

Sakura saw Campbell's nod, and the big man leaned forward. "What we might be able to do is combine the remains of the one wing, one of the drive systems, a bunch of superconducting power packs, and some self-designed Trapdoor coils to make an FTL distress probe. Send it up and have it fly straight to Orado, then broadcast a distress beacon once it gets in-system."

"Wouldn't that really require a nuclear reactor to keep the coils running?" Akira looked puzzled.

"Might not. See, the *size* of the Trapdoor field's one of the main power determinants. Plus, a ship for people needs all kinds of power to keep the ship comfortable and livable for human passengers. Our probe can be very small and won't need to maintain environmentals. So Xander and Tavana think it's possible."

"Do you think we should focus efforts on these possibilities?" Laura asked.

"*Mom!* Of course we do!" Melody said in a scandalized tone.

"There is no *of course* about it, Melody," Akira said. "And you will not use that tone of voice to your mother."

Melody opened her mouth, closed it, then looked down. "Sorry, Mom. But why isn't it 'of course'?"

"It's okay, sweetheart. Sakura, I see you looking at me. Can you explain?"

Ugh. I'd rather argue that we should. But Mom's right. "Um... because doing all that doesn't help *us* right here, building our colony, making ourselves safer and more comfortable, and it might all turn out to be a waste of time. So we have to decide whether doing that work's worth losing the other work and maybe ending up with having wasted all that time."

"Close enough," Campbell said. "It's not entirely an either/or choice. We could keep working on our escape or beacon plans off and on, but without a focused, dedicated effort that could take a long, long time. On the other hand, the people qualified to do the work at all are also several of the ones who'll be best at building up our colony—Xander, Tavana, Whips, and me, of course, with maybe little Sakura to help out too. And any time you split attention and focus across multiple problems, you'll end up wasting time and energy as your people change from one problem to the other.

"Still, if you were to ask me...I'd say we want to at least get to the point where we can say for sure whether either of them *can* be done with the resources and people we have here. But that takes a back seat to getting our group some permanent digs, I think."

"I agree," Laura said. "We need to think out where you're going to live—another column like ours? A tree? Build something on the ground?—and then get it done. Once we've done that, and set up some of the basic improvements for both homes that we can do with the supplies you've brought, then I think we should look into these possibilities."

"Have to keep us all fed and such, too," Pearce said. "Which means teaching all of us about your area—what we hunt, what we don't, what's dangerous, all that. You've been here a lot longer than us, and for my part I just woke up a few weeks ago."

"Tavana can come with me on the hunt tomorrow," Sakura said. "If we do a buddy system, teaching and safety combined, all of us will get up to speed pretty fast, right?"

Laura laughed, and she saw her exchange smiles with the sergeant. "Sounds like a reasonable plan to me, Saki. Maybe Whips and Mel can take Maddox fishing?"

"I love fishing! Can I go, Xander? Please?"

Even though the sergeant was clearly the leader of his group, it was just as clear to Sakura that Maddox looked to his big brother for a lot of things.

Xander smiled at his little brother, then turned to look at Whips. Sakura could see him pale slightly, but his expression stayed controlled. Sakura suppressed the anger that always tried to rise in her; it wasn't Xander's fault that his near-death at the hands of the raylamps had given him a phobia of things that had body-plans something like Whips'. Her mother was working out a program of treatment, and Xander certainly didn't blame Whips for his problem, but it was still hard to have someone looking at her best friend as though he were a monster about to spring.

"Whips," Xander said, "You're okay with that? You'd have to watch both of them, since you're the one safest in and near the water."

Whips did a rise-and-fall bow. "Mel knows the ropes pretty well. I'll keep a special eye on Maddox to make sure he stays safe."

"Okay." His eyes immediately shifted back to his brother. "Then you can go, as long as you *promise* to listen to Whips and do what he says."

"I will! I promise!"

"All right," the sergeant said. "Sounds like we've got some short-term plans as well as the longer-term ones." He looked down at Hitomi and Francisco, who were shifting in their chairs. "Let's not draw this out, then. Adults—that includes you, Xander, as well as Caroline—let's go have a powwow to hash out some details. Kids can have fun for a day before we get back to the grind."

"I agree," Laura said. "Tavana, Sakura, I'll expect you two to keep an eye on things for us, but if everyone stays in the clearing or Sherwood Tower it should be fine; we'll talk over in the shelter. Plan on a dinner in a few hours, Saki."

"Yes, Mom. I can do that."

She looked over at Tavana. "Now the trick's to convince the *kids* that we're in charge."

"*Vraiment*," he said with a grin. "That I leave to you!"

Chapter 8

"Hey, Tavana, can I ask you something?" Sakura had a note of hesitation in her voice.

The two of them were at a crude shooting range that the sergeant had designed, located in the long, low scar that *LS-5* had left when it crashed. The upcurved walls of the groove left by the careening shuttle provided good cover to minimize or eliminate the chance of wild shots hitting anything or anyone, and it was fairly broad and straight, allowing the sergeant to place targets (mostly made of leftover pieces of *LS-5*'s wrecked wings) at easily measured distances.

Tavana glanced over at Xander, who was overseeing the practice, then back to Sakura. *I wonder what she has to be nervous about. Me, I am nervous around her.* "Of course you can ask."

"Ha, yeah, that always sounds stupid, doesn't it? I mean, I just *did* ask you a question. Okay, it's . . . I know that Xander and Maddox were going to join their parents at Tantalus, and Frankie's—I mean, *Francisco's* parents ended up in a different lifeboat, but I never got why *you* were alone."

Tavana found himself unable to respond at first; instead, he raised the hunting rifle and sighted on the 50-meter target. He concentrated on slowly squeezing the trigger instead of yanking on it. The weapon kicked his shoulder but it was no big deal; neither was his aim, unfortunately, as he saw a tiny drifting cloud of dust half a meter to the right and above the target. *Ugh. I winced again instead of keeping my eyes open.*

But then, he hadn't really been concentrating on the shot.

Sakura was taking aim herself, but he knew she was still

waiting for his answer. He waited until she fired (and also missed, though it looked like she was a lot closer) before speaking.

"It is something like both of theirs," Tavana said finally. "My mother, Mahina, was one of the first wave of colonists, and my..." He paused, swallowed, then went on. "...the rest of my family stayed on Earth. *Maman* is a construction engineer and oversight manager for colonial construction, and she really liked what she heard about Tantalus; that was why she volunteered for the first wave, if they'd guarantee passage for the rest of us when the colony was ready."

"Something happened to the rest of your family?" Sakura asked quietly.

He looked down, set the rifle aside. "I...the outdoorsman, that isn't what I am, you understand? I mean, here I have been learning how to do many things I did not do at home. I was not sure I *wanted* to be a colonist. But I did not make a big argument about it; everyone else was excited about it, and it was not like I had much choice."

She had laid her weapon down too and was just standing there, listening.

"Anyway...it was half a year before departure, Papa and my brother and sister—Rainui and Aurélie—went on a fishing trip; I didn't feel like going that day, so I stayed home. I was supposed to study but, well...I didn't. Played instead. Then..." he took a deep breath. "Then the call came." He couldn't keep a tremor from his voice. "The fishing boat, it had disappeared. No one knew what happened for days."

"Days? My God, Tavana, that's horrible. With all the automated safety systems and—"

"Freak accident," he said, interrupting her but forcing himself to finish. *I didn't even tell the others on* Emerald Maui *about this.* "They never told us the details about how it happened, but one of the automated ocean sweeper ships, it mistook their boat for recyclable debris, and..."

The horror on her face echoed his own memories. Tavana was startled to feel the cool streaks left by tears down his face. *This is the first time I have let myself think about it in...more than a year.*

A faint crunching of gravel. Xander touched his shoulder. "Hey, Tav, what's wrong? Sakura?"

"Oh my *God*. That was *you*." Her voice was an appalled whisper. "The story was all over the news a few months before we left, everyone wondering how a sweeper ship could *ever* do that..."

Vaguely, Tavana was aware of Xander's face going blank with shock, even as Sakura continued, "...but they didn't use your real name and blurred out your face, so...I'm so sorry, Tav. I didn't know!" Her own voice wavered on the edge of tears, causing his own eyes to sting again.

"So *that's* why..." Xander murmured.

"*Oui*," Tavana finally forced himself to speak. "Yes, I had my, what was it...the fifteen minutes of fame?...from the accident. At least the privacy laws, they kept my name and face from being everywhere, but still..."

"How did *this* subject come up, Sakura?"

Sakura glanced at Tavana, the pain on her face a pure apology. "I asked him about why he was alone on *Emerald Maui*."

"Oh." Xander's brow wrinkled. "But you didn't seem *that* close to your aunt and uncle," he said hesitantly. "How did you end up with them—if you don't mind my asking now?"

"*Oui*, that I was not. They were not bad people, but they were from France and I had only seen them once before...before the accident. So I was to go to join my mother on Tantalus, but they do not like fifteen-year-olds traveling alone to colonies. Aunt Heloise and Uncle Francois wanted to go to the colonies, none of my Tahitian relatives did, so I went with them."

He managed a smile. "And then you see how *that* worked out—I am on my own on a colony anyway, as my guardians were at the same place as Francisco's when the alarm came."

"Lucky for us you came," Xander said. "I know you had some rough patches early on, but I don't know if we'd even have gotten here without you."

It was pretty obvious that Xander was trying to move the conversation away from the accident, to cheer Tavana up, but despite being obvious, Tavana found that it still *worked*; Xander really tried to be everyone's big brother.

"Well, maybe, maybe not, but the compliment, it is appreciated. And it is okay, Sakura; you aren't the news crews or someone just looking to hear nasty details."

She smiled and wiped away the trace of tears of her own, reflecting his own motion as he scrubbed his face dry.

"Okay," Xander said, looking relieved. "Now," he picked up one of the rifles, "Tav, I think you already know this, but you *have* to stop closing your eyes every time you go to shoot. Sakura, you're a little better that way, but you keep jerking the trigger."

"What do you mean? I just pull it when I fire," Sakura asked.

"You're pulling it like ... um, like you're yanking on a string or something. It shouldn't be a sharp, sudden motion, even though the *shot* will be sudden. You have to pull the trigger *smoothly*. Imagine, instead of pulling a trigger, that you're pushing a slide control back."

"Oh. Okay, I'll try."

"And," Tavana said, "I will *try* not to wince every time, but that habit, it is hard to break."

"It'll get harder the longer you let it go, so now's the time to fight it." He glanced at the two of them, and a momentary smile flickered across his face. "Well, I'll go back to watching. Keep practicing while you're talking, though; the sergeant wants both of you to finish qualifying as soon as possible."

Once Xander was back in his observing position, Sakura reached out and touched his shoulder. "Tavana ... thanks for telling me. That must've been pretty hard for you."

"It was," he admitted, picking the rifle back up after wiping his eyes on his shirtsleeve. "And now ... now it seems I may never see my mother again, either. For the first few months I was so upset ... so *angry*, at them, then at *myself*." Seeing her startled glance, he forced a sad grin. "The therapists, they say I had much 'survivor's guilt.' Is a very stupid thing to feel, but they say it is not unusual. I pushed it to the back of my head, avoided talking about it."

She fired, and there was a loud *whack!* from the target, which vibrated noticeably. "Wow! I hit it!" She looked back at him. "So ... how do you feel about having told me about this?"

He raised his rifle, took aim, and fired. This shot, too, went wide, but it was a lot closer. "It ... feels a little better, I guess. My grand-mère used to tell us that feelings sealed away can fester like wounds."

"I've heard Mom say things like that, too. I guess I really am lucky, though. You lost your family, Xander and Maddox got separated from theirs and then lost their uncle, Francisco's parents were in another lifeboat ... I've got my whole family, plus my best friend."

"I'm glad for that," Tavana said, though he felt more than a twinge of angry envy that he beat savagely back. *Concentrate on the good, not the bad. The bad is like a piece of rotting fruit in the middle of a bowl; it will ruin everything around it.* "And I was not so unlucky; I have new brothers, yes? Xander is a big brother to me, Maddox and Francisco my annoying little brothers." He grinned, and felt something genuine in that smile that eased his own anger. "And the sergeant, he is that scary-looking relative who suddenly comes over to take you to the park or something."

Sakura echoed his laugh. "Isn't he *exactly*?"

"And *mon Dieu*, am I glad he was with us when everything came apart. Maybe Xander is right that they needed me too, but the sergeant? He was the one who *really* kept us all alive." *Off to the right both times, so aim just a little to the left...*

The subdued hissing whipcrack of the shot was instantly followed by a loud *spangg!* of the bullet hitting the target.

"You *got* it, Tav!"

Tavana felt the grin on his own face spreading wider. "I did! But perhaps I should not be celebrating so soon; I do not think either game animals or predators will wait patiently fifty meters away while I take the time to sight in on them."

"You still hit it, which is a good step. I'm only meh with a bow, unlike Caroline, but guns seem a lot easier; I figure I'll get better if we keep practicing."

"I may try one of your bows too, but I expect I will be even worse. But now that I have hit the target, maybe I can make more shots today than you can."

"Ha! Not happening, Tav. What's the bet, though? No money here."

He thought a moment, then grinned. "The bet, it is simple; whichever of us loses, does the other's dishes after supper today and tomorrow."

Sakura bared her teeth in a challenging smile. "You're on!" she said, and took aim.

As he heard the sharp report of her shot striking the target again, he began to wonder if this impulse of his had been a good idea. But then he chuckled to himself and raised the rifle. *All I can do is my best. And if I wash dishes, then I will do that my best as well!*

Chapter 9

Xander forced his eyes to focus on the designs being projected in front of him by his omni. His mouth was dry and he could hear his breath coming more quickly.

"Do I need to move away?" a breathy, buzzing voice said, only a few meters distant.

Yes!

"No," he said. "No, we need to work together, me, you, Tav, everyone. Not letting this beat me." His heart vibrated in his chest with unreasoning fear—a fear that made him furious. *Whips is* not *a monster. He doesn't even look* that *much like the...* he shuddered, *the raylamps.*

His conscious mind agreed and could even specifically and in detail point out all the many differences, even in the feeding apparatus, between the native Lincoln scavenger-predators and *Bemmius novus sapiens.* His subconscious, however, was having none of it. Any sight of the front end of Whips triggered the fear and flashbacks to that horrific few minutes underwater when a horde of the raylamps had nearly dragged him down into the endless ocean.

"Then," Whips said reasonably, "show me you *are* going to beat it. Look at the designs and tell me if you've got any thoughts."

Xander nodded and clenched his jaw as he stared at the designs.

The one for the proposed probe was fairly straightforward. A long body, with a shape that oddly combined aspects of a cylinder and a rectangular cuboid, ending with a wedgelike nose, stretched to about three and a half meters in length according to the visible scale. It had an odd multiflanged tail assembly and an underslung scoop, and there were obvious separable boosters on each side of the device.

"Show cutaway," Xander murmured, and the view shifted to show a section cut down the longitudinal axis of the craft. He studied it a moment. "Jeez. It looks like most of it is battery."

"Superconducting storage batteries, ultra-high-power density exceeding that of any chemical fuel, yes," Whips said. "We'd be using a large portion of our larger powerpacks for this."

Now that he was really thinking about the design, Xander felt a little less shaky; his hands were still a bit unsteady, but he wasn't having to do any hand work right now, so that was okay. "Yeah, I get that. It's a heated-air hyperjet, right?"

"A noncombusting scramjet, yes. We'd be cannibalizing the one damaged thruster in the wing of *Emerald Maui* for that. Tavana?"

Tav moved up and pointed; since all their omnis were linked, they were all seeing the design as though it was physically in front of them, so Tav was actually apparently touching the part of the probe design that showed the engine. "It is fortunate, the damage to the engine? It did not affect the key parts for this function. I can salvage the high-efficiency heat transfer manifold and make it into the heart of the jet. I think."

Xander raised an eyebrow at that. "You *think*?"

"Xander, it is not like there is a manual for this, no? Whips, you, me, and even the sergeant have been combing through available data for the last week to put this together." He gave a quick grin. "And that is very, very fast; imagine if we actually had to do the design like in the old days, actually, you know, drawing it out ourselves, with every detail, instead of telling even the rather stupid automation we have to do most of the work!"

"Yeah, okay, you're right, sorry. The base design...looks *old*."

"Partly based on one of the oldest hypersonics we know of, the X-51 Waverider. One of my reference books, it had a whole lot on that one for some reason."

Xander tapped the projecting boosters. "What about these guys? They don't look like jets. I didn't work on this part."

"Those," Whips said, "are rockets."

Xander glanced at him, repressed the shudder, made his eyes meet those of the Bemmie. "And just *where* are we getting rockets? Unshipping some of the attitude reaction jets on *Emerald Maui*?"

"Screaming *Vents*, no. That'd be a crazy job and might end up damaging the hull. Well, this is also a crazy job but it's interior work. We'll cannibalize the ejection charges."

"The ejection—*what*? Are you telling me that *Emerald Maui*—"

"—has an ejection system? For the main control cabin and crash couch setup, yes, it does," Tavana said. "Required for craft of this class, though as Whips and I agree, it seems not likely to be useful in too many cases."

Xander scratched his head, looking up as he thought, and shivered slightly; the breeze seemed unusually cool in the clearing today. *Ejection charges.* A standard ejection charge, from what he knew, was basically a rocket tube with a method for igniting it in precise sequence with all the others. But they were strictly on/off things. "Are there enough? I'm guessing you want them to get the probe off the ground and going fast enough that the scramjet can take over."

"More than enough. The probe is three and a half meters long and will mass less than five hundred kilograms fully loaded; the ejection rockets were meant to eject something *far* heavier and get it clear of a disaster. *If* we can get the rockets out, and *if* our design can be assembled, and *if* everything holds together, the rocket boosters should be able to get it up to sufficient speed."

"Even a hypersonic jet isn't going to get this thing into orbit."

"Doesn't have to," Tavana said positively. "Once it's in space—enough so that the mass-fraction of air is below the critical value—the Trapdoor drive goes on for a few seconds. Then the auto-nav system—which is a pretty dumb autopilot we can cobble together—will lock onto Orado and then it starts doing jumps until it gets close enough to Orado. Then it starts transmitting distress signals until it runs out of power."

"That part of the Trapdoor feels like cheating."

Whips gave a rippling shudder that Xander knew was equivalent to a shrug. "From the naïve physics point of view? It went beyond cheating and into direct offenses against nature." A brighter flicker and pattern that was more a smile. "The physicists figured out how to reconcile it, but if you read the arguments I think there were some conferences where the attendees almost came to blows." He pointed at the projected design. "Questions? Comments?"

Xander studied the design again. *I still feel dizzy. I mean, even more than I did.* "Umm...the coils. Tav, we did some for

Emerald Maui when it was LS-88, but they gave us problems. How about—"

"It was my first try! Give me a break!" Tavana sat down with an uncharacteristic heaviness. "Sorry; feel kind of off today. I think we can do much better in winding coils for a hull we design ourselves. It will take months, but we are not pressed for time, yes?"

"No, I guess not. But if we're cannibalizing stuff like this, does that mean that building this probe probably means we're giving up the chance to somehow get *Emerald Maui* airborne?"

Tavana grimaced. "Well... *oui*, yes, it is that kind of tradeoff. If I am to attempt to salvage enough of the materials and components of *Emerald Maui* to make this probe, some of them will be parts I would have used in any attempt to repair *Emerald Maui*."

"Damn. Well, that kind of decision is for later anyway. You're working on *those* designs too, right? The ones to let us all get off the planet ourselves?"

"Oh, we are," Whips said. "And we'll keep both options open until we have to make a decision. We—"

"Help!" Hitomi was running towards them from near Sherwood Tower. "Something's wrong with Frankie!"

"Wrong? What happened?" Xander felt a quick, cold stab of adrenalin. *What could have happened to him?*

"He said he was feeling tired and dizzy, and then he just wanted to sit still, and now he's saying he feels sick. I'm worried!"

Tired and dizzy? He looked sharply over at Tav, even as he noted that his own thoughts seemed slower. "Tav, are you—?"

The big Polynesian tilted his head as he stood, and it seemed he, too, felt unbalanced. "*Merde*. The sergeant?"

"Yeah. No, wait—the doc. *Doctor Kimei! Laura Kimei!*"

"What is it, Xander?" Laura's voice was tense; she had clearly heard and understood the dread in his voice.

"I think something's wrong with Frankie, Tav, and me—maybe all of us from *Emerald Maui!*" He noticed with even more trepidation that his footsteps felt unsteady, the level ground not so level anymore.

Frankie came into sight, behind one of the many scattered patches of bushes. He was lying on his side now, shivering, and even though his skin was normally the color of coffee with cream, he looked pale, with hectic patches of red touching the cheeks. "Oh, crap."

"I'm on my way," Laura said. "It will take me a few minutes to get there, but I'm checking telemetry..."

The pause went on far too long. "Doctor?" he asked, realizing that his own heartbeat was still too fast, too hard, and his stomach was doing a slow, squirming roll.

"Sergeant Campbell, get your people to your shelter *immediately!*" Laura Kimei's voice was sharp, commanding, and utterly final as it cracked out over the radio waves.

Xander managed to lift Francisco up, and began to stagger towards the shelter. *I...don't know if I can make it,* he realized.

A forest of twining, bifurcated tendrils caught him as he stumbled, and prevented either himself or Francisco from hitting the ground. "I will carry him," Whips said.

The dizziness intensified, overriding the panic that tried to ambush him at Whips' nearness. "Thanks," he managed, and forced himself to his feet. *Holy crap, this is getting worse literally by the minute!*

By the time they reached the shelter, even Tavana was leaning on the doorframe. Half-supporting each other, Tavana and Xander made it inside and collapsed on their beds.

The pillow felt as though it were coated in ice—a strangely comforting ice—as his cheek rested upon it. "Doc," he managed, "are we...dying?"

Laura Kimei did not answer at once. Then she said, in a quiet, certain tone, "Not if I have anything to say about it."

Xander closed his eyes. *That wasn't completely an answer,* he thought. But he was astounded to find he had no more energy to even worry; uneasy darkness descended upon him.

Chapter 10

"What's *wrong* with them?" Pearce Haley asked, a tiny tremor audible in the normally-controlled voice. "And why hasn't it hit me?"

Laura shook her head, trying to banish any personal concern. That wasn't easy; anything that could take down the boys from *Emerald Maui* could presumably get her children, too. "I don't know yet," she said, following the projections and analyses in her omni. "Akira, how are you coming on the programming station?"

"It's operating, love, but the initial calibration and test runs will take a few hours unless we cut them short." Akira's low, grim tone held the unspoken question as to whether they could afford the few hours.

Maybe not. But even less could she afford to do any shortcuts *here*. There weren't any people or machines to catch her mistakes if she cut the wrong corner. "No," she said. "We have to be absolutely sure it's working at one hundred percent."

Ah. There's something. "A toxin. Complex protein structure. Catalytic inhibitor action on several nerve groups."

Pearce connected in; she could tell that the lieutenant had some medical training just by the way she was examining the data. "How do you mean that?"

"Many poisons—perhaps most—kill or injure by a direct chemical action; the poison reacts with some part of the body and damages it through that reaction, and the poison is generally consumed by that reaction." Laura had her medical library start comparing the structure of the new toxin with others. "But others are more efficient about their damage; they contact a particular type of nerve receptor, for instance, and cause some kind of shift in its response...and then move on, to the next receptor. They catalyze a damaging change, but they aren't themselves consumed in doing so, so that one molecule of the toxin can damage many nerves. Those require the active defenses of the body, or a direct antitoxin, to neutralize."

"That...sounds pretty scary."

"It is. Generally such toxins can be lethal at *much* lower doses than others. And this one seems to have something in common with the top-end bacterial toxins like tetanospasmin or botulinum."

"So it's a bacterial infection?"

"That's my guess. Something like that, anyway. Something that can be triggered by very small numbers of organisms, so the ordinary nanos didn't catch it right away. I found something like this in the early months when we were here, but it's obviously not identical or my quick patches to your nanos would have caught it." She shook her head. "But this incubation period... amazingly slow. Usually you see this in some forms of viral or even prion-based infection. Bacterial infections usually have a much shorter incubation period."

Pearce considered that. "Oh. And the reason it hasn't hit *me* is that I was in suspension for most of the time."

Laura nodded. "You may not even have been exposed; it might be something native to the island *Emerald Maui* landed on, and only those who went outside on that island would have run into it."

"But now that we know what's going on, they'll be okay." Pearce's green eyes looked at her sharply. "Right?"

Laura made sure the channel was sealed again; she didn't want this discussion available to the kids. "There's a good *chance* now. But it's not certain. I've got to design an antitoxin, and that's not trivial work. Oh, it's not too hard to make some kind of molecule that will break apart or disable the toxin, but you have to also make sure that *that* molecule isn't poisonous by itself.

"Killing off the bacteria—if that's what our source is—is something I'll also have to do, but make sure that it's done safely. In some cases—like shuddering fever on Vandemeer—the infectious agents release large bursts of toxin when they die, so the last thing I want to do is risk dumping more of this into their systems until I'm sure we can safely negate it all."

Lieutenant Haley's jaw set as she stared at the shelter where the rest of *Emerald Maui*'s crew were. "So we could *lose* them?"

"We could," Laura said bluntly. "But I don't think we will," she added, putting a hand on Pearce's shoulder. "One huge advantage we have is that the nanos can be used, at least for a while, to substitute for the absolutely vital nerve functions, so even with Franky—who's the worst off—he's not going to stop breathing or anything like that, at least not as long as I can keep the rest of the body reasonably functional."

"Why did it happen so *fast*?"

"It wasn't quite as fast as it looked," Akira's voice answered. "Undoubtedly there were small symptoms previously, but when you combine the significant reserves of healthy people with multiple changes of environment and unusual stresses, the incremental change of a slow-developing crisis can be overlooked until the situation reaches a critical point. Especially with nanos trying to compensate for small shifts; a slow, incremental change over weeks or months is easy for the systems to miss without constant baseline comparison."

"In a way, I'm relieved," Laura said absently.

"*Relieved*?"

"On human-compatible worlds, the single most common disasters are medical, usually diseases. Four or five major pathogens per world that present real problems is the rule of thumb. So if this is one of the big ones for Lincoln, I'm that much closer to getting us past the worst danger for our little colony."

Pearce stared at her a moment, then managed a smile. "I suppose I get that. But aren't there like, hundreds of terrible diseases on Earth? Why wouldn't there be at least as many on other planets?"

"Well, first, we evolved on Earth, so human-specific pathogens are only going to be found there, at least to start with. But more importantly, it's more a matter of how much better we are today at medical science. There are hundreds of dangerous pathogens on every world. But only a very few are sufficiently complex, subtle, or both that they manage to evade our modern medical prevention methods and require a doctor to actively figure out how to neutralize them." Laura leaned forward and found herself smiling again. "And *there* you are."

A dusting of faint blue shaded an outline of two lobes in a

human figure. "Respiratory. Probably inhaled while working out-side. If I had to guess, most likely during the excavation work, since that would have turned up almost everything in the dirt and thrown some of it into the air."

"And would fit with me not having any."

"Exactly." She studied it. "Hmm. Might be more fungal-related, if I insist on using Earth-standard nomenclature. Inhaled fungal-type infections are very nasty and often difficult to diagnose at first."

A faint chuckle was heard. "Serves us right," muttered Campbell.

"Sam! How are you doing?" Pearce said, brightening visibly at the sound of his voice. "And what do you mean, 'serves us right'?"

"How am I doing? Rotten, right now. Feel like utter crap. Better off than the kids, probably because of the military enhance-ments, plus I've been around enough worlds and had enough updates that my nanos are probably just that much better at the job." He gave a weary grin, visible in the omni's feed. "As for what serves us right? Well, it's not like we haven't had to learn the lesson about wearing dust masks over the last few centuries, is it? So we went around with our bare faces hanging out as we threw alien dirt into the air, and got about what you'd expect."

"Those kind of procedures always take a back seat in emer-gencies, and on new colonies," Laura said. "Maybe they shouldn't, but human beings haven't changed. And us colonial types are more risk-prone."

"Can't argue that; staying at home's so much easier and more comfortable, only us lunatics really want to come out here," Campbell said.

"I prefer to think of myself as curious," Akira said. "I can't do cutting-edge research on an alien world unless I'm actually *there*."

"Hah! That's what field expeditions are for. Leastwise that's one of the things my old commanders used to say; we were there to take the risks so you smart boys could get your samples without getting killed. And I'll bet you've got about eleventy-hundred other guys in your field that *do* stay home most of the time."

Akira laughed. "All right, I yield the point. Even after crash-landing on this most peculiar world, I still enjoy the thrill of walking through alien woods, never quite being sure something isn't around the next tree waiting for me."

"Lunatics all, then," agreed Campbell. He gave a big sigh. "Aaand I'm already running out of steam."

"Neurotoxic infections will do that to you," Laura said. "But while I'm not talking about the details to the kids yet, I *think* we're going to be all right. I've been watching your nanoresponse and it's already giving me some useful data on antitoxin design."

"Then," Campbell said, "Let's just hope nothing gets worse in the next few hours, 'cause then you should have your full medical nanoprogramming suite ready. Right?"

"Right," said Laura.

And I'm virtually certain I can keep everyone alive for days even without treatment. Now that I know the cause, I can stop this. She tried not to let the worry show on her face, but she couldn't relax yet. *The real question isn't whether they'll still be alive.*

It's whether I can fix all the damage . . . and how long it will take.

Chapter 11

"You're sure you don't want another column?" Whips asked, studying the various designs he had been contemplating in his omni view.

Campbell rubbed his chin, and leaned back in his bed. On his right, Tavana was propped up and trying to pay attention, but it was obvious to Whips that he probably wasn't going to stay the distance. Xander was more alert.

Tavana yawned prodigiously but focused on the projections. "Living in one of the columns, I like the idea, Sergeant. We have seen how very strong the islands are. Trees, even the biggest here—and they are amazing!—they have a history of rotting, burning, or falling in winds."

"Can't argue that," the sergeant conceded, "but after our little experience with getting our own island to half commit suicide because we were such bad tenants, I *really* don't want to do anything to mess things up here. The Kimeis already built a lot into one column, I figure the more of those we start plugging up, the more chance there is of drawing the wrong kind of attention. Xander? What's your take, Captain?"

Whips felt the shimmering ripple of a laugh play along his flanks, though he doubted any of them could recognize it, which was good. It might seem funny, but even in the few weeks the newcomers had been here, it had become clear that Campbell *meant* it when he called Xander Bird "Captain." And from their story, Whips guessed that Xander had earned it.

Xander plucked absently at the extra monitoring node Laura had installed on one arm. "Well...I'd say it's not just our call.

65

Dr. Kimei...I mean, our *bio* doctor, Akira Kimei—he's probably the one best able to tell us whether it's much of a risk. He recognized what was happening to our island, after all." Xander's gaze mostly avoided Whips, which wasn't a surprise, but he was getting used to it. Fixing that phobia wasn't happening overnight. "I can't argue Tav's points, he's right. These columns," Xander gestured at the shelter's window, through which Sherwood Column was just visible, "they're basically fortress towers that just need floors and amenities put in."

This time he *did* look directly at Whips, and met the gaze of Whips' top two eyes. "And *holy crap*, but I'm impressed by what all of you did there. I mean, even with the tools we've brought, setting up a column for living space won't exactly be an afternoon job, and you guys managed to pull it off with not much more than sticks and stones. And they tell me a lot of that was your work."

The prickly pattern of embarrassment stitched a clashing pattern across his skin, and he gave a shrug of all arms. "Oh, not a *lot* of it. I mean, it was really all of us together. Even Hitomi helped some."

"Jeez, Whips, take some credit once in a while!" Sakura's voice came from behind him. "Yes, it was mostly his design work. Sure, we all did the work, but he did most of the figuring out how to do the work."

Xander's face was slightly pale, but he managed a lopsided, amazed grin. "And you're, what, fourteen? Fifteen? I wouldn't have wanted to trust *my* teenage calculations anywhere near that far. Heck, I'm not sure I'd want to do it *now*." His gaze shifted back to the diagram of the interior of Sherwood.

A low chuckle from the sergeant. "Son, just goes to show how much desperation and necessity are mothers of invention. Or just mothers."

Whips gave a faint whistling *oof!* as Sakura plopped down on top of him. "Warn me before you do that!"

"I remember when you didn't even notice."

"You've gotten a lot bigger in the last couple years," Whips grumbled, but he didn't really mind; he'd been a sort of mobile couch as well as friend for Saki for a long time, and it was the closest to Bemmie communal contact that he was likely to get here. He cocked one eye in the direction of Tavana, expecting him to try to get his friend's attention, but saw that the French Polynesian boy's head had fallen back on his pillow. A faint snore emanated from the area.

"I guess," Sakura said. "So, maybe stupid question—why not just build something right here, in the clearing? A house or something?"

"Might could," Campbell said, "but leaving aside the tree-kraken, most of the dangerous wildlife—predators and the more irritable herbivores—hang out down on the forest floor. I don't see any percentage in putting my doors and windows where they can reach if I've got other options."

"Well, Dad'll be back in a couple hours, you can get his opinion then."

"Meanwhile," Whips said, "it's not like it's a waste of time to work on both sets of designs. Maybe one day other settlers will come and they'll have to find places to live too. And by the *Vents* does it make it easier to do design when I know all the tools you've got for me to play with!"

"What, don't want to try boring more holes in those things with fire and grinding?"

"I would rather cut off my top arm," Whips said earnestly.

The shelter door opened again and Pearce Haley came in. "Hey, everyone!"

"Well, good afternoon, Lieutenant," Campbell said, with a not-terribly-professional grin. "Back from the hunting trip so soon?"

"Give credit to Caroline," she said, hooking her thumb at the oldest Kimei daughter who was following her in. "She's a goddamn Robin Hood. I shot one capy, she got two with that darn bow."

"Well, they *were* in a group," Caroline pointed out.

"That wasn't from our—" Sakura began.

"No, not from our local herds. Trying not to spook those. There was a new herd coming in and encroaching on the territory."

"Local herds?" asked Campbell. "Trying to keep a good supply of game nearby?"

"That's part of it. Hi, Whips," Caroline said, stopping to give him a quick base-clasp of greeting. "Mostly though, we're hoping to get a couple herds used to us so that we can actually start domesticating them. Machines are great but they don't self-reproduce, at least not here."

"True enough. You think you can pull that off?" Campbell looked genuinely interested.

"Dad thinks it's possible," Sakura answered. "Says they show a lot of favorable characteristics for it. So for the most part we want to make sure they don't think of us as predators, or at worst as predators who focus well outside their herd."

"So we hunt well away from them, and make sure we clean up any blood or mess before we go anywhere near them," Caroline finished. She noticed the omni displays, since they were public-local. "Oooh, figuring out where you're going to live?"

"Deciding between the alternatives, yes," Xander answered. He'd straightened up and was now looking straight at Caroline, Whips noticed, and that triggered a Bemmie grin. Sakura noticed the shift in pattern, followed the gaze of his lower side eye, and grinned herself.

"Well, I hope it's not too far away," Caroline said, apparently oblivious to Xander's focused regard. "Don't want to have to hike through a kilometer of jungle just to visit."

"Doubt we'll have to worry about *that*," Campbell said, and Whips thought he saw a hint of a smile on his face that was aimed at Xander and Caroline. "Whether we choose a column or tree, there's *plenty* not far away."

Laura stuck her head into the shelter doorway. "All right, people, you've kept my patients up enough. Time for everyone to let them rest."

"*Mom*, I just got *back*," Caroline protested.

Laura gave a mock frown, then smiled. "Five minutes for you, then. The rest of you, out."

Whips looked up at Laura as they exited. "They are definitely getting better."

"Oh, absolutely," Laura agreed. "But they're not going to be nearly a hundred percent for a while, and they're still nowhere near there after two weeks. Seems to have hit the younger people harder, so I expect poor Francisco isn't going to make a full recovery until another month or so."

"Good thing they had the medical nanoprogramming unit."

"God, yes." She gave a shudder. "I might have lost Francisco if we hadn't, and they'd be looking at *much* longer recovery times."

"None of *us* will catch this, right?"

She gave him a reassuring squeeze at the base of his top

arm. "Not a chance. I don't think that exact agent lives on this island, and in any case I've made sure we're all immunized to it and its relations now."

"And they'll all make a hundred percent recovery?" Sakura asked.

Laura smiled. "A doctor doesn't like to make absolute statements, Saki, and you know that. But . . . yes, I expect everyone will be back to full capabilities eventually."

"Then I'd better keep working on these designs," Whips said. "Because it won't be long until we're *building* one!"

Chapter 12

"Huh," Tavana said, a questioning air about him, as he lowered himself heavily onto a stump at the side of the path.

Sakura had a momentary flash of annoyance that he'd stopped, but she suppressed it. Tav was still not fully recovered, and was just starting to get back to regular activity. "What's 'huh'?"

"The sun, I could swear that just the prior dawn, it was rising between those two trees, but now it is on the far side of the one," Tavana answered.

"Well, yeah," she said, after a moment. "Think about it, Tav."

The broad Polynesian face wrinkled for a moment, then Tavana smacked his head. "Stupid. The floating continent, it also spins. There is no really stable orientation here."

"You got it. I guess Caroline's having a ball gathering data on the planet with your satellite network. We didn't know hardly anything about Lincoln before we landed, and, well, until you guys got here we still didn't know much. 'Cept about the specific things here, anyways."

"Well, those were the things that mattered, yes? Aside from anything needed for survival, planetography would have not just taken the backseat, it would have been in a trailer behind you."

She heard her own laughter echo through the trees. "Yeah, exactly." She saw him glance up into the sky again, his brow furrow, then relax. "What is it this time?"

"Oh, that." He pointed into the sky a fair arc away from the sun.

Sakura could see a point of light, dimmed by the sky's brightness but easily visible. Concentrating, she could make out a faint mist trailing out to one side. "Oh, yeah, a comet. There's a *lot* of them here. I think there's only been a few weeks since we've been here that there wasn't a pretty bright one visible."

"*Oui*, I remember we saw two very large comets when we entered the system. Meteors are common too."

"Oh, you bet." She grinned, remembering. "When we were out building that dock for you, we hit a meteor shower that Caroline said outdid anything she'd ever heard of on Earth; it was like fireworks. And if you stay out at night and look up at any reasonable patch of sky you'll see a meteor pretty quick."

"Any actually fall around here?"

"We haven't *found* any meteorites, but there's bound to be some. But Caroline said that finding them would be tough; on Earth they used to go to places like Antarctica where there was nothing but flat ice and figure that if they came across an isolated rock, it pretty much *had* to be a meteorite, but here in a jungle? Not working so well."

"I guess so." Tav stood up. "Sorry to keep you waiting."

"It's okay," she said, even more annoyed at herself for her prior impatience. "You guys nearly died, I can't get mad at you for taking it slow sometimes. But this trip *was* your idea."

"Well, yes. I want to see how you do things here, and even if I am not up to helping much, it will be good to know how for when I am better."

Sakura couldn't argue that. "We're almost there, so if you can keep moving for about five minutes you'll be able to sit down and rest while I get to work."

They walked in silence for a few minutes; Sakura found herself very aware of Tavana being *close*, even though he wasn't really much closer than he was in a lot of other situations. *Does he feel the same way? I mean... What do I mean? Do I, well, like him?*

Tavana spoke suddenly, and his voice sounded unusually... tense? Nervous? It had a slightly higher, faintly strained pitch to it. "Um, Sakura, I was wondering, why here? That is, why is this the good place for your driftseed?"

The question relaxed her—to a startling degree. *Boy, I am nervous!* "Oh, well, that? It'll be easier to explain when we get there."

In a few moments they emerged into a semi-clearing along a narrow streambed. Across the stream, Sakura could see a strip of brilliant white, as though someone had taken a two-meter-wide paintbrush and drawn it across the jungle in front of them.

"What is *that*?"

Sakura studied the clearing and trees and stream for a moment to make sure everything was safe, then moved forward. "That," she said as she hopped across the stream, "is what we're here for."

As they got closer, the white streak resolved itself into what looked like a massive snowbank, a literal drift of white fluff. There were small animals, something like green-brown guinea pigs, moving in and around the fluff, but they scattered at the humans' approach.

Tavana surveyed the mound, eyebrows high. "Impressed, yes, I am impressed. So we use these rake-things to compress and scoop the driftseed into our bags, then carry it back?"

"Right. You can do as much as you feel up to, but don't push yourself."

She saw Tavana squint down the stream, then hold up his hand in the air for a moment. "Ah! I believe I understand."

"Thought you would!" Tav was smart, which was one of the things she really liked about him—that, and him being kind of quiet a lot of the time. "Prevailing winds get funneled up here from farther down, where it spreads out, so a lot of driftseed comes in here, and then it runs straight into this area where there's heavy growth because of the way the sunlight gets into the clearing."

"*Vraiment*, yes, but what about the turning of the island? We just mentioned that, yes? Will that not change the winds?"

"Some, yes, but so far it looks like our island continent doesn't just spin around like a top; it sort of wobbles back and forth but stays pointing in the same general direction."

Tavana scratched his head, then took the scoop-rake off his back and started trying to gather driftseed. "How is that? I mean, why does it not spin completely around?"

"We don't know," she answered candidly, dragging her scoop in what had become a practiced motion. "Might be the way the island's shaped that makes it stay in one general orientation, especially since it must dip *way* down to keep us all above water, or maybe there's some kind of active orientation guidance from one of its symbiote species."

Tavana was having difficulty getting the driftseed into the bag. "No, look, Tav, you have to scoop *more* first. Until it compresses enough it'll just puff right back up and fall apart. You have to tell by the resistance and the look. Here, let me." She took his arm and guided it through the scooping motion. He resisted at first, trying to anticipate her movements and failing, but by the second time through he had relaxed and just let her guide. "See?" she said finally. "Four, five good long scoops and it's squished itself down and if you turn it like *this*," she gave the scoop a sort of shaking half-turn, "It loosens in the grooves *just* enough. Now try putting it in the bag."

Most of the driftseed slid into the bag, with just a little of it fluffing and flying away at the edges. "Oh! *Oui, c'est facile,*" Tav said; his voice had that same strange, tense edge. She was suddenly aware of the warmth of Tav's arm, the hard-soft feel of muscle under skin.

She stepped back, letting go maybe a little faster than she'd originally planned. "So, um, you think you can do that yourself?"

"Yes, it is easy, yes? I said that." He laughed suddenly. "So, Saki, can I ask you another question?"

Another question would be good, she thought. "Sure!"

He hesitated, and she suddenly wondered if she did want another question. Or if she *really did* want another question. "So," he said again, and licked his lips nervously, then managed a smile. "The neighborhood, I did not see an immertainment complex or a performance hall or even restaurant around. So I was wondering, um, where would you go if you were dating?"

She couldn't help herself; the release of tension sent her into a gale of laughter. Seeing his wince-and-cringe helped get it back under control. "No, it's okay, Tav, jeez, I was trying to decide how I might ask *you*, and that was a pretty cute approach you tried, so the answer's yes but I don't know where!"

"Yes? *Vraiment*? Really?" He grinned, teeth flashing as bright as the driftseed. "Well, then we will think about the 'where' later!" The relief was as clear on his face as it had been in her gut, and then he went on, "Maybe the practice range? It is not so classically part of romance, but I had fun with our little contest before."

"Ha! That's not a terrible idea at all, but maybe we can come up with a better one. I'll have to talk to Mom and Dad, of course."

"*Oui*, and I with the sergeant. At least we have already met each other's family here."

She heard a giggle escape her. "Yeah, I guess we have. So, anyway, think you can help finish gathering the driftseed?"

"Now?" Tavana grinned again. "Now I could finish this whole *clearing.*"

Chapter 13

Campbell stretched, testing his body's sensations. *Mostly back to my old self, but still a little off. That damn disease really took it out of us.*

Still, he'd gotten off pretty light. He looked at Francisco, who was sitting in bed, trying to paint a picture of the view out the window, and shook his head. The little boy still had to pause every ten minutes or so to rest; Maddox was a little better than that, but even now after three and a half weeks he was only up to a little light labor.

"Is he going to recover all the way, Doctor Kimei?" he asked, voice low.

Laura bit her lip. "I...hope so. This was a complex disease. It actually started *adapting* to some of the nanotreatments, and I don't remember ever seeing anything like that in the literature before. If we had a full-scale hospital setup I'd be sure, but..."

He could see the dark doubts on her face. He put a hand on her shoulder. "What you're really telling me, ma'am, is that if we hadn't had the incredible fortune that you landed here, and that we were able to reach you, that little boy and the rest of us would be dead now. You reversed most of the systemic damage, including the neurological, and whatever happens, Franky's going to still be *himself*, and that's okay."

Laura shook herself and then smiled at him. "Playing therapist now, Sergeant?"

"Hell, that's the job of a noncom, isn't it? Half of your job's running out the recruits who really shouldn't have signed on in the first place, and the other half's helping build up the ones

75

76   Eric Flint & Ryk E. Spoor

who belong there. And the way you looked? Ma'am, I've seen that expression before, more times than I care to remember. In my line of work, you see a hell of lot of medics and doctors losing patients, haunted by *what-ifs* and *I should haves*." He frowned, remembering. "Sometimes the patient's only *one* of the victims that needs treatment."

Laura nodded. "They teach you that lesson in medical school," she said with a rueful grin, "but it's hard to keep in mind." She looked back at Francisco. "But...yes, I think he will. The nanos are working on the repairs and I don't think there's anything irreparable. It was *very* close, though."

"Too damn close. Your upgraded medical suite should keep that from happening again, right?"

"It should. I'm confident that it will. I had to do a complete wipe-and-reprogram on your nanos to enforce full compatibility and consistency, but that's done, so I think our little colony has full coverage on medical safety now."

She gestured upward. "And since you were saying how grateful you were for our presence, let me just add how grateful we are for yours. Those satellites are a godsend. Now we can talk to each other anywhere on the planet, and if there's a medical or any other kind of emergency we'll know about it right away, with all our omnis linked to the network."

"Well, now, I guess it's just that we're both groups lucky. Together I think we can really make a go of it here, even if we're never found."

She was quiet for a moment, and the two of them moved out of the doorway of the shelter to let Hitomi through; the little girl ran over to Francisco and dropped a flower chain on his lap. Campbell grinned at that.

"So, Sergeant...do you think that's where we are? That we'll never be found?"

He shrugged, and started walking slowly away from the shelter, looking up at the immense trees surrounding them. "Well, I'll tell you, ma'am; I was giving about one-in-ten odds a rescue ship would show up in the first six months—which time was actually spent while we were still trying to make our way here.

"Now? I wouldn't give you one in a thousand. The only reason anyone would have to come here is if they either suspect there are castaways on Lincoln, or if they notice something funny about this planet. The *star* someone might notice, but then they're not gonna be so concerned about the planets here, but on what it was that managed to hide a whole star this close to Earth. So they'll go looking in space along that line-of-sight. Only likely thing to draw anyone to Lincoln otherwise is if someone maps it with wide-baseline telescopes, and then notices the map ain't always consistent. But that's a matter of years at that distance."

Laura Kimei nodded; her thoughts clearly ran along the same channels. "So we're here for good."

"Unless one of those contraptions the kids are working on is built, and manages to make it to Orado. If *that* happens you can bet there'll be a big mission here straightaway."

A pair of arms slipped around his waist from behind and hugged. "And what do you think the chances are of *that*?" Pearce Haley asked, letting go and stepping up to join them. "Hi, Laura."

"Hi, Pearce!" Laura gave Pearce a quick hug. "That's a good question. I know Whips, Tavana, and Xander are spending a lot of time on those alternatives. What do you think?"

Campbell stole a quick kiss from Pearce before answering. "Well, first off, there's no problem with them trying to figure these things out. Chances . . . really hard to say. Engineers are usually either complete optimists or total pessimists about how something they designed will work."

"I like the idea of going home under our own power," Laura said after a moment.

"So do I. You can't beat ending a shipwreck story that way, with everyone hammering out a solution and beating the odds to get home on their own. Look at how many times they've dramatized the wreck of the *Nebula Storm* over the century and a half since it crashed on Europa." He swatted at a buzzbug that was flying too close. "But they'll have to do a hell of a job of convincing me that they can get that hulk skyworthy again before I greenlight that. Doing the separate probe might permanently ground *Emerald Maui*, but it won't risk any of *us*, and honestly I like that a lot better."

"I agree," Pearce said. "But we'll decide that when the designs are all done; have a family conference about it."

"Sure thing."

He took Pearce's hand in his as they walked around the clearing, and noticed Laura's expression. "What are *you* grinning about, ma'am?"

"Oh, seeing the two of you and then remembering Hitomi running in with that flower chain."

"Ha! Though I think the ones you need to keep an eye on are Tav and Sakura."

"Oh, I *am*," she said, "but Tavana seems like a very nice young man, and it's not like Saki can't take care of herself. Mostly the problem is keeping them from distracting each other now. Tavana especially."

"I hear you on that," he said with a chuckle. "Especially Tav; when he came to us to ask about what a guy might arrange to have a date, he was practically incoherent. But what about Xander and Caroline?"

"Honestly? I don't know if there's anything there or not. They're clearly friendly, but I haven't got a sense as to whether they're interested in each other."

"I hate to say it," Pearce said, "but right now it's *Maddox* who's interested in Caroline."

"What? He's only, what, fourteen?"

Campbell heard his own laugh echo across the clearing. "And she's eighteen, which is only four years apart. Looks like a big separation *now*, of course, but it doesn't mean much to a young guy. Or gal, for that matter; can't tell you the number of young ladies I know who got crushes on older teachers. Yeah, I've seen Maddox sneaking looks at Caroline myself. Tries to hide it. Kinda like Xander and Pearce."

Pearce boggled at him. "*What?*"

He laughed again, reflecting on how good it was to laugh now, after all the prior months where good laughs were in short supply. "What, you never noticed him staring at you back on the ship? Or sometimes giving me the narrow side-eye when he thought I didn't notice? Think he's pretty over it now, but he had it pretty bad for a bit."

As Pearce chewed on that minor revelation, Campbell looked to Laura. "Anyways, one question I gotta ask, have you got the critical issues on this covered? The emotional ones they'll have to work out on their own, but..."

"Oh, I *absolutely* have that covered. None of us—not me, not Pearce, and not any of my girls—will be having children unless and until it is decided they will. Obviously, if it comes to that,

Pearce, it's completely your decision; you're my patient but not my responsibility."

The redhead gave a grin up to Campbell that jolted him and sent his heart racing as though he was a teenager again. "Oh, maybe it *will* come to that. But not just yet."

"Uh, yeah," Campbell said, noticing that his own conversation wasn't as sparkling as it ought to be. "Hm. Not yet, that's for sure. We'll need to finish getting established and comfortable before we worry about *that*."

There were, of course, other problems with the long-term viability of their colony, but for now the real problems were simple: make long-term homes, secure long-term food sources, keep improving their resources and capabilities...and be ready for anything Lincoln threw at them.

Because even now, with all of them together, Samuel Morgan Campbell could still feel it. Lincoln had more surprises in store for them.

And some of them could be lethal.

Chapter 14

"You're sure this is a good choice?" Campbell directed the question to Sakura, even as he stared up at the column.

Having Campbell ask *her* sent a maybe-unreasonable thrill of pride through her. "We're pretty sure, Sergeant. Dad's been doing as much studying of the ecology here as he could, and it seems that some of these columns aren't used as much. We already chose one that *is*, but this one's actually got a floor on it. For some reason the continent's sealed it off."

"Really?" Campbell rubbed his chin, still studying the concrete-like tower in front of him. "Why d'you suppose that is, Akira? I mean, sounds ideal for us, and your own tower's working out well, but I'd hate to buy into something that turned out to have problems that even the *continent* rejected it for. Not like there's a building code around here."

"I don't think it's for anything to do with structural integrity; you know that I borrowed Xander and Maddox and went over this one in detail with some of your equipment last week. My best guess is that as the continent grows, the needed number and placement of vents changes, and ones not needed are simply walled off."

"Hmm. And yours is active, but this one isn't. Could it be unwalled off later?"

Sakura nodded. "We saw how the structure of your island responded to thinking you were a threat; probably the same kind of thing happens, more slowly, as the island adapts to change. So it could probably reopen this one."

She saw Campbell's gaze run up the column into the canopy

and look around. He nodded thoughtfully. "Well, Saki, could you and Tavana start checking out the configuration on the 450? Looks like we're gonna start cutting soon."

"*Me?*" Sakura said with surprise. "But Xander and Maddox know a *lot* more than—"

"Exactly why you and Tav should do it," Xander said, somewhat abruptly. He was also looking up, studying the column and the canopy. "Maddox, you can help out. We've got plenty of time, so this can be a lot of learning as well as working. Right, Sergeant, Dr. Kimei?"

Her mother had frowned when Xander interrupted, but her face cleared some when Xander directed the question to her. *He may be their captain, but my mom is* boss. "I suppose so. Yes, go on, Sakura. It can't hurt for all of us to understand how to run all of our equipment."

Sakura didn't mind, to tell the truth. The JD-CAT 450 Universal Excavator, to give the machine its full name, was a really impressive and *massive* vehicle, with a fully-shapeable "blade" that could be anything from a bulldozer to a bucket loader and more.

As she and Tav, along with the smaller Bird brother Maddox, headed towards the big yellow-painted machine, she heard the sergeant say, "and Whips, maybe you could work with Mel to figure out how we could put in a floor at the bottom level that'll support itself, just in case the island decides to pull the rug out on us?"

"Sure thing, sir!" Whips said cheerfully, and Mel followed him over to a large exposed rock which the Bemmie liked to sit on; it was smooth and comfortable for his belly-pad.

Sakura was glad they didn't have to watch the younger kids; Caroline had stayed behind in Sherwood Tower with both Hitomi and Francisco.

She felt a faint, welcome tingle go up her arm as Tavana took her hand while they stood for a moment, looking at the 450. Maddox glanced at that and just grinned at them; Sakura smiled back. "So what do we have to do here?"

"Okay, well, we need to cut holes in that column, right? So that means the 450 needs a cutting array."

"*Oui*, that is clear enough," Tavana said. "But can it *do* that? Bulldozer blades and excavators, that is what we have used it for. The cutting, I did not know it could do this."

"I'll bet it can. JD-Cats are used for road work, and you have to cut up roadways sometimes, right?"

"You sure do," Sakura said. She remembered seeing such a machine with what looked like a huge rotary sawblade slowly grinding its way through the pavement, back on Earth. "So is that just another mode we have to switch on?"

"It is not an option in the menu," Tavana said after a moment of staring at the interface; Sakura brought up the same connection; there were a lot of configurations but not that one.

Tavana grinned. "But then, I do remember having a tool that lied about what menu options it *could* give me. Maddox, is this another handholding limit?"

Maddox laughed. "You don't get fooled twice, huh? I'll bet it is. Let's start digging into this interface!"

Sakura tried to watch what Maddox was doing, along with Tav, but she wasn't really an engineer or an interface jockey, so some of it was out of her league.

She glanced over at the others. Mel was waving her arms animatedly as Whips projected something in front of her; Pearce Haley was using what Sakura thought was an acoustic echo probe on the column, probably gauging its thickness at the bottom, while Mom and Dad looked up at the column itself, talking. Xander was staring up into space, maybe looking at an omni projection, while Sergeant Campbell had stepped back about ten meters, taking a different perspective of the column.

That was why she was looking straight at him when, without warning, a tree kraken plummeted from the branches, heading straight for the sergeant.

Before she—or anyone else—could cry out or even break their shocked paralysis, Sergeant Campbell whipped around, the automatic rifle that had been slung over his back suddenly in his hands, and a chattering snarl ripped through the sunlit green air of the little clearing.

The details of armaments had changed over the centuries, but chemical propellants shoving carefully-designed pieces of metal down barrels was *still* one of the most devastatingly effective ways of stopping anything hostile. Sergeant Campbell fired in three-shot bursts, one set after another, and alien blood and flesh and bone spattered from the impacts.

The creature stumbled and crashed to a halt, giving a whining screech of pain, fury, and dawning fear. Even as it turned to flee, Campbell raised the rifle, aimed, and fired a final burst that took the thing through its tiny head, dropping the tree kraken like a load of cement.

No one moved as the echoes of the shots dwindled away into the distance; the forest of Lincoln was unnaturally silent, still, shocked into quiet by the violence of that unknown sound.

Akira Kimei was the first to speak, as the sergeant slowly lowered the weapon. "My God. Are you all right, Samuel?"

Campbell grinned as he re-slung the rifle. "Never got close. Been watching it stalking me for the last ten minutes, as you know."

Sakura was relieved and puzzled. "But Sergeant, then why didn't you *tell* us? We could have tried to discourage it, maybe run it off."

"He did tell us," her mother said. "Over the private circuits, which is why the rest of you were moved well away from the column. I *would* like an explanation for why you didn't scare it off earlier, though, rather than letting it try to attack you. That scared the daylights out of me, even though I knew it was coming."

"Scared me more than that," Tavana said, with a frown. "My heart, I thought it would stop."

"Same here," said Pearce. "What about you, Xander?"

Xander's cheeks were touched with pink. "Well, it *did* scare me, even though Sergeant Campbell had warned me too. As his captain, silly though that still sounds."

"The explanation, Samuel?" Akira said, in the deceptively gentle tone that told Sakura that her father was near the boiling point. "I hope it is a good one. We just scared almost all of us, and killed an animal that we could have, in all likelihood, chased off without injury."

"And we'd have had to do that again and again and again," Campbell said bluntly. He was examining the corpse carefully. "You've probably studied colonial operations, Akira, Laura, but— no offense—you've never *done* the initial colony setup, and sure as hell none of you were in on the first landings and clear-cuts.

"One of the *first* things you have to do is scare the living *hell* out of the predators that have a chance of learning to stay away from you. You have to establish that your people are the biggest, baddest living things on the planet, and you do that by killing the ones that come too close or—especially—the ones that try to attack any of you. Sometimes you have to wipe out the entire population in range of your people."

He looked at Sakura's expression, saw it mirrored on a lot of the others, even the people from his own crew, and shook his head. For an instant, Sakura saw his age on his face as it went both stony and somehow sad. "Yeah. I know. Back on Earth we just about wiped out not just the predators but thousands of other species, but you have to understand this: we could start trying to save them, to conserve and protect them, because we ended up *dominating* that planet. We *became* the danger, to pretty much anything else. That was a *long* time after we had to spend our waking hours wondering if we were gonna be someone else's meal."

Akira bit his lip, then gave the most reluctant nod Sakura had ever seen. "I...I believe I understand, Samuel. And...much as it pains me...I am afraid I have to agree with you."

"Akira!" Sakura felt a pang near her heart; she'd never heard her mother sound so shocked. "Are you serious? We have ways of setting up safe perimeters, we could have chased even *this* one off with—"

"It's establishment of territory," Akira said bluntly. "Predators rarely attack each other unless they have no other choice; the potential cost of attacking something that is as well armed as you is far too great. But we are new creatures; we are not clearly recognized as what we—honestly speaking—are, the greatest apex predators in the Galaxy. Samuel is right. We have to treat any incursion into the territory we intend to live in as any predator would—driving off or killing any intruders that might threaten us and our children, until they learn to fear and respect us as a group."

Tavana stared at the still shuddering corpse and nodded, muttering something in French. The running translation from her omni showed that it was mostly curses.

Pearce Haley drew in a deep breath. "Well, that was sure a good first lesson. You'd killed one before, right?"

"Yes," Sakura said, overriding her embarrassment at the memory. "Twice, actually. But the first was more a matter of running into the middle of something without thinking, and the second we'd started it by bashing the column they were in. We've just kept away from the krakens as much as we could."

"Well, given the weapons you had to hand, that was probably the right approach," Campbell said. "But now there's more of us, better weapons, and we're going to need more space. And since we know from our prior island and Akira's studies that we'd be *really* ill-advised to go around doing a clear-cut and burn to make a perimeter, that means we gotta establish ourselves as the most badass things on this continent so we don't have to do this more often."

Thinking about it, Sakura realized he was probably right. "I guess. But I still don't like the idea of just killing things, even the krakens."

Campbell's smile was more natural and sympathetic. "Saki, I hope to god you never like the idea. I don't particularly like it either. But I don't know any good alternative, and I think we all agree that we'd rather shoot a few hundred of these things than let one of them get the drop on Hitomi or Franky."

Sakura had no disagreement with that.

"All right then," Akira said briskly. "Let's get back to work, shall we?"

Chapter 15

Whips pulled himself up as high as he could, then dropped back to the floor in a flopping landing that stung his belly pad. The *thud* transmitted itself loudly, echoing up through the column. "How's that?"

"Looks great!" Maddox said, squinting at the readout in his omni. "Mel?"

Melody Kimei—almost eight centimeters taller but just as thin as she'd been when they had landed—nodded. "Well within strain parameters, and Whips outweighs any two or three of us. That floor will hold just fine."

"How far below it is the column floor?" the sergeant asked, sticking his head in the newly-cut doorway.

"About half a meter," Mel answered. "Makes sure we weren't relying on it even indirectly for support."

"Still nice to know it's there. Will we be able to check on that if we have to?"

"Oh, easy. We had to make a hole in it anyway," Whips answered, gesturing with a flick of tendrils at a large tube already in place at one point of the floor. "Some of the Nebula Drive dust was perfect for monitoring stuff like this."

"What'd we need a hole for . . . oh."

"Unless you want to have a lot clumsier waste disposal, this is the best we've got," Whips confirmed, flickering his own colorful grin at the sergeant. "Dumps everything into that hundreds of meters deep volume inside the island. We've been doing that all along in Sherwood Column."

"And with the screens and monitor dust we can make sure

87

nothing comes *up* in either column," Maddox said proudly. "Added some of that to Sherwood Column's disposal, too."

"Good work. How long you figure before we'll be ready to move in?"

Whips checked the display in his omni, ran some work calculations, and blinked, then checked it again. A rippling laugh emerged. "Wow. You have *no* idea how long it took us to build the first one, but with the tools that *Emerald Maui* brought, and the extra manpower, and all . . . I think if we all pitch in and follow the plan, we could get everything else set up in a week and a half, two weeks tops. Then put together stuff like additional furniture, stuff like that, over the next week."

"Then we stow away the shelter, huh?" Maddox asked.

Campbell rubbed his chin, then shook his head. "You know, I don't think so. Not yet."

"Why not?"

"Well, once we have our own tower, then each of us has our own home, but even in small towns, it's nice to have gathering places that *ain't* home. I figure we'll build us a town hall or market or church or whatever, but until then, a full-size shelter'll do just fine. Enough room to have a few different setups—little gaming room, a theater, something like that. Okay, so our choices of social partners might be a little limited, but the more stuff we can do, the more it'll *feel* like we're living somewhere civilized."

Whips had to agree, though a part of him felt more left out than ever. The arrival of the survivors from *Emerald Maui* had been a godsend—that much he couldn't argue. But none of them were *Bemmius*. A lot of socializing of *his* people took place in the water, and even the best of the humans—Sakura and, to his surprise, Francisco—couldn't even *begin* to keep up with him in the ocean. He'd spent more time on land, dragging himself from point to point, in the last year than he had in . . . well, probably the whole rest of his life.

True, that did mean his arms were stronger than ever, and his belly pad was so tough it was practically armor plate by now, but it just wasn't the same, and what was *really* annoying was that Sakura wasn't around nearly as much, hanging around almost all the time with Tavana, which was . . .

He froze, unaware for a few moments of what everyone around him was saying, as what he was *feeling* finally broke through his thoughts. *Vents Below and Sky Above, am I...am I feeling jealous about Sakura?*

He hated that thought, but as soon as he allowed himself to recognize it, the truth was there, staring him down with the human's metaphorical bright green eyes. Sakura had been his best friend since they were both so much younger. He remembered her even as a toddler, walking in a confident but stiff-legged thumping gait ahead of him as he tried to drag himself after her, his second-growth griptalons not even in yet, and then her turning back, draping his arms over her shoulders and *pulling*, dragging him along so they could both get where they were going.

And they'd always been that close. They played together, and worked together, and...

It occurred to Whips that even back home, he'd spent more time with Sakura than he had with anyone outside of his own family. He'd hardly ever gone for even a casual swim with some other of the people. He'd never thought...never thought of a time where she *wouldn't* be there.

Depths, I'm going to have to think this out.

He became aware that something had called Campbell back out. Mel and Maddox were checking the floor mountings one last time and arguing about the details of the next steps, even though the basic plan was already set. Whips undulated over to the exit and saw Campbell talking with Akira.

"What's up?" he asked. "You look serious, Akira."

"Well, yes," Akira said. "In the last week or so I've noticed a marked downturn on traffic along our accustomed gametrails. I *think* I've noticed some others, but they're farther from where we currently are, which means a longer walk to get there and back."

"Well, a lot of animals ain't dumb; if you're killing them at the same general place, they'll tend to stop going there," Campbell pointed out.

"But we've been doing this for, oh, six months at least, and I've been careful to avoid making it obvious. Give me some credit, Sergeant; I may not be a hunter by training, but behavior of alien species *is* my specialty."

"Oh, sure. No offense. So you think something else is up?"

"I'm fairly sure of it. The problem of course is that we haven't been here nearly long enough to understand the long-term behavior of species. We've been here slightly longer than one Lincoln year now, but that's hardly a guarantee that we've seen anything close to all their typical behaviors. Various species on Earth and other planets go through cycles that are multiyear in span."

"You know," Whips said slowly, "things...*smelled* a little different this week. When I was in the water, I mean."

"Day before yesterday? When you dragged in that golden-sided fish thing?" Campbell asked. "You did mention you hadn't seen one of those before."

"I hadn't. And Finny and his friends seemed a little more energetic. Though it's hard to tell with them."

"Finny" was the name Campbell had given to a streamlined predator which seemed to include a large streak of curiosity in its makeup; Finny and some others of his species had followed Campbell's crew all the way from their doomed island to the Kimei's floating continent, and now stayed in and around the semicircular bay that *Emerald Maui* had arrived at. Whips didn't think the "Finnies" were actually intelligent, any more than the capys probably were, but he wasn't sure. They *were* smart for animals, that much was for sure.

Campbell laughed. "Yeah, 'energetic' is pretty much their default. But when you say it smelled different, you mean the water wasn't the same?"

"Yes." He thought back. "Might have been a little different in temperature, maybe warmer?"

Campbell rubbed his chin again, then suddenly looked at Akira. "Oh."

"Easily checked," Akira said at almost the same moment.

Whips looked between the two, and suddenly got it. He sent a query up to the satellites, and displayed the data on his omni.

What he saw made him draw in a breath with a faint hoot. "Oh," he said, unconsciously echoing Campbell.

The outline of the floating continent they were on had moved. For most of the prior time it had been monitored—several months now, since the *Maui* crew had dispersed its cargo of satellites into space—it had wobbled back and forth but stayed, generally, in the same general latitude, straddling the equator.

But now it had *drifted* noticeably, heading northward at a slow, but definite, pace. Already the northern edges of the island were edging towards the borders of the tropical zone. Enhancing the image in different spectra confirmed what Whips was now suspecting.

"We've moved into some kind of current," he said finally. "It's taking us north—not very fast, the currents here are going to be pretty slow given the depth of the ocean and other factors—but definitely north."

"Ahhh," Akira said. "And we know most animals on the islands are adapted to be able to evacuate the islands, move from one to another. It would be unsurprising to find that there are entire *populations* that move as landmasses enter other climatic areas. That is, our familiar flora and fauna may shift as we move."

"Or it may just *leave*," Campbell said, "meaning we'll be most of what's left here."

"I would tend to doubt that. As is said, nature abhors a vacuum, so a big empty landmass is a huge vacuum begging for new animals to fill it up. But either way we have to be ready for changes."

"Big ones, maybe. Wonder what would happen if we end up going *far* north? Think these trees will survive?"

"Hard to say," Akira admitted. "They have thus far seemed to be tropical in their type and behavior, but if they cannot move and such movements of islands are common, they must have some form of adaptation to such extremes."

"Either way, we should prepare for significant changes," Whips said, thinking about what he knew about different biomes and the challenges of survival in territory you didn't know. In this case, the island might suddenly become territory they didn't know.

"Damn," Campbell said with a slanted grin on his face. "This world's quirks keep throwing funny curveballs at us. Akira, how about the island continent *itself*? Is it going to be okay if things get colder?"

Akira didn't answer at once, and Whips recognized his expression: he was considering a whole host of possibilities at once and trying to get an answer out of them.

Campbell apparently recognized that expression too, because he didn't prod; just let Akira Kimei think.

At last, Akira nodded. "I think it should be fine. We have evidence that these islands persist for extremely long time-scales when left unmolested, and given the nature of wind, currents, tides and such, I cannot believe that these islands do not commonly wander across the globe. While the population of the island's top *surface* may well change, I suspect the core animals, including key symbionts, are well able to adapt to wide changes in temperature, some in salinity, and so on. They may reinforce areas prior to entering colder waters and then go dormant, but the drift patterns likely take them out of very inhospitable waters in reasonable time."

"What's 'reasonable time,' though?"

"Hard to say. Caroline and I will have to work on that, see if we can get a model going now that we have more data on the whole planet. It's not out of the question, though, that we could spend a year or three in high latitudes before exiting them. I doubt we'd spend decades there, though."

"Why's that? Not that I *want* to spend decades up north, but why do you think we won't spend lots of time there?"

"I can answer that," Whips said, and the omni displayed the whole globe, rotating. "Take a look; most of our floating land-masses range from the equator through the subtropics; you don't see too many of them far north or far south."

"Huh. Currents?"

"It would have to be, I should think. Wind naturally will play a part, but the vast majority of these islands' mass and area is underwater." Akira tapped the side of his omni absently. "The physical topology underwater would ultimately guide a lot of the currents and their courses, but as that is tens of kilometers down we have no way of knowing what that topology is and modeling it, thus we're going to be discovering its effects, well, this way."

Sergeant Campbell studied the display for another moment, then nodded sharply. "Right. I'm with you two, we *do* need to prepare. Stockpile, in case some of our food sources dry up. Figure out heating options for our columns—we can stock up on firewood but since wood's the minority population in this forest, we don't want to overharvest. Have to watch that."

"Find a good way to ensure water sources, too," mused Akira. "We have no certainty that we'll have regular rainfall if we're in different latitudes. Weather patterns will undoubtedly be disrupted by something this large entering different climatological boundaries."

Whips was playing worst-case scenarios in his mind. "Can I make a suggestion?"

"Of course, Whips," Akira said.

"Well...I don't think there's any immediate danger of anything, but it occurs to me that if the worst does happen—I mean, maybe the island separates into chunks when it gets too cold, or island-eaters get it, or something—we should be ready to move. We'd all fit on board *Emerald Maui*, right?"

Sergeant Campbell looked at him with a bemused expression, then grinned. "Son, you *are* thinking with Murphy in mind, aren't you? I like it. Sure, those shuttles were meant to carry up to fifteen plus a pilot. Plenty of room for emergency evacuation and moving."

"And if we keep some of the equipment on the island, and some onboard, we'll have space onboard for survival supplies," Akira said. "Excellent thinking, Whips. I think you should take point on that project."

"Me?"

"Sure thing, son," Campbell said, still grinning. "The reward for thinking of more things that need to be done? That's you, getting more work!"

Chapter 16

"I don't see anything," Xander whispered.

"To the right of that big white rock," Caroline said quietly.

Xander concentrated on the indicated area and his omni activated his retinal displays, causing the metamaterial lenses to realign and provide an effective ten times zoom. At the same time, it shifted the viewing spectrum slightly to take advantage of the dim light of Lincoln's night—mostly provided by one of the huge comets that currently stretched across a quarter of the sky.

Shadows lightened and Xander suddenly saw motion. "I think I see! One . . . two . . . um, about five?"

"I see six," Caroline said. "But the sixth is off to the side."

"Got him." The lone capy, a bit larger than the others, stood on a small rock, his forequarters raised up rather like those of a rat, sniffing the air. "Sentry, I bet."

Caroline nodded, then looked at him expectantly.

Xander called up the map overlay. "Yeah . . . they're almost to the edge of that rocky area that borders the swamp. If they keep going they'll have to trek right through the bogs, and from what you told me that's not safe."

"Not if the hillmouths are still there. And I think they are."

Xander remembered the briefing on the various dangers of the Kimei's continent; the hillmouths were semi-crocodilian ambush predators, massive things that could disguise themselves as small hillocks of marsh vegetation. A capy would barely make a decent meal for a small one.

On the other hand, the tree krakens apparently stayed in forested areas when they could, so it might be a case of trading one predatory threat for another. "But this *is* part of the same group?"

"Sure. Here, call up the reference patterns. See?"

"Hard to make out in this light. Um...oh, okay, yeah. Pattern matches on these three, that's for sure. So they're part of the herd you usually saw near your column area?"

"Yes. And now they're almost out of our walking range, and moving at night as well as day."

Xander grimaced. "Slow, but even if they only do a short distance every day they'll still be moving a long way in a few months. Guess your dad was right, they're migrating."

"Looks like it."

"Are we taking any more of them before they leave?"

Caroline pursed her lips and pushed her brown hair back as she studied the group. "We could use more supplies, but it's a *long* way back home from here. We'd have to clean the carcass quick then make the hike back, and there are nocturnal predators around we *don't* want to meet up with if we can avoid it."

And if we're carrying a lot of meat, a predator's going to smell it. "So no?"

"So I think we need to think hard about it. Dad hasn't seen any replacement species show up yet, but that's probably more a matter of months. There's still plenty of fish and other sea creatures around, but capy meat's one of the most nutritious things we've found on Lincoln, and it's pretty tasty too."

"No argument there!" Xander actually thought capy steak might be one of his favorite foods.

But his stomach wasn't the most rational decisionmaker; the real question was whether it made more sense to kill one and take the time and effort to dress the carcass and haul it home than to forego the opportunity but be able to return more quickly and safely.

"I'll leave it to you," Xander said finally. "You guys have lived here the longest."

"Thanks, drop it all on me," Caroline said, but the visible flash of white teeth showed she was smiling as she did so. After a few moments of silence, she sighed. "There's only six of them in that group, and I have no way of knowing how many of their herd's around. I think we'll have to let these guys go."

"Okay." He stared after the little herd, which was moving off into the shadows. "Just as well. I dunno about you, but I'm not sure I'd be able to make the shot from here, at night, even *with* my omni helping."

"Oh, I'm sure we could. I could do it with a *bow* if I had to."

"You've gotta be kidding me. They must be close to sixty, seventy meters off."

"I didn't say I'd *want* to do it," Caroline admitted, "but with a good bow like we have now, I'd try anything up to a hundred meters if I had to. Rather be a lot closer, though. If we were going to do it, we'd stalk the herd until we got closer—ideally about thirty meters or less."

"You think we could do that?"

She scanned the terrain and seemed to sniff the air. "Probably. I'd head down the hill, that way," she indicated where the ridge they were on curled slightly southeast, "which would keep us out of sight, and once we were at the bottom we'd be downwind, so we could work our way up to the next ridge and a better vantage. Maybe get into one of the trees."

She definitely knew what she was doing. No surprise—they'd told him that Caroline was one of their best hunters. Xander could tell he had a lot to learn. "You'll have to show me someday. But since we're not doing it tonight, maybe we should head back?"

A few quick flashes of light—meteors—illuminated her as she nodded. "Sure. We've found out what we wanted to know."

They made their way back through the darkened jungle carefully; Xander remembered Sakura recounting her terrifying run through this forest after her mother was hurt, and her heart-stopping encounter with a creature like a cross between a hunting cat and some kind of predatory beetle. It wasn't likely such a thing would come after them, though; there were two of them, adults, and armed.

That did trigger a thought. "Caroline, there's something that's been bothering me about this island."

"Yes?"

"Well . . . it definitely has a lot of life on it, of all different types, but somehow it seems to me—especially after all the scary stories you guys have told us—that there's, well, *too many* predators. Are there really enough prey animals around to sustain all the things you've talked about—these tree krakens, hillmouths, that panther-insect thing that Sakura ran into, the," he gave a shudder, "raylamps?"

Caroline laughed softly. "You'd think not, wouldn't you?" she said. "Dad thought the same way, but it's not that simple, it turns out. The raylamps were actually the clue. There weren't *that* many of them, and then they just kept *coming*. They're opportunistic predators, but they're also scavengers, something like pretty dumb sharks. They were coming in to attack us from a long way around, probably out into the ocean nearby. We started keeping track of individual predators when we could, and you'd see a pattern of them coming in, and then *leaving*."

Light dawned. "Oh. You mean, their hunting grounds aren't all that limited. Because they're aquatic—well, amphibious."

"Right. They get to use the ocean to move around the continent better than they could on land, they can hunt (at least some of them can) in the water as well as on land, and they can even go to other nearby islands or other faraway parts of this floating continent, way far away from us."

"So you're saying that some weeks or months there's probably hardly any big predators around, and others there are way too many."

"Something like that. At least, it makes sense of what is, as you say, hard to explain."

They walked a bit farther in silence. "So..." he finally said, "how do you feel about staying here? I mean, if we're really marooned here for good?"

An indrawn breath and a pause answered him. He could see her profile, silvered by comet-light in the night, turn to him and then away. "Well, if we're really marooned for good, what does it *matter* what I feel about it?"

He grinned. "I suppose it doesn't make a difference to the world, but it still matters to how we think about it. Right?"

"Hmm. Yes." She was quiet a few moments. "I don't think I'd mind it too much, as long as things keep going pretty much as they are."

"How do you mean that?"

"I mean...well, recovering as much civilization as we can, building more of a sort of community than just surviving." Another flash of her smile in the dark. "I mean, we were proud of discovering iron ore and making our own metal on this floating coral-continent, but having you guys come in with all your equipment and extra know-how? Boy, does that make a difference."

Xander hadn't gone through all that with them, but he could remember everyone's relief at knowing there was a real doctor available. "Yeah. Like...your family proved you could survive without anyone's help, if you had to. But you don't want to go back to having to."

"Right! That wouldn't be fun." Her voice was serious now. "It...almost broke us, once. I remember that. We hit a low point that really *did* feel like we were shattering into pieces. As Sakura said to me later, from outside it might have been almost silly; after all, human beings on Earth lived for generations without even as much as we were shipwrecked with."

Xander nodded. "But they hadn't lived their lives the way *we* do, so it's a lot harder on us to go back; we expect so much more as, um, just normal life."

"Something like that." She paused, glancing around.

"What is it?"

"Something *was* following us. But when I stopped and looked at it, it gave ground."

"Should we run it off, or what?" Xander squinted in the indicated direction; the omni's enhanced vision showed a faint infrared glow, but he couldn't really tell much about how big or what shape the creature was.

"Let's see if it follows us any farther," Caroline said. "It did back off when I looked at it; maybe letting it know we're aware will be enough to make it go elsewhere."

Continuing to walk with the knowledge that *something* might be following them gave Xander an itchily creepy feeling between his shoulderblades, but if Caroline could walk on as though nothing bothered her, so could he. "Is it still following?"

"A little longer." They went on for a few more seconds, then she nodded. "It's gone."

"You've got really good ears or something. My omni wasn't showing me much of anything."

"Good hearing and more practice. I'm still the best hunter here, and if you don't get good at listening and hearing in this jungle you'll end up dead."

"I'll have to practice more, then. We can't afford to lose any of us, that's for sure."

She was quiet for a while. He noticed her looking up often. "What are you looking at?"

"The place where the Sun should be," she said.

For an instant he wondered what she was talking about—it was the beginning of Lincoln's extra-long night, so the sun wouldn't be up for a long time. "Oh. That's right, Sergeant Campbell said that Lincoln's star wasn't visible from Earth."

"Which seems *really* odd to me. Maybe a small nebula, at *just* the right distance, could be blocking the light without heating up and giving away the fact that there was a star behind it... but that seems really unlikely to me."

Xander thought about that. "Maybe unlikely, but what other explanation is there? Aliens like the Bemmies hid it somehow? Why? And if you were going to do that, wouldn't you try to hide it from *all* directions?"

"I... don't know. It just seems awfully unlikely to have happened by accident."

"True," Xander conceded, "and we do have proof there *were* ancient alien civilizations, but even so... everything in life's pretty unlikely, right? You and me having this conversation, for instance; means that all the factors in the universe came together to have *me*—and not all my parents' other possible kids—be born, the same thing happen for you, both of us to end up on the same colony ship on the same trip, both of us to be on *separate* shuttles that somehow survived and made it here... right?"

Her laugh had a faint embarrassed air to it. "Yes. And the fact that our Earth has a moon that's *just* the right size and distance from it to provide a perfect eclipse is pretty unlikely too. Your point; the fact that something's unlikely isn't a great argument. But I would like to know what it is that's blocking that light. I'd *really* like to know."

"If we're ever rescued, I'll bet we'll have a chance to find out," he said. "But we didn't bring any astronomy gear with us, so I guess we're stuck not knowing as long as we're here."

"Unless," she said slowly, "it *does* have something to do with Lincoln itself."

He looked at her; in the dimness he almost missed the slight turning-up of her lips. "Stop that! You're *trying* to creep me out."

"Maybe just a little," she said, and laughed.

A distant spark of light caught his eye, a momentary flicker as it became visible then hidden behind the trees. "There's Sherwood Column," he said.

"Oh, good, we're almost home!" He saw her touch her omni. "Hi, Mom? Yes, we're not too far out now. What? Oh, goody. See you!"

He found himself walking faster, trying to keep up with her. "Hey, what's the rush?"

"Mom says there's dinner waiting for us—plus some hedral-and-vineberry pie!"

That sounded delicious. He started jogging. "First one there gets the bigger slice!"

"What are you, *six*?" she demanded, but she was laughing. And then she was sprinting ahead of him, her omni's vision letting her avoid obstacles as though it were daylight.

"Hey!" Xander took off after her, laughing himself.

Chapter 17

"That's good, Francisco, Hitomi, keep doing exactly that. We're making great progress," Whips said.

Hitomi flashed one of her bright smiles and Francisco nodded seriously. "*Si*, it is going well."

Now that he was finally recovered, Franky had really wanted to show he wasn't lazing around anymore; that, along with the real need to move emergency provisions and stow them inside *Emerald Maui*, provided a perfect opportunity to let him and Hitomi work together. Whips was supervising them while he worked on carefully removing the damaged propulsion unit from the former lifeboat.

Whips watched as the two youngest colonists continued to carry in rations and stow them away in their assigned crates. Franky's artistic eye for detail and Hitomi's obsession with precision were actually very useful here; together they would make sure every package was stowed *exactly* the way it was supposed to, they wouldn't forget to secure the layers as instructed, and they wouldn't move to the next storage crate until the one they were using was full and properly secured. Whips would, of course, help them whenever something really large needed to be moved or carried.

He turned his attention to the crumpled drive jet. "All right, Sergeant Campbell, Dr. Kimei, this is the last chance. I am about to cut one of the main supports. Once I do that, this thing is *never* going back on *Emerald Maui*."

"Just to verify," Laura's voice responded, "nothing you are doing will reduce *Emerald Maui's* seaworthiness. Correct?"

"That's right, Mom...Laura," Whips said. "Had Xander and Tav check me on the cutting plans three times. It might actually make things better; this engine's basically dead weight and the outrigger morph has to work around it right now. It can probably morph faster and be a more unified outrigger support once the jet's gone."

"Then I say go ahead. Sergeant?"

"I concur. Honestly, even your best models didn't convince me ol' *Maui* was ever gonna fly again. Take the parts we need for the distress probe."

"All right! Proceeding."

The last permission acquired, Whips turned his focus to the engine's supports and fastenings. *Have to be* really *careful with this,* he reminded himself for what was probably the fifteenth time. *This is the heart of the distress probe.*

More accurately, it was *one* of the key pieces of the distress probe, but probably the one with the most uncertainty to it. It had been agreed upon fairly early that they could afford to remove the ejection charges from *Emerald Maui,* and the maintenance manuals had shown that those were surprisingly easy to access (for heavy manual labor and a lot of cursing values of "easy"). Testing on a couple of them had verified both the power and reliability of the self-contained rockets. A triad of the bare-bones omnis found in a case aboard *Emerald Maui* made up a sufficiently powerful and self-monitoring control and sensing "brain," and a careful repackaging of the power coil stack from one of the three excavators (which would henceforth serve as a spare parts source for the other two) had provided the energy storage for the probe; it was currently hooked up to the main reactor output, to verify the maximum capacity storage and internal discharge rates.

My job's still easier than making the Trapdoor coils. Whips had one eye check on the kids' progress—still going well—and then returned to focus on the support. The precision laser cutter glowed in readiness, and Whips' omni projected the exact cut path for minimal structural impact and maximum usability. He gripped the customized handholds and began the cut.

The cutter proceeded smoothly through the extremely tough carbonan and titanium matrix. "Tav, how're the coils coming?"

"Now that the doctor is helping? Very well!"

"Did you thank Melody for the suggestion?"

"*Oui*, many times. She is watching now, even."

"Glad it looks like it works," Melody said, with an audible attempt not to sound *too* proud of herself. "I just thought of it when you said that usually coils are laid down and customized with nanomanufacturing approaches."

That was true enough, Whips thought. But making the jump from "nanomanufacturing" to "my mom the doctor could program nanomanufacturing devices" was a little different.

She'd been right, though. The rather stupid nanodust available from the Nebula Drive, combined with some of the internal nanorepair installed on the heavy machinery, provided the potential foundation for assembling high-precision coils with nanomanufacturing. What Mel had seen that no one else had quite put together was that a modern medical professional had the tools and knowledge to specify nanooperation on a detailed and very tiny scale—a scale more than sufficient to produce the coils in question. With Tavana, Xander, and even Whips to help, it had turned out that Dr. Kimei's expertise could transfer to that domain very well.

The main support gave forth a musical chime as the last portion of it was severed. Whips stopped and evaluated the situation. *One more cut on the other side, and then I can unfasten the rest with less destructive approaches.*

"Whips, can you move the next box closer?" Hitomi asked. "We just emptied the last one."

"Down in a second," he answered. He inactivated the laser cutter and put it down safely on the upper wing before he let himself slide down to the ground, using his two long side-arms to grip and slowly ease him over the edge; when you massed as much as he did, even short falls were to be avoided.

He did his usual grab-slide-grab walk to the loading area, and tossed aside the empty box. A quick movement wrapped his arms securely around the next crate, and he was able to use his rear gripper-pushers to help drag it up the ramp. "This one's heavier than the last," he muttered. His griptalons hooked into the top and pulled it off, and he lifted his body to get a glimpse of the inside. "Oh. Dried and smoked capy. No wonder. That's a lot of meat."

"Thanks, Whips!" Francisco said. "These go in the red-marked storage areas, right?"

"You got it, Francisco," Whips agreed. He snagged one of the broadfront-wrapped packages before he headed back down the ramp; as an omnivore with a marked preference for meat, this kind of thing was his favorite snack.

Feeding the woodsmoke-flavored meat to his grinders a little at a time, Whips clambered back onto the damaged wing of *Emerald Maui* and resumed cutting.

It took about an hour to finish. He felt the universal tool in its wrench configuration suddenly exhibit more resistance, and knew he'd reached the last few turns; the stress was torqueing the bolt in its threads. "Hitomi, Francisco, you both still inside *Emerald Maui*?" he called.

"Yes," Franky answered. "We are resting right now, on one of the cases."

"Okay, stay there. I'm almost about to finish this, and when I do the jet engine will fall straight down. I don't want anyone getting hurt."

"Okay, Whips, we'll stay here. Can we watch through the port?"

"Of course you can. Let me know when you're there, then I'll do the last few turns."

"Wait . . . okay, we're both at the port!"

Whips gripped the wrench tightly in both arms and pulled. The bolt turned grudgingly, a faint screech and vibration warning Whips that they were deforming and stripping the threads. He winced, his engineer's instincts jabbing at him, even as he reminded himself that it didn't *matter*, they weren't going to be using that hole for anything again.

Without warning, the wrench swung around, there was a sharp *snap!* sound, and the heavy engine assembly plummeted with a *thud* into the mound of soft dirt that had been placed to catch it. "Done!"

"Our engine?"

"It's out. We'll have to get one of the excavators to haul it to our work area, but I think it's all intact."

"What, you can't carry it home yourself?" Sakura's voice asked over the link.

He gave a hooting chuckle. "I might *drag* it a little ways, but no, it's way more than I could really carry. If Maddox wants to—"

White, harsh light suddenly flared behind him, so bright that the daylight looked dim and he had dark, dark shadows standing out before him; the protective ports of *Emerald Maui* had gone black in automatic response.

Slewing around, Whips shuttered his eyes to slits to see a massive, brilliant streak of light brighter than the sun curve down and across the sky; there was another flare visible over the rim of the horizon, and then the sky was clear, with a whitish trail marring the blue above.

"What the *hell* was that?" Campbell's voice demanded. "Whole forest lit up!"

"Meteor—biggest I've ever seen," Whips said. He triggered a query to the SC-178 satellite in best position to observe the area. "Wonder if it hit anything."

The satellite responded immediately, giving a clear image of the area.

Whips blinked. It looked like a bullseye, with rings around it.

Rings that were *expanding*.

"Oh-oh," he heard himself say, then commanded the software to perform some quick estimations.

He looked at the results. "Screaming *Vents*," he whispered. "Everyone," he began quietly, then triggered a full emergency alert. "Everyone, listen! That meteor must have been *huge*. We have incoming waves that are...ten meters, maybe higher."

There was an explosion of color from the forest; dozens, hundreds of the quadbirds were taking flight, heading away from the impact point.

"Mother of God," Campbell said. "Get back here *now*."

"No time," Whips said, feeling a sense of terrifying unreality washing over him as he realized the full situation. "We'd never get to either of the columns in time. There's...five minutes, maybe less, before it gets here!"

"The kids—"

Whips looked around. "The only chance is for us to ride it out in *Emerald Maui*."

"You'll have to throw off the mooring ropes," Xander said. "Don't make *Emerald Maui* have to fight against the water, it'll lose."

"Right," Whips said.

"Whips, what was that? What's happening?" Hitomi was standing at the base of the ramp, looking in the direction of the impact, where the white trail was slowly twisting. *Was there a wrinkle on the horizon already?*

"Hitomi, Francisco, get back inside the shuttle *now*," Whips said. "Choose one of the acceleration couches and strap in. Strap in *right*, like we were taking off."

"*¿Qué?*" Francisco asked, a touch of fear in his voice. "What is happening?"

"A big, big wave is coming and it's probably going to wash us out to sea," Whips said, as he slid quickly off the wing again. "It'll be fine if you're strapped in, so *hurry!*"

"Do what Whips says, Francisco," Sergeant Campbell's voice said over the omnis. "You too, Hitomi. He's in charge there. Do *exactly* what he says."

The two swallowed visibly, but ran back up the ramp.

Whips turned and got all three arms around the jet engine. Digging his grippers into the soil, he heaved, yanking it a meter towards him. *Stretch* and pull, another meter, though his support segments were complaining.

"Whips, what do you think you're *doing*?" Laura said after a moment.

"Trying to save our chance to send a distress call," he answered.

"Don't be stupid!" Sakura snapped.

"I'm watching. If the waves look like they're getting too close—"

"—Then it might be too late," Laura interrupted. "Get inside that shuttle, *now*."

"Only a few more meters to go," he said, stubbornly hauling on the heavy engine.

"Whips, you will need time to *secure* that damned thing," Campbell said emphatically. "You can't have it banging around inside the shuttle when those waves hit!"

He felt his hide ripple in chagrin. He hadn't *thought* of that, and Campbell was right.

But still, there might be enough time. He knew where the holdfasts were, and there were securing lines right there, and . . .

"Whips, your responsibility is for Hitomi and Francisco," Laura said, and her voice was hard and cold. "You will *not* take a chance on leaving them alone in *Emerald Maui!*"

Sky and Vents, she's right, and I can't argue it. With a hooting groan of frustration, Whips let go and whirled around, squirming toward the fore end of *Emerald Maui*. He hit the quick-release hooks on the mooring lines, all five of them in sequence, then headed towards the ramp as fast as he could go. *Vents, I almost forgot.* He sent another command to the shuttle, and saw the outrigger-wing and the tail-vanes reconfiguring, folding up, melding as closely as they could to the hull.

In the distance, there was a vague hissing sound, and he glanced over with one eye, to see water streaming *away* from them, towards the horizon—a horizon that didn't look quite *right* anymore. "Oh, *crap.*"

The water level was actually *dropping*; he remembered that this happened sometimes on Earth, but he'd thought that a floating continent wouldn't show *that* kind of effect. As he reached the loading ramp it dawned on him; this was, compared to the floating continent, a *local* event.

Water could recede. And it could come *back.*

Or, a part of him thought in calm horror, *the part of the continent that's now* above *water might just snap off in time to be hit by the wave and dragged across the rest of it.*

"Are you both strapped in?" he shouted up the ramp. Even as the two called back "Yes!" he was triggering the ramp to raise and seal. *Was the front airlock... no it was still open!* He sent another command out, saw that one closing too.

Have to strap myself in fast. The external monitors now showed the approaching wave, something that might well subside to invisibility, a ripple, in a hundred kilometers or so, but not now, not yet, and with the massive skirt of the pseudo-continent to guide and raise and focus it...

He gave another Europan curse as he realized that *Emerald Maui* had never had any of its hold-downs configured for Bemmies, unlike LS-5. He began feverishly dragging out the straps, rehooking and distributing them for his very inhuman body shape.

There was a rumbling whisper in the air now, and the water was rising back to the shore. Rising *over* the original shoreline, foaming around *Emerald Maui's* keel. "Get ready, Francisco, Hitomi!"

He had one line fastened across himself, but there were two more to go. The water rose swiftly, streaming around the aft part of the ship, making a rippling fountain where it struck the mostly-circular casing of the removed jet engine.

Whips ground his interior masticatory array in frustration as the engine began to slowly move under the pressure of the water. *So close. Just* five more meters *and it'd be inside.*

But there *hadn't* been time, and while Whips yanked the next securement line tight he admitted that to himself. He'd have been *maybe* to the base of the ramp before the water started to hit, and then...

The light dimmed, and his gaze snapped towards the porthole. Francisco looked too, and screamed.

A massive green-and-white-and brown *cliff* of water towered above *Emerald Maui*, blocking out the brightness of sun and sky.

Whips twined all three of his arms around the third securement line and gripped *hard*. "Hold on!"

And then the world spun and whirled and heaved as the *tsunami* smashed down on *Emerald Maui*.

PART 3

POSSIBILITIES

Chapter 18

Sue Fisher leaned back in the bath, luxuriating in the hot, soapy water and the fact that after tomorrow she'd have seven glorious days off. Orado Station had gone back to the old routine in the months since *Outward Initiative* had staggered its way into the system, and she happily embraced routine after *that* disaster.

Seven days would be more than enough to go planetside, visit Mom and Dad and maybe her brother if he wasn't somewhere on the other side of the world by then, and hit the beaches before going inland. She'd already talked with her friend Kate about doing some mountain-climbing in the middle of the week. And some nightlife afterwards sounded *real* fun.

She chuckled to herself. "Boy, sounds like I've planned a lot of work for my vacation," she admitted, and stretched a bit in the water—that stayed in place courtesy of the carefully-controlled spin of the station providing a good ersatz version of gravity.

There were, of course, fun things to be had in her job, apart from the long, slack periods that let her catch up on all the reading and viewing she might want—fun things like the letter she was reading through her retinal display. One of the fast couriers had brought back the latest edition of *The Journal of Interstellar Spaceflight*, which featured the final version of "*Analysis of an in-flight malfunction of a Trapdoor drive system: implications for the structure of Trapdoor space and the potential for self-reinforcing resonant field disturbances*," which was the long-winded title of the article she had authored with Numbers.

The letter was from Dr. Helen Glendale, current Director of the Board of the Interstellar Flight Foundation, which published the JISF. Dr. Glendale—a sidewise descendant of *the* Dr. Glendale who had been instrumental in the initial colonization of Earth system way back when—expressed her reaction to the paper:

"...a startling set of claims bolstered by some solid theoretical and practical research. The Kryndomerr Resonance is an invaluable discovery in the purely scientific sense; all the reviewers agree that this discovery is almost certain to provide us with insights into the actual nature of Trapdoor space and, perhaps, higher-order spaces beyond it.

"In a more practical vein, of course, this discovery will undoubtedly save countless lives. On the basis of this paper a detailed Industry Safety Bulletin was prepared and immediately dispatched to all colonies and relevant organizations. We already—"

ERRRT! ERRRT! ERRRT! ERRRT!

Sue froze; reminiscing about the prior disaster and involved as she was with the letter, she thought for a moment she was flashing back to the earlier alarm.

Then it penetrated. *Another emergency alert?*

She lunged to a stand in the tub, comfort forgotten as she hit the *drain and dry* control. Hot air blasted from the side vents, scouring the water from her body and her hair; she ran her fingers through the shoulder-length brown waves and they dried swiftly, even as she triggered the connection to Orado Port's AI control.

A shiver of déjà vu sent goosebumps chasing themselves across her body even in the hot-air blast, hearing the received transmission.

"Mayday, Mayday, Mayday," it began—and like that other time, the words were not those of a controlled automated system or the self-assured confidence of the command crew of a vessel, but the exhausted, frightened, but somehow victorious sounds of a living human at the end of their endurance but not of their hope. "Orado Port, this is *LS-42*, lifeboat off of *Outward Initiative*, out of Earth. If anyone can hear this...please send help. We are out of food. Multiple systems failed. Mayday, Mayday, Mayday..."

LS-42? One of the lifeboats arriving *now?* It should have arrived months ago, if it was going to come at all! "Orado Port, what resources do we have in that area?"

"The nearest vessel to *LS-42* is a manned construction and mining vessel, the *Bill Williams*. The nearest official Orado vessel is the OIS *Zenigata*."

"Do either of them have a good intercept vector for *LS-42*, and if so, how long until they can reach the lifeboat? Or would I be better off taking *Raijin*?"

Orado Port could calculate all the variables involved faster, really, than Sue could possibly have spoken the question; it was more programmed courtesy than anything else that made the system wait for her to finish the query before answering it. "If you pilot *Raijin* with your customary skill, you would arrive with emergency supplies approximately thirty-one hours before *Zenigata* could intercept and forty-seven hours before a best-case maneuver by the *Bill Williams* could bring them in range."

So much for the vacation, she thought with a touch of ruefulness—but only a touch. This was what she was employed for, and no one would kick about her having to reschedule in *this* situation. "Transmit to *LS-42*: Mayday received, *LS-42*. Help is on the way. Emergency Watch Officer Susan Fisher, Orado Port. Repeat message until you get an acknowledgement or I have arrived at *LS-42*, whichever comes first. Who's the medical officer on watch?"

"Doctor Haven, but he is not cleared for emergency flights at this time. Doctor Ghasia has been alerted."

She nodded. *Buriji Ghasia . . . he's good enough.* And almost as small as Carolyn Pearce, so that would help in the transport area. "I'm getting ready. Can you make sure *Raijin* is loaded with food, clean water, and medical supplies, as well as basic repair materials?"

"Already underway," Orado Port replied. "Do you intend to undertake a tow?"

"Advice? You can run the numbers a billion times faster than I can."

"*Bill Williams* will bring them in faster than you could manage the tow. *Raijin* could be used to transport critically ill patients if it was necessary to do so faster than the tow could manage, but the OIS vessel has a good infirmary on board so this may not be necessary."

She grimaced, looking at a secondary display of data she hadn't read in months. "But it might be, at that. Given the passenger and crew complement and the known supplies on that ship, they should all have starved to death at least two months ago." She stared at the faint moving dot in another display. "I don't know how *any* of those people could be alive now."

Chapter 19

The stench was the first thing that struck Sue as the airlock door finally opened, a smell that combined the worst features of sweat, bad breath, mildew, and rot. She coughed, almost gagged before her nanos cut in and damped the reaction, and hesitated for a moment at the threshold. Modern ships and space stations had highly advanced filtration and atmosphere reclamation systems which were designed to remove even the worst odors from the air and leave it with only the faint background scents that had been determined to make air smell "fresh." Even *Outward Initiative*, cut to pieces by its own Trapdoor field, multiple systems failing, had mostly cleansed the stench of smoldering insulation and other damage by the time it had arrived in Orado.

What that implied about the conditions in *LS-42* was horrific.

"Hello?" she said.

The interior lights of *LS-42* came on, low, and Sue sucked in her breath, even in that miasma.

In some ways, it wasn't as bad as she had feared. Despite the smell, the cabin wasn't strewn with rotting litter. But what *was* there was still heart-wrenchingly, nauseatingly bad.

The majority of the acceleration seats were occupied, by what looked like half-mummified corpses. Dressed mostly in the simple two-piece ship undergarments, ribs and hips and shoulder bones jutted out under skin somehow both slack and taut. Most of them had their eyes closed, but though they seemed either unconscious or dead, there was no sign of relaxation; the faces were lined, even with the skin tighter against the bones, with fear and exhaustion.

The normally bright surfaces of the shuttle were dimmed, scummed over with thin but definite traces of mold or some other growth. *The air in here feels humid; that must have promoted the growth. Water reclamation falling behind?* Sue's analytical, professional brain was assessing the situation, even while the remainder of her was screaming in sympathetic revulsion.

Doctor Ghasia stepped in behind her; his low voice murmured something she thought sounded like "Besime'ābi!"—almost certainly a prayer or expression of shock.

At the pilot's position, one figure turned its head. Long hair straggled, brittle and dull, around the woman's skull-like face.

But then the eyes widened and the faintest smile appeared on the cracked lips. "Oh, thank *God.* You're here. You're real, aren't you?"

"Yes, we're real." The faces she could see were vastly distorted from those on file, but she thought she could make out key features. "Josephine Buckley?"

"That's ... my sister." It was clear even this much conversation was exhausting. "Jo ... Jo died last week."

One week too late. And that would make her ... "I'm sorry. Jennifer Buckley, then. How many ... ?"

"My omni ... says five of the nine of us are still alive."

I wouldn't have bet on one. "All right. Just ... relax, as much as you can. This is Doctor Buriji Ghasia. He's a fully qualified surgeon, general practitioner, and nanomedical technician. He's going to take care of you all."

Sue keyed up the system overrides they'd established in the rescue of *Outward Initiative* and managed to link up with the badly-damaged shuttle, as well as the local nano-net, and hook that into her own and that of the doctor.

"Well, now ... astonishing. This is some kind of nanosuspension. But ... it appears to be a sort of *ad hoc* design," Dr. Ghasia said after a moment, frown lines appearing on his ebony brow. "Nothing standard at all."

"No one ... had any suspension applications available," Jennifer said.

"No need to talk," Ghasia said quickly. "There's nothing *wrong* here, though obviously it's not an ideal solution in many ways. But ... I *think* we have a good chance of saving the rest of you."

"I could get back to Orado Port in a few hours," Sue said. "Should I take one or two of these people with me?"

"Give me a few minutes to do an actual *evaluation?*" the doctor said, a testy edge to his accented voice. "It is possible that will be necessary, yes, but for now begin bringing in the supplies. The most important thing to do is to get proper nutrition started, and to improve the conditions in this cabin."

"Got you." Sue sprang back easily through the airlock back to *Raijin*—whose air-recycling systems were already noting the offensive material from *LS-42* and responding with nanoelectronic speed—and grabbed the nutritional nanomedical packs in one hand and her engineering troubleshooting kit in the other. Another quick bound brought her into *LS-42's* cabin, where she locked the case of nanomedical packs to the chair nearest Dr. Ghasia, and turned to the main control panel.

As they'd deduced would be the case, the board had switched over to almost entirely manual systems, and was showing vastly more red and yellow than functional green. Her access codes allowed her to query the systems that remained at all operational.

Jesus. Reactor's working, but only on low-power mode . . . why would that be? It seemed obvious that the *passengers* had no reason to throttle the power down, so some aspect of the disaster must have caused it. That partly explained the condition of *LS-42* right there; virtually all of the reactor's low-power mode would have gone to recharging the Trapdoor drive for the allowable periodic jumps. In fact . . . Sue nodded, feeling her lips tight with empathic understanding. The low-power mode wasn't even *quite* enough to maintain the jumps. They'd have had to stretch out the recharge interval. No wonder it had taken so long; not only had these people had to—somehow—get the landing shuttle working after the Trapdoor pulse shut down multiple shipboard systems, but also they'd had to make the Trapdoor drive take far longer to get them anywhere.

She shook her head slowly as the data from the shuttle and her own engineering diagnostics built up the whole picture. No, it wasn't surprising it had taken this long. What *was* surprising was that they'd gotten here at all. Multiple system failures, several of which could have—*should have*—proven fatal, and none of the crew were on record as having any of the relevant skills needed to diagnose and repair those failures.

But the fact that this shuttle, with apparently no trained engineers *or* medical people aboard, had somehow ended up here *did* add a new mystery, a mystery she'd thought of as solved by default months ago:

Where are LS-5 and LS-88?

Chapter 20

"Jennifer?" Sue said softly.

The young woman's eyes opened and looked around; for at least the third time, Sue watched the tension in Jen Buckley's face ease into relief as she took in the clean brightness of Orado Port's main medical facility. "I still keep thinking I'm going to wake up on *LS-42*."

"I can't blame you. You spent a bit over a *year* on that ship. But you're safe now."

"How are the others?"

"All five of you are making a good recovery, Doctor Ghasia assures me. The four who...didn't make it have been preserved for whatever their next-of-kin want done."

Jen's brown eyes closed, a flash of pain. "Jo..."

"I'm sorry." Sue reached out and touched the too-skinny shoulder. At least now there was starting to be a feel of some muscle underneath, a living tension in the skin instead of the horrific half-deadness of the people they'd found on the shuttle. "The doctor says you're well enough to talk for a while, and as the Emergency Watch Officer responsible for addressing this situation, I need to start getting to the bottom of what happened. We can't just drag people's private data out of their omnis without permission, so that means we need personal consent, at the least."

"Oh." Jen Buckley got a distant expression on her face, then laughed. "God, where do I *start*? None of us ever had any idea we'd be..." She trailed off.

"I know. Let me give you a starting point. We know what happened to *Outward Initiative*—and why. We know—"

"You know *why*?"

"Yes." She outlined the solution she and Numbers had come up with in those days following *Outward Initiative*'s arrival.

A hollow chuckle from Jen. "Well, I guess we can't sue them for negligence. They were so careful that they almost killed us all. Without knowing it."

"Basically, yes. I don't know it it helps, but because the crew *did* get *Outward Initiative* back to us reasonably intact, we were able to make this discovery and by now most of humanity's faster-than-light fleets know about it. With luck, this won't ever happen to anyone again."

"I hope to God not," Jennifer said. "Sorry I interrupted you."

"No, its fine; you've got far more to bother you than I have. Are you ready to talk?"

"I . . . guess. Yeah, I suppose. The others aren't ready?"

"Your father and mother are still in serious recovery. That level of starvation causes biochemical changes that nanos aren't programmed well for, so getting them back in functional shape is taking time. Barbara Caffrey should be well enough soon, although she was also in pretty bad shape. William Fields seems okay, but he, well, clams up and seems nervous about saying anything to us about what happened."

"Bill? Not talking?" For a moment, Jen looked puzzled. Then a look of comprehension spread across her face. "Oooohhh, I get it. He's afraid that he might be held *responsible*."

"What? Why?"

"Umm . . . Okay, so if you know about the disaster, I guess you know that when we got cut away from *Outward Initiative*, just about everything shut down *hard*?"

"Yes. Primarily caused by the Trapdoor radiation pulse."

"So, yeah. Everything shut down and we were all freaking out and I was screaming and I think my sis . . . Jo was too."

"Were you the pilot?" Neither of the Buckley sisters seemed old enough, but she *had* ended up in that chair.

She shook her head. The dead-dry hair had been cut off; the new fuzz starting to replace it was a glossy brown, the best sign of returning health Sue had yet seen. "No, I . . . well, I sort of was later but that was because our real pilot, Mr. Costigan . . ."

"He didn't die *en route*?" The detailed examination of the bodies had taken a back seat to the care of the living, and the forensic specialists from Orado itself had just arrived.

"No. He seemed okay for the first few days, then he got really sick." Her quick description of the symptoms confirmed Sue's immediate guess.

"Was he out of his chair when the accident happened?"

"How did you know? Yes, he was in the airlock, trying to check on a warning light, when it happened."

Sue nodded. None of the actual acceleration berths were in line with the airlock, which meant they were all more-or-less shielded from the radiation pulse that would have come straight down the access tube. "That makes sense. Trapdoor radiation pulse. The rest of you didn't get enough of a dose." She brought up visuals of parts of *LS-42* in her omni, linked it to Jen's. "What I'm interested in, really, is how you *got* here. For instance, do you know why the reactor was in forced low-power mode? What about these indications that the Trapdoor coils here and here," she pointed to one section towards the front end of the shuttle, and another underneath, about halfway back, "were accessed? The coils obviously worked to get you here."

"Well, they weren't at first," Jen said. "Bill said they'd, um, microwelded themselves together at points around the windings. So we had to take them out and make new ones."

Sue blinked. "How did you know *how*?"

"Well, Barb—Barbara Caffrey? She's a research information specialist. She was bringing a whole technical library with her, and once Bill figured out how to trick the rear door seal to open, she was able to get it activated."

"Mr. Fields did that? He's listed here as a minimum-technology mechanical specialist—the kind of person who does things like simple plumbing, non-autoassisted electrical wiring, and so on."

Jen grinned; that still looked unfortunately skull-like in her current condition. "Well, yeah, but he tinkers, you know? He did a lot of stuff in his spare time—he talked a lot about it while he was showing us what to do. He'd ask Barb about something and she'd look it up, like the manual for the reactor, and then he'd dig into the diagrams and logic and figure out something. The low-power mode was because we couldn't operate the reactor on full power anymore."

"Why?"

"Because we needed to take out some of the coils for the wire, to replace the wire on the old Trapdoor coils."

Sue blinked at that. "Wait. You mean Mr. Fields *disassembled* some of the harvesting coils in the reactor and then started it up again? And it *worked*?"

Jen nodded. "Is that hard to do?"

Sue bit her lip. "In *theory* . . . well, you'd have to remove *just* the right coils. In *just* the right positions. Or you'd end up with an imbalance in the fields keeping the fusion reaction stable and the whole thing would shut down." *No wonder they were kept on low-power mode.* "And your research specialist Caffrey and Mr. Fields did the other repairs?"

"With the rest of us helping." She took a deep breath, and the reason for her nervousness was suddenly obvious with her next words. "Um . . . I did a lot of the coding for them."

"You coded the suspension app?"

"Well, with help from the database. Yeah."

"So you're an application oversight specialist? That wasn't on your file."

"I just did it as a hobby. I didn't mess it up, did I?" she asked, and swallowed. "I mean . . . people *died*."

Sue considered the answer carefully. Technically . . . yes, of course Jen had messed up parts of that design. Even with the best database to help, suspending the function of the supremely complex machine that was the human body—and especially the brain—was one of the most delicate and difficult tasks known to humankind.

But that wasn't the right answer. "You did an astounding job, Jen. It took you . . . months, I guess, to do the repairs, and by then, even with rationing, you knew there wasn't enough food. All of you would have died—*all* of you, Jen, without question—if you hadn't done what you did. The fact that more than half of you got here alive tells me that you may not have done something *perfect*, but you did something more than good enough."

Jen's eyes were haunted. "But . . . I lost *Jo*. And Zahir and Alia."

"Even professional doctors don't save everyone, Jen. And there are trained doctors who wouldn't have *tried* making suspension code like that—and they'd have lost everyone." Sue made sure Jen's eyes focused on her. "Be *proud* of what you accomplished. You're not going to be in trouble over this, and neither is Bill Fields."

"You can't *know* that."

Sue grinned herself at that. "Oh, yes I *can*. Because it is my job to decide where the blame goes, and I'm not dropping any on people who managed to pull off a miracle. How did you navigate home?"

"Oh," Jen said, "that was the easiest part. Once we made sure we were going towards the right star, it was just sleep a long time, wake up and check that Orado's star was still pretty much in the centerline of our course, and sleep again." She looked sad for a moment. "The only person worried about it was Alia."

Alia Manji had been an astronomer, one of the few pure science types headed for Tantalus (although she had a number of more practical skills that made her a good candidate). "Why was she worried?"

"Because of the extra star. Said it shouldn't be there. But that wasn't a problem, if you just ignored it you could tell that all the other stars were just where the databases said they should be."

"Wait," Sue said. "What do you mean, *extra star?*"

Chapter 21

"No offense," a sleepy-eyed Portmaster Ventrella said, cradling his coffee in his hands like a precious jewel, "but this had better be *very* good, Sue."

"You know I wouldn't drag you out of bed for anything that wasn't," Sue said. Then her conscience poked her, and she said reluctantly, "Well, it's not life-or-death...not directly now, I think, but..."

The Portmaster sighed and gave a weary grin. "Ehh. You've got me up, let's talk about it. I'll decide whether I'm docking your pay or something later. Has to do with our most recent survivors of shipwreck, eh?"

"Indirectly. It started with Jennifer Buckley mentioning something that sounded very odd, and so I went to check it out. She said that their onboard astronomer was concerned about an 'extra star.'"

"What did she mean by that?" Ventrella took a sip of coffee, looking slightly more awake and certainly intrigued.

"Literally that—a star in the sky they could see that wasn't on the charts."

He frowned. "Well...we're fifty light-years from Earth, and the charts are almost entirely put together based on Earth data. Surely there must be *some* stars in our skies that aren't visible from Earth."

Sue shook her head. "Not...really. Modern telescopes, especially the wide-baseline scopes that turn large chunks of a solar system *into* a telescope with an effective mirror diameter of millions upon millions of kilometers, can spot even brown dwarfs at ridiculous distances. Oh, there are stars we humans see in the sky that we wouldn't be able to see with our naked eyes from Earth, but there's pretty much nothing in our sky that some Earth-system telescope didn't spot decades back."

Portmaster Ventrella scratched his beard and then nodded. "And this star...?"

"...would be a problem even from the naked eye point of view. They said it was the brightest thing in the sky, and that Alia estimated it was a fraction of a light-year away from them. A G-type star like the Sun, or Orado's own star."

"Oh. Oh, my. We can spot the Sun—not easily, but with good viewing—with the naked eye from here. And you say this mystery star is, what, about ten light-years from here?" He obviously remembered the distance that *Outward Initiative* had been when disaster struck. "So it should be easily visible to us, then."

"Once I *looked*, yes. It's about a magnitude 2.26, but mostly visible from the non-settled hemisphere of Orado. Nothing extraordinary about it—there's plenty brighter—so it didn't really call attention to itself. I'm still surprised it didn't get flagged by any astronomers, but that's a mystery for later."

"But that means that Earth should have seen it *easily*. It should have been in the naked-eye catalogs. Yes?"

"It *should*. But it wasn't. And I've checked actual images of that area of the sky from Earth. This star *does not show up*."

There was no trace of sleepiness in Michael Ventrella's eyes now. "But *we* can see it."

"Yes."

He regarded her for a moment. "All right, give me the rest."

Sue laughed with an embarrassed edge. "You do know me, I guess."

"You wouldn't have come here with just that, strange though it is. So...?"

"So I slightly abused my authority and hijacked a few minutes from the Orado Wide Baseline to take a quick survey of that star and surroundings." She triggered her omni to dump the key images to a display.

The Portmaster stood slowly, gaze riveted on the brilliant green-white-brown marble in front of him. "My...God. Is that..."

"A planet. In the Goldilocks Zone. Spectroscopy says positive for free oxygen in an oxy-nitro atmosphere, water, and chlorophyll."

"My God," he said again. "So this sometimes-invisible star

has a *habitable* world around it?" He gave a grin that was filled with a tense disbelief. "Isn't this the kind of thing that should have ominous background music as an accompaniment?"

Sue Fisher shrugged. "It is creepy, yes."

The sharp eyes appraised her. "You've got more."

"Well, more what I don't have. I don't know what's hidden it from Earth, or whether it's still hidden—though it probably is, since the latest data from Earth I have is only about seven years old and it still doesn't show this star. But we also are still missing two lifeboats."

Ventrella stared at her. "You cannot be serious. Why in the name of all that's holy would any of them have headed for some unknown star when Orado was only ten light-years off? Isn't it much more likely that, for whatever reason, they just didn't make it here? After all, *LS-42* barely did."

"I know, Portmaster. I have no idea why they might go towards a different, unknown star. Well, one, perhaps, in the case of *LS-5*; they had limited consumables and one of their passengers was a Bemmie who simply wouldn't survive a long trip without appropriate water treatments that they couldn't give inside the craft, and that family had a particular connection with that Bemmie. That would still seem crazy to me, but then, I know all sorts of things the passengers of those two shuttles might not have.

"And yes, of *course* it's much more likely that they simply didn't make it—died minutes or hours or maybe weeks after most of their systems went down and they just couldn't make enough of it work to get home on." She drew in a breath. "But maybe... just maybe... they didn't."

"I can't authorize a faster-than-light jaunt on 'just maybe,' and for something like that, you'll want something like..." his eyes narrowed, then a grin flashed out. "Oh, clever."

"I thought you'd like it."

"You want to send a survey team there, ostensibly to examine this impossible new system and see if they can find out anything unique that might explain why it's been apparently invisible for centuries, but also because a survey team's going to have the best chance of finding any trace of castaways."

She nodded.

"Well... that *is* a thought. And I suppose you want to go with the survey group."

"Technically it could still be a search-and-rescue. Though I'd be the only person who officially *knows* that."

"Hmph." He couldn't hide the smile that remained behind the neatly-trimmed beard and mustache. "I will...consider it. You've got a decent case. I'll see if there's the right personnel for this wild-lifeboat hunt, and the resources to support it."

"It might be possible to—"

"Officer Fisher, don't say anymore. Let me look at the possibilities and figure things out on this end on my own."

"Yes, sir."

Ventrella gave her another smile, though a small one. "I'm on your side, Sue, but even if you're right, this isn't a trivial expedition you're talking about. I'm not sure we've got an appropriate Trapdoor-capable vessel around right now, and outfitting a new one would take months. We might have to wait that long before it's practical."

"All right, Portmaster," she said, and forced herself to relax. "There's no rush; If they made it to a livable planet and they're still alive *now*, I can't imagine a few days or even weeks make much difference."

Chapter 22

Even without Whips' terrifying message, Laura would have known that something was horribly wrong. With no visible warning, the quadbirds and other flying creatures suddenly burst from their perches and flew away, whistling and hooting and screeching, all in a mingled, multicolored mass that arrowed off to the south.

Almost in the same moment, she could see movement on the ground and the trees—animals large and small running, scuttling, swinging through the branches, and all going in the same direction. A herd of capys hurried straight through the center of the clearing. As Akira came up next to her, she saw a tree kraken bound through the area from tree-trunk to tree-trunk. She released her grip on the sill, realizing her hands *ached* from the tension. "The other girls—"

"All safe." She heard the rapping of feet coming up the stairs; at the same time she heard the rapid dialogue between Whips and his crewmates.

Then she couldn't believe what she was hearing. *That crazy boy is trying to save the engine when a* tsunami *is coming!*

It took both her and Campbell to get Whips to accept that there was no sense in this quixotic attempt and concentrate on getting himself inside and strapped down.

Sakura was next to her now, and her face was white under the dark tan. "Whips..." she whispered.

"He'll be okay, honey," she said, trying to convince herself. "Those shuttles are tough and he knows enough to strap in well."

"*Emerald Maui* isn't configured for a Bemmie passenger," Akira said quietly. "I hope Harratrer had time to—"

"*Hold on!*" came Whips' voice—and then a rumbling roar that cut him off.

Sakura didn't scream, but her grip on Laura's arm was tight as a tourniquet.

Then Laura heard a noise—a hissing that became a rattling, rushing sound, and a deep rumbling underneath.

A brown-gray carpet burst into view, enveloping, tearing and crushing the undergrowth, grinding it down and sweeping the remains up into the tide of destruction that was already more running mud and debris than water. Laura heard screams of disbelief, some of them her own, as the tsunami surged across the clearing below. The temporary shelter that had been their town square, their meeting place and theater, was torn from the ground, its solidly-anchored pegs no more able to resist that savage torrent than they could a bulldozer. Over the public channel she could hear Tavana's disbelieving curses in three languages; Xander was murmuring "no, no, no" over and over, and she could hear Pearce praying.

The tsunami flood reached Sherwood Column, and Laura gripped the sill harder as she *felt* it, felt the vibrating impact of water, mud, and debris being dragged and ground against the base of their home. "My God, Akira, will the column hold up?"

Akira's face was pale, but he answered, "Of course it will. Remember how hard it was to cut into."

But his eyes met hers, and Laura shivered, seeing the real answer: *I don't know.*

The water was *roaring* now, a snarl and a deep basso thunder and a shrieking hiss all combined. The level rose higher, a wave in truth, driving hard against the trees and columns, sending fountains of spray a dozen meters into the air. There was a groaning crack, then another, and now trees were falling, torn from their roots and then dragged down, to collide with other trees or the bases of columns and be stuck, barricading the flow until its implacable force tore the trunk to splinters.

A screeching, grinding sound from below, and with horror Laura saw the ramp-door to the column ripped away, drowned and destroyed in the black-brown flood. "Is everyone upstairs?" she demanded.

"We're all here, Mom," Caroline said, her words shaking like the column itself.

The sound of rushing water was coming from *inside* now, the water pouring into the lowest section of their house, the foyer. "If this keeps rising—"

"—then there's nothing we can do," Akira said grimly. "All we can do is—"

There was a sudden shock that transmitted itself through Sherwood Column, and now the water was *thundering* inside. For a crazy instant Laura harbored the insane conviction that the water was coming up the stairs, charging up for her and her family.

But the water levels weren't nearly that high yet, so what...

"The bottom floor—it's gone!" Melody shouted. "We're hearing a waterfall going down through our house into the island!"

"Naturally," Campbell's tense voice said. "Get that many tons of water and who-knows-what on that one floor, it had to give way."

"Ours, it has a solid bottom," Tavana added. "That will not happen here."

A third time the water rose, and more of the trees—wooden and otherwise—leaned and fell with groaning, splintering sounds that blended with the growling thunder of the *tsunami*. A writhing shape was briefly visible in the horizontal cataract—an immense wormlike thing, twin to the creature that had nearly killed Whips on one of their first nights on Lincoln. But huge as it was, its strength meant nothing to the meteoric flood; it was dragged back under, hammered against stumps, crushed and swept out of sight, farther into the flooded woods.

Sherwood Column thrummed like a bass string being struck by an angry god-child; another of the columns they could see shuddered visibly and then tilted, fell. The girls screamed, even Caroline; Laura only kept herself from doing so by clamping her mouth shut, and she could see the fear in Akira's eyes when she glanced to her husband. *None of us will survive if the column falls into the flood...*

She closed her eyes and held on, hoping that she would not feel the terrible disorienting sensation of the room she stood in *tilting...*

Then Laura became aware that the roaring was diminishing, more a grumble and hiss, and even that fading. She opened her eyes and looked down.

The water had stopped its headlong flight; for a few moments it eddied in seeming confusion, and the sound of their indoor cataract ceased. Then the water began to recede, flowing away, dropping down.

In a few minutes, there were only scattered pools across the devastated floor of the forest.

Laura glanced around, assuring herself that all of her family—minus Hitomi and Whips—were there and safe. "Sergeant, are you all okay?"

Campbell's shaken voice replied after a moment. "Except for our boy on *Emerald Maui*, all present and accounted for. You?"

"Everyone's fine here."

"Then we'd better go check out our columns pronto; you saw that one fall, right?"

Laura understood his point. "All right, everyone grab your go-bags and get outside now . . . wait." Realization struck her. "Sergeant, we may have a problem."

"Dammit, yes," Campbell said. "You might not have a floor to walk out with, just a long drop to nowhere."

"I'll go check it out," Sakura said.

"*I* will do it," her father said, his voice iron-hard in a way it very rarely was; Laura saw Sakura freeze, then nod.

In a few moments Akira was back. "The whole bottom floor is gone, including storage. The steps end hanging in midair, a long way from the entrance."

"You have any rope?"

"I will check, but most of that was stored on that floor."

"We've got some, so no biggie. You'll have to go out your largest window. Wait a few and we'll be along to help."

"Understood. We'll wait." She raised her voice. "Whips? Hitomi? Francisco? How are you?"

Moments stretched out, and there was no answer.

"Whips? Answer immediately! Hitomi, are you there? Francisco?"

But no matter how many times she, or the others, repeated the words, the airwaves remained silent.

Chapter 23

Hitomi gripped the arms of her seat tightly, focusing on the panels in front of her. She had to concentrate, because if she didn't, she'd skip from thought to thought to thought in a blur, and it would be scary. Way too scary.

Whips was still out there, and the wave, the wave was coming, a *big* wave, they said. No, wait—she heard the dragging sound of the big Bemmie moving fast behind her.

"Are you both strapped in?" he said, his voice having that hooting undertone it got when he was breathing hard.

"Yes!" Hitomi answered, feeling relieved that big brother Whips was onboard. She heard Francisco also answer, from his acceleration seat nearby.

"Good," Whips said absently. She heard him fumbling with the straps, and for a moment she could see the straps in her mind, remember the exact position of every strap and fastener, and she swallowed hard. They weren't right for a Bemmie.

She heard a rippling rumble that she knew was a Bemmie bad word, and the whispering of the straps and the muffled jingle of fastenings intensified. She tried to turn her head to look, but the seat wouldn't let her. *Of course not,* she thought, remembering the diagrams in the emergency courses, arrows and vectors showing how sitting the wrong way in the seat could hurt you bad.

"Get ready, Francisco, Hitomi!"

Hitomi heard it now, a faint whisper like a stream...but a stream that from the sound was passing *under* them. She couldn't see it, not from where they sat, but the water was coming. But this didn't sound so bad...

The light from the port dimmed, and her gaze snapped up to look.

Her first thoughts were that it was beautiful; a massive green wall streaked with foam moving in almost-patterns across it. The focused part of her started trying to count the lines of foam and see if they came in patterns.

But then Francisco screamed, and suddenly Hitomi felt as though something had switched on in her, and her focus was gone. Now she could see it coming, a monstrous wave that was blotting out the sky. A spurt of cold-spiky terror ripped through her, stealing her breath; she couldn't make a sound.

Lines creaked behind her, the sound of Whips' arms entwining themselves tightly around them. *"Hold on!"*

The wave began to curl, and Hitomi's terrified memory replayed another book, a chart of a wave, hitting shallows, *oh, yes, the skirt-shelf that sticks out from the island*, and at the same time all she could do was gasp in and then hold her breath, redoubling her hold as the whole world turned green-white-black—

A gigantic hand slammed into *Emerald Maui*, skidding the lifeboat sideways with a grating, ripping screech, but still, that wasn't so bad, if the hull held out everything would be fine—

And then *Emerald Maui* tipped and began to spin, tumbling over and over, smashing randomly into things now caught up in a murky blackness that enveloped them. Hitomi did scream now, feeling the pain of the high-pitched sound in her throat but hearing none of it over the roaring, grinding, grating thunder that beat on the ship's hull from every direction.

Something flew over her head and hit the wall with a thud that was barely audible in the din, and then it flew past again, striking with a deep, pained *whoop*.

It's Whips! He's . . . he didn't get strapped down enough! She cringed as far down into her seat as she could, trying not to think about what would happen if Whips fell on her.

The tumbling and crashing went on, spinning them around and around, and Hitomi was getting dizzy, her stomach starting to protest as the ship not only rolled but whirled around, nose to tail again and again and then flipping end over end before going back to rolling, and all the time *hitting* things, grinding-growling battering, and poor Whips tumbling around like a pebble in a can.

Then, without warning, the tumbling slowed, steadied. The

ship was still careening and bounding along, but she rolled once more, righting herself, *Emerald Maui* finding her natural pose. She was rolling and rocking in what had to be waves, but smaller waves, waves *underneath* her. Light began to return, the splash and ripple of waves clearing the blackness from the front port.

But...

But there was *nothing out there*. With a creeping horror Hitomi stared at the port. Instead of waves or the waving trees of the island, or even wreckage, there was *nothing*, just a...a milky whiteness. For a moment she wondered if it was a cloud, fog, thick fog, but the day had been clear. And this didn't have the look of fog. It was somehow swirled yet unmoving, her eyes just able to sense some kind of texture to it, but it was a texture that looked like...like...

"The port," Francisco said, and his voice seemed loud in the ringing silence. "It has been clouded. Like the glass on the shower doors at my old house."

Hitomi gave a huge sigh of relief. Now that Francisco had said it, it was obvious. The front window of *Emerald Maui* had somehow become the color of milk. Light sort of came through, but not images.

And hearing Francisco talk made her feel better too. They'd come through that disaster. "Whips? Are you okay?"

Silence.

She remembered the thudding tumble and swallowed, then unstrapped herself. "Whips!"

The Bemmie was sprawled against the back wall, arms splayed and crumpled under him. She could see that he was badly hurt, there were lumps and twisted parts that just didn't *look* right, and...

"Hitomi...he is not breathing," Francisco whispered.

"Oh no...Mom. *MOM!*" she shouted. "Mom, Whips is hurt, he's not breathing, what do I do, Mommy?"

There was no answer. Hitomi heard herself starting to breathe faster, panic creeping up behind her like a monster, as she realized that her connection was dead. Her omni showed the red slash symbol that meant no connectivity to the main net. And a red slash through all her family's icons. Only Francisco's and Whips' were still green and ready.

"They can't hear us," she whispered, and heard her voice squeak as she did. "Whips isn't breathing and they can't hear us!"

"*Dios mio,*" Francisco said. "Then...then we're alone."

That thought, and the terror in Francisco's voice, was almost enough to bring the monster panic down on her. Alone, with Whips dead or dying, no way to talk to anyone...

But then she remembered all the other scary days, and Mom and Sakura and Dad saying that the most important thing was not to panic...and most of all she remembered her sister Sakura on one of those days—sitting herself in the pilot's chair and trying to land *LS-5* by herself. She remembered every detail of that moment, just like she could remember almost everything, and she saw her sister's face, turned to look to the side, so pale it was almost white, and it finally really dawned on Hitomi how scared Sakura had been.

So scared.

But she had done it. She had taken *LS-5* from the depths of space all the way to the surface, flown them through a storm, and landed them. Crashed...but they'd *lived*. Because Sakura hadn't let being scared stop her.

Hitomi closed her eyes. *Focus. Focus on something. Think. Think. Think. What do we do?*

It was hard. It was so, so very hard to focus, her mind wanted to run in all directions at once. But that was why she needed to focus, why she did focus so much when she could, because if she didn't find something to concentrate on, her mind skipped all around from one thing to another. It didn't bother her but it confused everyone else. And it did make some things difficult—*stop that. Concentrate. Whips, we need to focus on Whips.*

She swallowed again, then moved to Whips' side.

Not breathing. Francisco's right. A flash of a medical manual, saying two minutes without breathing or heartbeat would result in brain damage...

No, wait. That's humans. *Wasn't there something about Bemmies? Mom...*

And suddenly she had it, a talk that Mom had given them on first aid, on emergencies...

"...now for one of us two minutes without breathing or heartbeat is very bad," her mother said. "But with Bemmies it's different. If they're not breathing on land that is a bad sign, but it's not quite that desperate. Bemmies are mostly aquatic creatures, and they store up extra oxygen in what we call Klugman's

Organ—sort of a specialized liver-type organ which is solely for binding oxygen in a highly concentrated manner that can be released back into the bloodstream."

Hitomi had never felt so thankful for her peculiar memory as she did then. She shushed Francisco as he started to say something, and listened *hard* to her mother. "So you have at least half an hour, and maybe as much as an hour and a half, before you need to worry about oxygen. Even if the heart stops, the brain and other organs have protections against low oxygen conditions. Ten minutes without heartbeat is about the limit, though."

"But Mom," Caroline said, "You can't give a Bemmie CPR, right?"

"Not the way you do to humans, no," Mom said. "But there is a way..."

Hitomi straightened up. "There's a way to help Whips!" She looked around desperately. "If we can just figure out *how*..."

Francisco looked at her, then nodded. "You tell me what we need to do. We'll figure out how." He nodded again. "We will."

Chapter 24

Harratrer was rising through a nightmare. The Europan sea surrounded him, filled with darkness and menace. There were no Vents in range, and with horror Harratrer realized he was *alone*. He was in the high waters, nearer the Sky than the Earth, away from all safety.

And there was something coming, behind him even as he fled. Something huge and swift and *hungry*.

An *orekath*.

He jetted as hard as he could, but the water seemed to have turned to gel thicker than a stickyseal. He moved forward centimeters at a time, forcing his trembling body to drive forward, but instead of a dozen meters he covered perhaps one, and the hunting bellow of the creature was upon him.

A tentacle shot out from the darkness and caught at him, two of them, gripping him hard. Harratrer wriggled desperately, felt the crushing grip sliding down his body in a wave of stretched and bruised ligaments and shift-plates, but he was moving forward, he might just—

And then a *second* set of tentacles caught him just as he escaped the first. Once more he drove forward, almost escaping, but *again* he was caught, the *orekath*'s mighty grip squeezing him, releasing, then constricting again...

He gasped suddenly and gave a hooting cough that echoed through the cabin, a cough driven by something pushing with emphatic broad force on his back, then withdrawing.

"*Whips!*" Hitomi nearly screamed. "Stop, Franky, stop, he's waking up!"

I'm...I'm on Emerald Maui, *not in the ocean,* Whips realized fuzzily. Agony rippled through his body. "What...happened?" he managed to force out.

"Oh God, oh GodOhGodOhGodOhGod I thought you were *dead* and we didn't know what to do and everything was rolling and then it stopped but no one answers and then I remembered the treatment Mom told us about once but neither of us was *strong* enough to do the compression because you're so big and—"

"*Hitomi!*" The sharp bellow turned into a gasp as pain lanced through him at even the simple motions of speaking loudly. "Hitomi," he said again, this time as quietly as he could, "Slowly. The wave hit us, I remember. But I..." the terrifying moments came back to him. "...but I hadn't finished strapping in and I started slipping out as we rolled and banged against things, and then..."

Francisco nodded, coming into Whips' view, his usually chocolate-olive complexion slightly grayer with worry. The light itself seemed somewhat washed out, misty, as though the ship was caught in a fog. "Then you *did* come loose and you tumbled around the inside of the ship," he said. "You missed hitting us by *centimeters*. More than once."

"You weren't breathing when we got to you," Hitomi said tremulously. She swallowed and went on, "and we tried calling Mommy and Sergeant Campbell but no one answered and we both almost panicked but I remembered what Mommy and Saki said about panicking so we tried to think. And I remembered Mom and Dad showed us what first aid for a Bemmie was, including Bemmie CPR. So we tried to compress your body the right way—"

"*Si*, but we were not strong enough," Francisco said. "Then Hitomi thought that maybe we could do it with the adjustable seats."

"Seats?" Whips managed to reach back with his top arm and feel the reclined back of the seats above him. "Oh. Oh, that was *clever*, Hitomi. You dragged me over behind one of the rows of seats and reclined and raised them in a wave."

"Franky got the rhythm," Hitomi said. "He called out one, two, three, and we would hit the raise and lower controls like he said."

Probably overcompressed and torqued plates all out of place—the rear contours of those seats aren't anything like the right shape.

But it did *work.* "Good work," he managed to say. "But all that tumbling did hurt me."

He turned his attention to his interior nanos, and even though it hurt he sucked in a breath. *Screaming Vents, I'm in bad shape.* His lower left arm was broken in three places—the shift-plates not merely dislocated or torn from their muscle-ligament joins but cracked across. His top arm was mostly functional. The lower right arm didn't have any actual breaks but a lot of dislocations.

But the rest of him...he shuddered and had his nanos trigger a surge of both emergenine—his people's equivalent of adrenalin—and pain suppression before he dared look again. His mind cleared temporarily, but that didn't make things look any better.

His right bottom eye didn't respond at all. If it was still there and working, the exterior cover shutter was too badly damaged to work, and while he wasn't in any way a doctor, if he read the nanosignals right the eye itself was damaged. His beak and masticators had been struck a few heavy blows; they'd probably work but it would be really, really painful. His main body structure...was hurt. Hurt bad. Some of the damage was new—the improvised CPR *had* done damage, some of it significant. No point in telling the kids that, of course. But he was bleeding internally in at least three places. Several organs were damaged, though he thought the nanos were getting that under control.

But overall...*I...I don't know if I'm going to survive this.*

Whips saw Hitomi and Francisco looking at him with terrified, tense faces, and knew that that didn't matter. As long as he was alive and conscious, he had a job to do.

"Okay...kids," he said. "First...good work getting me awake. I'm getting my nanos on this. Hitomi, there were nanopacks stored onboard. I know your mom tailored at least a few of them for me. Do you know where they would be?"

"Ummm..." Hitomi closed her eyes and visibly calmed herself. Whips crossed two of his functional fingers in the gesture Sakura had taught him long ago; if Hitomi could focus enough to get into the right mindset, she'd be able to recall the exact location of everything she'd seen packed on the ship. That was one of her talents, even if the obsessive focus had previously gotten her in trouble.

The little girl's face lit up, the blue eyes snapped open. "*Duh!* They're back in storage, port side, rack seven, shelf three!"

"Rack seven, shelf three," Francisco repeated and dashed unsteadily back.

Unsteadily? Oh. Now that he thought about it, he could feel *Emerald Maui* rocking back and forth in a significant swell. Whips triggered a connection to the ship, was relieved to sense its immediate response. The main operating systems still working, at least. He sent the reconfiguration codes, and those, too, seemed to be working. He felt *Emerald Maui*'s motions flatten out noticeably as the rear rudder-vanes and the outrigger extended themselves to operating dimensions. *That will make it easier for the kids, anyway. And reduce the amount of motion my body has to put up with.*

Francisco came back with a nanopack. "What do I do with it?"

"Let me look at it first." Sure enough, there were the markings on the green-blue gel pack that showed that Laura had tweaked the performance of this healing pack for Bemmie biology. "Take about half of it and smear it on my face, including near my eyes. Then I guess I'll have to swallow the rest." He didn't look forward to that; nanogel had a particularly *nasty* texture for swallowing and the taste was not anything he'd recommend, either. But if even half the nanos could get on the job, he'd have a better chance of living.

The two children carefully applied half the gelpack to his face area, then Hitomi squeezed the repulsive ooze into his mouth. Somehow Whips kept his throat from sealing itself shut and forced the vile sludge down. Ideally it would be injected into him, but the pack wasn't injector-equipped and he wasn't up to instructing either of them on locating, identifying, and applying Bemmie injector assemblies.

That's about all we can do right now. I'll have to wait and see if I need more packs . . . or if the packs can't do the job. Without a doctor or at least trained medical nanotechnician to direct the nanos they had to rely on general programming, which might not be ideal for this situation. So much damage in so many areas . . . maybe he *should* do another pack right away. But there were only so many of the packs available at all.

He gave the rippling Bemmie equivalent of a shrug, and winced as that reminded him of just how widespread the injuries were. He'd rolled around and around in the cabin, bouncing off almost every hard surface. It had been a minor miracle that he hadn't landed on Hitomi or Francisco.

"Okay. First thing...we're stable, we're not sinking, I can get a response from *Emerald Maui*, so we're not in immediate danger. Air processors are working fine, reactor's online. So next thing is getting contact with the others."

The fact that the children hadn't been able to make contact didn't mean much. Inside the ship, the omnis depended on being able to make a good relay connection with *Emerald Maui* and her inlaid antenna arrays, and there were plenty of reasons that might not happen in an emergency. Whips engaged the shuttle's main transmitters. "Sherwood Tower, Sherwood Tower, this is *Emerald Maui*, come in."

There was no response, and Whips noticed there were a couple of yellows and reds showing on the comm board. "I couldn't get Mommy or the sergeant on the line. Neither could Francisco," Hitomi said.

No connectivity with the array? How in the depths did that happen? The array's molded into the hull, multiple wavelength support inherent to the design, just tune and transmit. I'm not seeing any damage in the actual structure of the ship, and the actual connection cable's also molded in, so...

Whips froze, and the tension sent sparks of pain dancing along his body. *Oh, I have a* bad *feeling about this.* He saw the misty-fog light illuminating the cabin, a light that came from the forward port—the internal lights dim or off because they weren't needed.

With an agonizing effort, Whips pulled himself forward a meter or so, giving him a chance to look directly forward.

For an instant, he thought they were in a fog, for there were only faint shadows visible in the port, most of it a pearlescent, almost featureless white. But then he was able to make out a dim but visible pattern within the white, a pattern of an innumerable set of lines and streaks large and small that covered the entire port—a port whose exterior had a hardness equal to diamond.

"Oh, *Vents*," he sighed.

The *tsunami*. It had picked them up on the north side of the continent, then dragged and tumbled them across *kilometers* of the semi-landmass, in what had become not water but churning mud filled with fragments of natural carbonan fibers and spikes that were the key reinforcement and strength of the floating continents.

Emerald Maui had been literally tumbled through a gargantuan grinding and polishing cycle driven by the power of a small asteroid impact. The diamond-hard dust and mud had scoured the exterior of the shuttle to the point that its reinforced viewports were almost opaque...and had scraped and gouged at the rest of the hull until, undoubtedly, the antenna array had been ripped off or ground down to the base hull, completely eliminating it as a functional connection to the world.

There was no way to communicate from inside the hull. And Whips knew that he was in no shape to leave.

Which meant that he was going to have to send one of the kids outside.

Chapter 25

Sergeant Campbell surveyed the forest from ground level and found himself shaking his head. *Doesn't stink* too *bad yet, but it will, and that'll be just the beginning.*

If their columns had been located on the northern edge of the continent, it might have been better in some ways; the wave wouldn't have had a chance to pick up much debris, it would have been more water than anything else. But they'd been kilometers inland and south, and what had reached them had been a set of massive waves of mud and wreckage. Mud, filled with broken rock and torn branches and dead creatures that had failed to flee in time, was many centimeters deep, in some places maybe a meter deep. Undergrowth had been completely stripped away or crushed.

At least getting the Kimeis out of their possibly-dangerous home had been easy; plenty of rope had been stored in an upper room of Campbell's column, so it had just been a matter of throwing it up, getting it braced in the largest window, and letting everyone slide down carefully.

He turned back to contemplating Sherwood Tower, and saw Xander coming back from his inspection. The expression on Xander's face told him what he didn't want to hear. "No good, huh?"

Xander screwed up his face. "I...don't know. The real damage is near the entrance, where the water came in, ruined the floor, and then started pouring through. Stuff would get jammed in the opening and then broken by the force of the water running behind it, and that kept stressing and wearing at the column..."

"Will the column repair itself? I know there's some parts of the island that do that, right?"

"Dr. Kimei—Akira, I mean—isn't sure. There *are* living cells in parts of the column, but we've seen these islands weaken and try to cut out dead parts before, so if the columns do that..."

He remembered their island practically drawing a dotted line labeled *tear here* around where they'd settled and imagined the equivalent on the Kimei's column. "Damnation. Then they *do* have to move out."

"I think so. We made ours pretty roomy, so they can probably squish into a few rooms for a while."

"A while, yeah, but we've got to get things working again fast. What about equipment and supplies? What'd we lose? Everyone?"

Tavana's voice replied. "Sakura and I, we have finished the hike to the shore along the line we guessed. There are small pieces of the shelter but nothing worth keeping. The excavator... we cannot find a trace of it except a few drag marks we think it made, but even that we cannot be sure."

"So it's down and out in the sea. Never getting that one back," Campbell said. "Anything at all we can recover?"

"Nothing," Sakura answered. Her voice sounded numb, a tone of shock the sergeant remembered hearing on other disaster-struck worlds. "Nothing that was below about three, four meters. You saw what happened inside your column too. The shelter and everything in it... gone." She went on in a whisper he didn't think they were meant to hear: "It was all so beautiful and *alive* and now..."

"It will be again, Saki," Laura Kimei said. Her voice held less shock and more determination. "In fact, it *is*, not that far from us. Compared to the size of this continent, that impact wasn't all that big. Our real problem was that we were very near the point of impact and we're on the very narrow end of the continent. The modest ridge of mountains to the west of us broke the wave's impact on everything past that; there's only minor damage beyond the mountains."

"Well, that's encouraging," Campbell said. "Means that if we have to we can mount expeditions to go there to get supplies. Or move there, if there's no other choice."

"There are a lot of downed trees," Pearce said. "If we have to move, we could probably build rafts to transport everything a lot easier than walking."

"Good thinking." Campbell took a breath and asked the

question he'd been dreading. "Dr. Kimei, what about the medical equipment? Your nanoprogramming station and such? Last I knew it was in the shelter."

She was silent for a moment. Then she sighed. "Yes, the station's gone. And I don't think there was a spare in the cargo."

He closed his eyes, gave a quiet curse.

"But," Laura went on, "Xander and Tavana had managed a backup download of the station's programming, and the nano-packs I'd already produced and programmed were either in the upper storage area of Sherwood Tower or were on board *Emerald Maui*. If we can find—"

"*Got them!*" came a shout from Melody.

"What? Who? You mean Hitomi, Whips, and Franky?" demanded Sakura.

"I mean I've found *Emerald Maui*," Melody said. "It didn't sink! It's in what looks like mostly one piece, anyway."

A connection ping later, everyone's omni displayed a satellite image. Magnified to the limit of the SC-178's admittedly inexpensive and small telescopic capabilities, in the very center of the image was a tiny shape, a blunt streamlined shuttle-shape with a long outrigger sticking out from one side.

"Where are they, Mel?"

The image zoomed out, showed a blinking red dot where *Emerald Maui* was. The dot drifted to one side of the display as the scale increased, and then the edge of their own continent came into sight. "They're about a hundred twenty-seven kilometers from us, almost due south right now."

"If they're alive, why haven't we heard from them?" Laura asked tensely. She paused, then asked quietly, "Do we have any evidence they are alive?"

Campbell frowned. *Emerald Maui* didn't seem to be damaged enough to make it likely its passengers were dead, but things that would kill humans—or Bemmies—didn't have to hit hard enough to break the hull of a landing shuttle. "I... don't know, Ma'am. I wish I did."

"Wait, Sergeant," Tavana's voice said. "Until the wave hit, we had telemetry from the ship, yes?"

"Yes. But we're not getting anything now, is that it? What would that mean?"

"Well, that is a different point than I was going to make, but yes, there is something in that as well. But what I meant was, I am reviewing the data, and I see that Whips triggered the outrigger morph and tail morph to retract."

Xander grinned. "Ha! And since we can see they're extended *now*, at least one person—probably Whips, since he was hooked up to the ship with authorization—*had* to be alive after everything was over, to extend them again."

"Yes, that is what I think."

Campbell felt a tiny trickle of hope, and heard a deep, shaking breath being taken by Laura. "Then why aren't they answering?"

"That's what's got me worried," Akira said. "Someone was alive enough and conscious enough to extend the outrigger; why in the world wouldn't they make contact?"

"They would," Maddox said promptly. "So they can't, somehow. Sergeant, you've been in ships like that a lot of times before, what could make you unable to talk to people outside?"

"Huh. Lemme think. Honestly, the only times I remember we couldn't do it was when someone couldn't *talk*, or where for some reason there wasn't power to the comm unit." He rubbed his chin, thinking. "But if they got the outrigger extended, there's power. Can't imagine the main ship comm's wrecked—how you could have that happen without killing everyone inside I just can't figure, at least not when we're talking about a tsunami and not a freak accident like what happened to *Outward Initiative*." He thought back over his career. "I remember a few times when we couldn't call out, but that was when we were underground, usually inside some building without molded multiresonance antennas. But that doesn't apply to *Emerald Maui*."

After a pause, Sakura—her voice slightly more engaged, less dead-sounding—spoke. "Maybe it *does* apply. The antennas have to be on the outside of the ship, right? Wouldn't that mud-wave and all the bashing around strip the antennas?"

Campbell blinked, then grinned. "By God, you might have it, Saki. Xander, could you do a model with Tav's help? Could a wave like that damage the exterior antenna integrated array?"

Xander was smiling, shaking his head. "Count on Saki to see the obvious. No, I don't need to model it, Sergeant. The conditions it went through, I'd *bet* on it. That's the answer. They're almost certainly alive, but they can't talk to us."

"Great!" Laura said, and Campbell could *hear* the relief in her voice.

"Not so fast," Caroline said. "I'd really like to believe that. But...if that's the case, all Whips has to do is get outside and his omni will be able to connect. Why hasn't he done that?"

Campbell's feeling of relief faded, and he saw Xander's smile dwindling. Because that *was* the question, wasn't it? There was no way that Whips wouldn't want to contact them as soon as possible.

So why hadn't he?

Chapter 26

The problem, Whips thought, wasn't that he had to send out one of the kids; it was that he had to do that and accept that if something went wrong he could not do anything about it. Sky and Earth knew that there were dangers to going out on a rocking ocean vessel—especially in this ocean. After the tsunami there would almost have to be a huge number of dead bodies, animals that hadn't been able to escape in time, and that meant that the water for many kilometers around, maybe hundreds of kilometers, would be filled with more predators and scavengers looking for an easy meal. Maybe even an island-eater, checking to see if the damage was enough to make the area hit worth tasting.

He looked over at Hitomi, who was carefully laying out a meal on the floor for him, and two more—one for her and one for Franky—on the seats. Francisco was working with his omni, but as Whips watched he shook his head. "I cannot get a connection, Whips! No satellite, no one answers!"

Bite the bullet, as the sergeant would say. "No, Francisco, I can't get one either. I'm pretty sure that the exterior antennas are gone."

Francisco thought about that for a moment, then noticed the food and came over to help Hitomi finish putting the meals together. "Then we have to go outside. *¿Si?*"

"Right," he agreed. "Or rather...one of you has to. I can't go out. Honestly, I can barely move. Yes, in the water I could probably move better than I can out of it, but I would be so injured any predator would sense it."

Hitomi and Francisco exchanged glances, and Whips could

see Hitomi go pale. Francisco's olive-dark skin didn't show the change so obviously, but he could tell both of them had suddenly realized the truth: it was up to *them*.

Slowly, Hitomi put down the sandwich and stepped closer to Whips. "Whips . . . Harratrer . . . you're not . . . *dying*, are you?"

The fear and fright in her voice was so intense that Whips wanted very much to lie, to make her feel better . . . but in these circumstances, he couldn't. "I might be, Hitomi. Even if I'm not . . . I'm not going to be much help for a long time. I might be able to tell you what to do, or how to do it. But actually *doing* things, that's going to be up to you two."

The tiny golden-haired girl stayed bent over for a moment, and he saw a shiver go through her. But then her back straightened and he saw her jaw tighten; for just an instant, despite all the difference of coloring, he could see that she *was* a Kimei. "Like Saki when we landed. She wasn't ready. She was scared like me."

"Just like you."

"Like Tavana. And the rest of us. We did not know how, but we had to," Francisco said. "Your parents, the sergeant, Xander, they are not here." For a moment his expression was touched, not just with fear and uncertainty, but wonder. "*We* have to be the grown-ups, Hitomi."

She nodded. "'Kay. So one of us has to go out."

"That will be me," Francisco said at once.

"Why *you*? I can go outside just like you!"

Whips almost intervened, but stopped himself. Better to see if they could resolve it reasonably themselves; if they couldn't . . .

"I'm taller," Francisco said. That fact was inarguable, as he'd grown three centimeters in the year since the accident, which made him thirty centimeters taller than Hitomi—despite Hitomi having grown twice as much in the same time. "If I have to jump or climb on things, I can reach things better."

"I can swim better than you," Hitomi said. That, also, was inarguable; Francisco could now manage something better than a dog paddle but not much, while Hitomi could swim about as well as any human her age could ever expect to manage.

Instead of immediately arguing, Francisco looked thoughtful. "Hm. But the idea is just go out and try to make sure our omnis talk, right?"

"Right, but what if we fall off?"

"That would be bad, and yes, swimming would be important. But if you are not tall, maybe you could not reach the right part of *Emerald Maui* to climb back up and you would be stuck in the water."

Hitomi blinked, clearly not having thought about that. And Franky was right, Whips thought. Climbing back on *Emerald Maui* from the water would not be easy even for the taller boy; he wasn't sure that Hitomi could do it at all.

"Well...a *rope*! Then you can't fall!"

"But if I can't fall, it doesn't matter who swims better!"

Hitomi opened her mouth, looked offended, then stomped her foot. Then she laughed. "Okay, you go out. If we can find a rope. If we can't, *I* go out."

"It is a deal!"

Whips grinned—a rippling color pattern that probably wasn't visible to the two kids. *Smart. Of course, they've been living with everyone in survival mode for all this time; they've seen a lot of these kind of arguments. They've learned to stop and think.* Even through the aches and dizziness that was trying to assail him, that was a warming thought. *They* can *work together. Without me pinging in their direction every ten seconds.*

It didn't take too long for Hitomi to locate a rope in the rear storage area. The two of them tied off the rope to the base of one of the crash seats, then Hitomi looped it back and around one of the armrests before giving the end to Francisco.

"Why did you do that?"

"Saki showed me that this gives me leverage," Hitomi answered, pronouncing the last word very carefully. "Means I can pull harder."

"Oh. Yes, I see that." Francisco wrapped the rope around his waist, tied it off, then had Whips check the knot. Then, without being told, he took one of his belt loops, opened the clip, and then clipped it onto the rope.

"Very good, Francisco. Never trust one way of fastening a lifeline," Whips said, forcing his voice to sound as normal as possible even though it hurt to talk. "Now, if it starts to come loose, which way will the rope be going?"

Francisco studied the rope, and then pointed.

"Right. So put another knot in the rope before the belt loop clip, so that the rope can't go through it if the main knot comes undone."

Francisco frowned. "But that means I have to untie it now!"

"Yes. But it will be much safer that way. Otherwise the belt loop won't do much to hold it."

After a momentary hesitation, Francisco nodded and, with difficulty, unknotted the rope, tied a simple stop-knot into the rope near the belt-loop, and then retied the rope together. "Is this good?"

"Perfect! Now, let's test how hard Hitomi can pull."

With the leverage, braced feet, and a look of grim determination, Hitomi showed she could drag Francisco backward all by herself.

Whips gave a sigh of relief. "All right. Good. Time to go out. Francisco, before you go, listen to me. The outrigger is below the airlock on that side, but with luck you shouldn't have to get on it. The farther out you go on the outrigger, the more things will move and the harder it will be to walk, so try to just go out on the ladder and make the call." His last sentence trailed off in a sort of hiss.

"Whips, are you all right?" Hitomi asked.

"No. But I'm not feeling much worse yet. Let's get this done." He looked back at Francisco. "Franky—Francisco—look out carefully before you actually step out of the airlock."

Francisco suddenly looked less eager. "Oh. *Si.* The raylamps."

"Or other things." The boy's grim expression reminded Whips that he'd seen Xander almost dragged down and torn apart by the creatures, so his associations with the black stingray-shaped things were about as bad as Whips' memories of them.

Francisco went back into the storage area and came back with a long bush knife, almost a miniature machete. "If one comes at me when the door opens, I will be ready."

All that said, Whips thought there wasn't too much chance of danger in this case.

He was wrong.

Francisco was only starting to lean forward to look out the lock when he jerked back. A black tendril had whipped around the doorframe, and with a wet plop a meter-wide raylamp flopped onto the floor of the airlock.

The little boy didn't hesitate. Instantly his long knife plunged into the thing and ripped back, tearing most of the creature in half. It gave a thin whine, but Francisco danced back out of the way of its thrashing tentacles and then kicked it hard, shoving the slick creature's body out the door. With quieter, damp sliding sounds, two other raylamps dropped from the top hull of *Emerald Maui* and began to feed on their fallen comrade, which was still struggling.

Whips was speechless; he had not expected that. By her expression, neither had Hitomi—and Francisco had now clearly risen in her estimation. "Well...well done, Francisco. Is everything clear now?"

Francisco's hand was shaking with obvious adrenalin reaction, but his voice was *almost* steady. "It looks so. *Si*, it is, nothing else on the hull I can see." He looked around, at areas none of them could see from inside. "Nothing anywhere near me now, except in the water. Which I am not going into."

"No, not time for a swim."

Francisco nodded, then raised his omni to his mouth. "Sergeant? Xander? This is Francisco, on *Emerald Maui!*"

Chapter 27

Relief and fear speared simultaneously through Laura. "Francisco? Thank God! Are all of you all right?"

"Hitomi and I are good, yes. Whips... Whips is not good. He cannot move much."

Then Whips' voice—weak and with the burring undertone of pain and exhaustion—came on the comm. "I'm here... Mom," he said. She smiled and felt tears start from her eyes at the same time. "Relaying through Francisco's omni—I can link through the open airlock door."

"I'm here, Mommy!" Hitomi said. "Whips is hurt bad, can you help him?"

"I'll do what I can, baby girl. Francisco, are you all safe right now?"

"If nothing big comes after *Emerald Maui* we are," Francisco answered promptly. "There are raylamps crawling on the outside here, but if I watch them they aren't too dangerous." She could hear the tension in Francisco's voice and knew he was more frightened than he wanted anyone to know.

"The important thing," Campbell said, "is that you're alive. Thank God for that. Whips, we—well, Saki—already guessed the *tsunami* stripped the exterior antennas. What's your condition otherwise?"

"Most internal systems..." Whips trailed off, took another breath, continued in what was a clearly weaker voice. "... most of them are okay. Life support, power, base controls, even the comm if it had antennas. Haven't tried the jets yet."

Laura had managed to link to the telemetry from Francisco's omni, and through that she could connect to the other two.

159

She heard herself gasp. "Shit."

"*Mother?*" The shocked, half-accusatory cries came from all four of her children—five, actually, since she heard Whips echo it.

"Sorry," she said. "But...Harratrer, you are in worse shape than I thought. What happened?"

A brief explanation clarified it. "No wonder. You look as though you were in two or three wrecks all at once."

"Can you help him, Doctor?" Campbell asked, on a private channel.

"I'll do what I can, but there are things that nanos can't do without outside support. Like moving and resetting bone or, in this case, broken plates. They're not good with draining fluid fast, either."

"How bad is it, Laura?" Akira asked, linking in with his own channel.

She connected the two channels and added in Xander, since he was explicitly in command of *Emerald Maui* by the sergeant's choice, and Pearce Haley. "Very," she said quietly. "His oxygen-exchanging manifold got crushed internally; it's functioning at an acceptable level in air because the major damage is *after* the air-water bypass. But if Whips went into the water and tried to breathe, he'd be running saltwater over an open wound and probably be close to drowning."

She continued, trying to sound dispassionate, clinical. "The impact also badly damaged his Sutter Organ—that's something like a combination of our liver and kidneys—broke multiple internal plates, ripped tendons and ligaments and muscles in multiple places, damaged one of his eyes maybe beyond repair, and he's bleeding internally in at least three other places. He needs surgery, not just nanorepair, and he needs it *soon*. His digestive system's mostly—but only mostly—intact, so he's getting nutrients into the system, but at the rate he's bleeding, even with the nanos trying to shut it down..." Her voice was still calm, but she felt two tears splash down on her arms, which she'd folded across her chest in tension.

"Damnation. How long?"

"If he doesn't get treatment? A day. Two days, at the most."

"Xander, can we run *Emerald Maui* back here by wire?"

There was a pause as the younger man looked over the data they had. When he answered, his voice was grim. "Not a chance.

Without external antennas we can't link directly into the shuttle systems, and the drive systems won't engage with the airlock open—at least not without someone overriding a lot of the safety protocols, and I *think* the interlocks require that someone to be on-site, not remote."

Laura understood what that meant; they couldn't use the omnis to relay remote-control instructions to *Emerald Maui*—at least not without some very clever programming to get around safety features that normally prevented people from doing very stupid things with the shuttles.

"Not that it would matter anyway," Xander went on. "The exterior cameras are completely gone. The antennas also provided the satellite navigation link, so *Emerald Maui* doesn't have that. Internal camera feeds show that even the front port is almost impossible to see through."

"That's something we can work around," Campbell said. "We've got satellite feeds, they've got omnis, so do we. Between all that we could navigate *Emerald Maui* pretty well, good enough that we could get her back here and board her. The problem's those damned interlocks. How long for us, together, to hack a way around them and let us run her with that door open?"

"I really hate that idea, Sergeant Campbell, because I can just *see* a big wave—or nasty animal—coming through that airlock. But..." He thought, then she heard him talking quietly to Tavana, Sakura, and Melody for several minutes. Finally he came back onto the private channel. "Days, probably. At least two or three days, maybe a week."

"At least? No way to speed it up?"

"I'm *assuming* your codes speed it up already, Sergeant," Xander said. "You're talking about disabling some pretty solidly-written safety precautions and not screwing up all the other associated systems. That's not simple work. We can't afford to mess up here; we could brick whole sections of *Emerald Maui*'s systems if we do."

Laura was silent for a moment. *Days. Whips does not have days. If I was there I could help, give him more time...*

"Doctor Kimei," Pearce Haley said, "could you suspend him? The way Samuel did for me?"

Laura closed her eyes and whispered a prayer. "Maybe. Yes, maybe I could. I was looking into that off and on since you arrived. Xander, can you and the others search the archive you have from the medical station, see if you can find my notes on suspension of *Bemmius Novus*?"

"Right on it!"

She switched back to the public channel. "Whips, Hitomi, Francisco, we're working on ways to help all of you. For safety's sake, I'd like you to go back inside, Francisco, and call us back in... in one hour, all right? We've got a little work to do before we figure out how we will get you home. But we *will* get you home, understand?"

"Yes, Mommy," Hitomi said.

"Understood, Dr. Kimei," Francisco answered.

"Got... it," came a weak response from Whips.

In a moment the transmission cut off. "Tavana, Saki, has Xander told you what we need?"

"Yes," Tavana said. "Your archives, we need to find the right material in them. Melody, this is something you can do well."

"Should we start on the safety overrides?" Xander asked.

"Only if that will not in *any* way affect how long it takes to find the nanosuspension data," Laura said. "Understand, everyone: if we can't find that data and I can't apply it in the next... twelve hours," she hesitated, not wanting to say the words. But there was no avoiding the truth. "... if we can't, then Harratrer is going to die."

Chapter 28

"I'm dying, aren't I?" Whips asked over his private channel.

He was pretty sure what the answer was going to be.

Laura was silent for a moment. Then, very quietly, she said, "Yes. Yes, you are, Harratrer. I'm sorry."

"Thought so." He tried to say it casually, but he could hear the pain in his voice too clearly.

"We're working on it," she said. "We're not giving up, and you shouldn't either."

"Got . . . too many things to do to give up," Whips said, studying the side display in his omni. "Franky and Hitomi are getting home and I'll make sure of that, Mom."

The way the sound cut out for a moment told him she'd started to cry. "I know you will, honey. None of my children would let anything happen to them."

"Mom," Whips said, then hesitated. Then he took a big breath—even though that hurt, a lot—and went on. "Mom . . . Laura . . . I love you, you know. All of you."

"Of course I know that!" The flash of anger wasn't directed at him, he knew; it was at the universe that might doubt it.

"Then . . . look, is there *really* a chance to save me? Really, not just . . . hoping?"

"There is, Harratrer. They've dug up my work on suspension of *Bemmius*, and I'm putting together the nanoinstruction set now, with help. I can do the updates to your nanos and the gelpacks with your omnis to transmit. It . . . it *should* work, at least for a while."

"How long?"

Laura's voice shifted to its professional mode. "Estimating the effectiveness is not easy, but...I think we can slow your metabolism and other processes enough to make it possible to successfully revive and treat you...oh, for at least a week and a half, maybe up to two or three weeks. If the suspension works."

That last line told him how much Laura was pushing the edge of their capabilities. *But... that's not so different than what we were doing for the last year, is it?* "If you get it in time, it'll work. How much worse will I make it if I move?"

"*Can* you move? With those injuries—"

"Very slowly, yes. With lots of rests. If I use my nanos to reduce the pain and shock I can do some stuff for a while, I think."

"I...I really do not like the idea of you risking any movement. Why?"

"I need to work on what's going to get us home. There are links that need to be set up for omni access to the ship controls, and I don't want to try to talk Hitomi or Francisco through it by remote. Maybe we won't need that access, but I'm betting..." he took another breath, fighting off the haze that had risen to cloud his thoughts. "...um, betting...yeah, betting that we will. I can't see a way around doing *something* that connects us remotely, and the manual controls will be *really* hard for either of them to use."

She was quiet for several moments; Whips took the time to recover his strength, focus attention on the jobs he was going to have to do. Finally, he heard her sigh. "Harratrer, I've said I don't like the idea...but I know you're right. Just...be careful. Too much effort, the wrong *kind* of effort, could make things worse. And we really don't have much margin for 'worse,' hon."

"I know. Thanks, Mom. I'll be careful."

He switched to the public channel, even as he sent signals to his internal medical nanos to start reducing pain signals and prevent shock. He also, reluctantly, set up a bunch of interlocks that would cancel the analgesics if there were indications of significantly increased damage. *Have to give Laura her chance.*

As the pain ebbed, his mind sharpened slightly. Gingerly he tested his ability to move. His rear "pusher" manipulators were in better shape than his front ones, so he could probably push slowly forward. One of his arms was able to move halfway decently. Two of three eyes were usable. "Okay, everyone, this is Whips on *Emerald Maui*. I'm going to be surveying the nav and comm systems and seeing if I can get them both set up for omni access."

"You sure you can do that?" Xander asked.

"Sure I have to, so I'll do it somehow," he answered.

"We were talking over here and Pearce asked why we couldn't just coach you near to shore with some dead-reckoning—compass on *Emerald Maui* still works, we've got magnetic poles here, we could give you directions and you stop every so often, open the lock, and let us update the navigation. You wouldn't have to leave the lock open until you got real close."

"No can do," Whips said after a minute. "Here, look at these clips from when Francisco was outside." As they looked, he began the slow process of inching around the crash couches and heading for the control panel.

"*Merde*. I see what he means, Xander."

"Yeah," came the sergeant's voice. "You've got a damn good point there, son. Too much debris of all kinds floating in your way. You'd have to either take major risks or move forward at walking speed. And the currents ain't helping you."

"Right. And we can't see the stuff in front of us with the window scoured the way it is." The port was a milky-white; Whips wasn't sure if they'd be able to see an *island-eater* through it.

"No way to clear the forward port? If you could just *see*, someone like Francisco with Hitomi to help would be able to get back to our area pretty easy."

"We'd need a bunch of nanorepair dust to fix the scratches, or maybe a portside polishing rig." He thought a bit. "Maybe, if we could reprogram some of the Nebula Drive dust, but that'd take a while, right?"

"Hold on." There was a flurry of conversation between the more nanoprogramming-conversant members. "About a week and a half is our guess. If it'd work."

"So that's a maybe." He finally pulled up in front of the console, lifted his one arm and, with difficulty, managed to coax the panel to open. "I have to get as much ready here now, before... um, before Laura puts me in suspension."

"Right," Campbell said. "You need my auth codes?"

"I had a subset...but yes, sir, if you could give me the whole set...?"

A low laugh. "Sure, why not? It's not like I have to worry

any of you are out to steal the silverware. Stand by for encrypted transmission," he continued on a private channel.

Whips signaled his Omni to be ready. "Secured reception ready."

It was a quick transmission, relayed from a no-frills spare omni that Franky had stuck on the hull just outside of the currently-open door. Whips tested the codes, saw the proper responses. "Got them. Thanks, Sergeant Campbell."

"No problem. Let me know if there's anything else I can get you."

"Intact antennas?" he asked.

"Ha! Fresh out, I'm afraid."

He narrowed one eye and adjusted focus. Yes, that was the right set of panels. *Just have to make a few switchovers.* He reached out, but his arm was not responding well. His extended fingers brushed the edges of the sunken panel, rebounded. He tried again, found himself almost missing it entirely. After several more attempts, he gave up. "Hitomi, can you help me?"

The little girl was there almost instantly. "What, Whips?"

"See inside that panel?"

She leaned over and looked. "Lots of lights and switches."

"Right. So I'm projecting that into your omni as an overlay—got it?"

"Got it!"

"See the switches I'm marking in red?" It was astonishing how much effort it was taking him to do even simple commands to his omni now.

"Yes."

"Push those switches, and *only* those switches, over to the left. I mean right! Right!" He felt a twitch in his damaged gut from the surge of emergenine as he'd caught his mistake. *If I told her to do it wrong and didn't catch it, it might take a long time to realize why things weren't working.*

"You *sure* you mean 'right,' Whips?" Hitomi was looking at him, worry writ large across her tiny face.

"Absolutely sure. All the way to the right." He managed to make his one arm touch her right. "This one."

"Okay." A few moments later she stepped back. "Did it!"

"Francisco, see if your omni can connect to the nav controls now. Just connect, don't do anything yet."

There was a pause, then Francisco said from his position near the airlock, "Yes! It shows me controls are unlocked!"

Thank the Skies and Vents. Every time we fiddle with things on Emerald Maui *I'm afraid I'll find something else our misadventures have ruined.* "Great!"

Whips took a few moments to refocus. Even with the anesthetizing nanos, his body was telling him how badly injured he was. His mind was sluggish and his motor control wasn't as good as it had been only half an hour ago. "Okay. First things to do. Check integrity of systems. I have the codes, comm systems are now unlocked for full omni access. That one didn't need any physical override switches."

In a voice that was just a little too filled with casual interest, Sakura entered the transmitted conversation. "So why is that, Whips? I mean, why are there physical override switches on the shuttle, instead of just programming?"

"Hmm. You know, I'm not sure. I just know it's true of every vehicle I've ever seen. I think it has something to do with safety. Sergeant?"

"Huh. You've got me stumped too, Saki. Got the same impression as Whips, but can't quite pull it up."

"Goes back to the twenty-first century," Pearce Haley said. "The first fully automated vehicles that were deployed were all-computer controlled. And it turned out they could be hacked and controlled from the outside, which got people killed in at least three instances. Resulting law required that there be a physical layer isolating any vehicle meeting certain standards from external signals that could in any way affect the direct operation of the vehicle. In general there are good reasons to keep it that way. For things like *Emerald Maui*, there are dedicated external communications for automated landing and such, but the bands and communications protocols of omnis are physically excluded, which prevents accidental interference in operations, too."

"Wow," Whips said. "Where did you pick that up, Lieutenant?"

"One of my degrees is actually in criminal justice, as Samuel could tell you, and one term we reviewed the criminal and civil suits surrounding those events."

"*Another* degree?" Xander sounded both amazed and amused. "I knew you had some military training with the sergeant, and a lot of medical technician training, and then you surprised us by advising on the best way to extract the ejector charge, and now you're a lawyer?"

Whips felt a little better, having sat still for a few moments. He closed the panel door with only two tries and then keyed in his omni to run the shuttle systems, as Pearce replied "Not a *law* degree. Criminal justice, which meant for me that I was qualified for law enforcement and private security positions. Good additions to have in my career."

"Sure seems like it," Whips said. "How'd you end up with the ejection systems knowledge?"

"Studied shipboard systems for crew support and safety as part of my training to work aboard *Outward Initiative*. Meaning mostly environmentals, but the safety ejection systems of all types were part of that."

"Ooooh," Maddox said with a tone of sudden understanding. "And that saved our lives, didn't it?"

"What...oh. Well, yes, I suppose...yes, I guess it did." Pearce sounded bemused.

It took a moment, but Whips finally understood what Maddox meant. When *LS-88* (later *Emerald Maui*) had been cut loose from *Outward Initiative*, part of the boarding tube had remained connected to the shuttle, and it had been Pearce Haley who had figured out how to force the detach by detonating the charges meant for emergency launch. Had she not done so, many of the shuttle's systems would never have switched to internal control.

"Okay, everyone, could we be quiet for a few?" Whips asked. "I've...got a few tests to do here. Need to concentrate."

The others went silent. "Franky...Francisco, Hitomi, I'm going to test the drive systems. Just in case, I'd like you to come inside and close the door, Francisco."

"I will." Francisco reached up and removed the communications omni from its temporary perch, then triggered the airlock to close. Once it was fully closed and Francisco sitting on one of the seats, he said: "Done! Go ahead, Whips!"

The first test was to make sure the rudder worked. It turned exactly as the designs, and prior experience, said it should, so next he checked the jet condition. All indications seemed to be positive, so he activated the jets for a quick burst—not enough to move them more than a few meters, but enough to show they were working.

Instead of the smooth whistling hum, however, there was a buzzing, whizzing noise and an uncomfortable *jolt* through the cabin. "*Vents!*"

"What is it, Whips? What's wrong?" Francisco was obviously trying not to sound too worried; Hitomi wasn't saying anything, just watching with her full intensity.

"Not sure..." He forced his brain to clear for a moment. "Ummm...hm. So that's okay. But that means...*ugh*."

"Should we open the hatch?"

Whips heard the words, but for a moment he couldn't quite figure out what they meant...and that scared him. "I...yes, Franky. Open it and, um...put out the comm omni."

Now what was it...oh, yes. "Something's jammed in the portside jet." More buzzing rumbling. "Aaaand it won't come out easily."

"Okay, we'll look over the data, see if we can figure out what it might be and how to deal with it," Sergeant Campbell said. "What about the comm system?"

The world looked...*different*. Kind of...ripply, even inside the cabin. *That's...not good.* "Comm system. Right." He triggered the omni to give a status scan. "Huh. Um...Yes. The comm system's still mostly, um, running. Antennas are clearly missing. But no shorts, no malfunctions."

"That might be salvageable, then."

"Think...maybe, yes." The strength of a few minutes ago had already entirely drained away.

"Harratrer," came Laura's voice. "Your vitals are not good. It's time to try to put you in suspension."

"You...ready, Mom?"

"Almost. Can you move yourself away from the control area, just in case?"

"Sure." His rear pushers still worked, but they were even more sluggish than they had been a little while ago. Nonetheless, Whips was finally back near the securing points that could be used to lash him down. "Moved."

"Francisco, get one of the Bemmie nanogel packs and bring it over to Whips," Laura said.

"Thought...you could do it to my nanos."

"I can and I am," she answered, "but adding more can't hurt."

"They taste *terrible*."

A laugh that had an edge of tears answered him. "Yes, I know. We don't like the stuff either. But...it works."

"I guess. But couldn't...um, the kids, couldn't they work the injectors?"

"I don't want them trying injections on you when there are so many injuries all over. This will work well enough, and having a heavy coating of nanos on your internals won't hurt at all."

Francisco was back, though his shape looked strangely *dim*. Were the cabin lights on? They seemed to be, yet Franky and Hitomi just looked so far away. He did something with his omni—Whips heard, but couldn't quite understand, Laura's instructions—and then brought the pack towards Whips' mouth.

Whips tried to grit his beak shut and the twinge of pain through the anaesthetic momentarily cleared the fog. "Ugh. Okay, just open the top...yes, like that." He forced his mouth open. "Just pour it in, I'll swallow."

That was one of the hardest things he'd ever done, he decided. Swallowing nanogel really, really sucked.

Slowly, he felt a sort of strange, distant warmth beginning to envelop him. "M...mom?"

"Shh, Harratrer. It's all right. You're going to go to sleep now."

"Franky... 'tomi..."

"We'll take care of you, Whips," Hitomi said, tears standing out in her eyes even through the rising haze in his mind. "*Promise!*"

"Promise!" echoed Francisco.

With that word as a talisman, Whips allowed the soft heaviness to claim him and quiet darkness became his world.

PART 4

RESCUES

Chapter 29

Sakura tried to ignore the telltales at the corner of her omni's display. *Maybe I shouldn't leave them there at all.*

But the idea of *not* having an eye on her best friend was intolerable. And really, she just had to remind herself that there wasn't any reason to keep checking every second. Whips was in suspension, his metabolism slowed to something like a hundredth of normal. That didn't entirely apply to other aspects of his injuries, of course—he wasn't going to live a hundred days, or even half that, in the suspension—but they had time now, and that was what they needed more than anything.

What was important was to figure out how to get *Emerald Maui* back.

"Ready, Hitomi, Franky?"

"Ready," the two said. Francisco didn't even complain about the shortened nickname, something he usually did without fail.

Sakura triggered the engine cycle, forward, back, forward, back, as fast as the motor could safely shift direction. The idea was to unstick the, well, whatever-it-was that was currently jamming the portside jet.

Unfortunately, even after several different cycle patterns, there wasn't much sign of change. Whatever was caught in the jet was tough, and wasn't going to be easily dislodged. She sat back in frustration and drew in a breath.

She regretted the deeper breath immediately. The mud and wreckage, filled with innumerable corpses of creatures large and small, was acquiring an increasingly terrible stench. "Ugh. Mom, can I adjust my smell nanos again?"

"Go ahead, Saki. Though even with the best discrimination work, that means you'll lose more of your sense of taste too."

She grimaced. Taste and smell were so closely intertwined that you couldn't mess with the one without affecting the other. So dulling your senses to all the organic components of that vile smell...

"Well...for now, anyway. I need to focus on the work. But we can't stay like this forever, Mom."

"Hate to say it, but Saki's right, Ma'am," Sergeant Campbell said. "We don't have the cleanup crews a city'd have to get this muck out of here, and it's going to be months before it starts to get better on its own."

"We have to *leave Sherwood Tower*?" Melody's incredulous shout made Sakura jump, as it came from right behind her.

"Jeez! Don't do that, Mel!"

"But we did so much work," Melody said. It was a mournful sound, so like a dirge that Sakura almost laughed; Mel had gotten a lot better at throwing herself into projects and actually putting forth effort, but that wasn't her natural tendency, and the old, unreformed Melody's voice was the one lamenting all the hours of effort put into Sherwood Tower.

"I'm afraid the sergeant's right," Pearce said. "We've already seen a couple of those giant worms coming up to scavenge, and the combination of new scavenger threats and whatever this... mess is going to do in terms of disease and such? We'll have to move; we won't even be able to rely on our earlier sources of water—look at Blue Hole."

Sakura bit her lip, nodding involuntarily. From one of the windows of the Tower they could sometimes see Blue Hole Lake, which—before the tsunami—had been a beautiful pure blue, one of the deepest lakes on the explored section of the continent, with at least twenty to thirty meters of pure fresh water overlaying less palatable stuff below.

Now it was a filthy, stinking mud-brown eyesore, no better than the wreckage visible in all other directions. "It's not going to clear up?"

"Eventually, of course," her father answered, obviously listening into the conversations as many of them did. "But this event completely disrupted the balance of Blue Hole and the other two similar lakes on this section of the island. The mud cascaded into them and overturned the thermocline and density barriers; they're not only contaminated, they're brackish. It will be a matter of years, I would guess, before they're back to what we remember."

"I remember how hard it was to make Sherwood Tower the first time," muttered Caroline. "Not looking forward to that again."

"I don't think it'll be that hard," the sergeant said. "Remember, there's still another excavator, and a lot of other stuff, on *Emerald Maui*. If we get them back here, it'll solve a lot of our problems, not the least of 'em being safe, clean, accessible shelters, not to mention tools. We've lost a lot of stuff, no arguing that, but we're a long way from having to go the way of re-inventing civilization from the stone age again, like you folks had to. God forbid we ever have to."

"Saki? What about our engine?" Hitomi asked.

Her lips tightened, and she looked up, seeing Tavana across from her in the little room. He didn't look any happier. She cut out the transmission to *Emerald Maui*. "Tav? Any other ideas?"

He shook his head. "No, Saki. And from what they've been saying, neither do Xander or Maddox or our adult friends. The thing stuck in that engine, it is staying there until someone pulls it out."

Sakura swallowed hard. "You mean Hitomi or Francisco has to go out there and *dive*? That's..." she remembered the story of Xander's near-death experience, and her own family's siege by the raylamps. "That's crazy."

"Crazy or not, he's probably right," Laura said. "None of us can get there. The only one of us who could have reasonably safely gotten to them on his own was Whips."

"But that, it is not entirely true," Tavana said. "We could make a raft, or maybe an outrigger canoe, like my own ancestors did. It would not be an easy thing, but we could get there fairly quickly."

"Hmmm. Maybe, Tav," Xander said. "But first, with the limited tools we have left, it'd take quite a while to make a seaworthy canoe or raft, and second, *Emerald Maui*'s in a current that's taking her in a different direction from our continent. So you'd have to either have good winds for a sail, or be able to paddle like mad to catch up to her."

Sakura saw Tavana's face fall. "It was a good idea, Tav, but I don't think we have the time to try it," she said, trying to comfort him. "But that reminds me—how's it possible that *Emerald Maui* is in a current and we aren't? Shouldn't we all be drifting the same way?"

"You'd think so," Caroline spoke up. "But I think you're forgetting what we're really drifting on. This floatcoral continent is like an iceberg—there's a lot more below us than there is above the water. So my guess is that the lower parts of the continent—the keel of our boat, you could say—are in a deeper-water current that covers a lot more area, or maybe is stronger, than the surface one that *Emerald Maui* is caught in."

"*Oye*, everyone, we still need help here!" Francisco's voice was sharper than usual, and Sakura smiled ruefully.

"You're right, Francisco," she said. "Okay, first we'll need to get a look at what you're dealing with. That means someone's going to have to go out and put an omni or some other camera into the water near the rear jet that's not working. If we get some good imagery we can figure out what needs to be done."

"That's me," Hitomi said.

"Why you?" Francisco asked.

"'Cause you've been doing all the outside stuff, and now it's *my* turn," Hitomi said reasonably.

She could see Francisco turning that over in his head in the view from Hitomi's omni, then he grinned and shrugged. "Okay, yes, we all have to do the work. I will hold the safety rope and you will put the camera in the water." He looked at the tiny girl with a concern that echoed Sakura's own. "But are you sure? If you're out there, one of the raylamps might come for you."

"Francisco has a point, Hitomi," Sakura heard her mom say. "Honey, no one doubts you're one of the bravest here, but Francisco's a lot bigger than you."

"Mr. Sergeant Campbell—"

A snort of laughter. "That's Mister Campbell *or* Sergeant Campbell, honey, not both mashed up together."

"Sorry," said Hitomi, sounding genuinely contrite. "I thought Sergeant was your first name, Mr. Campbell."

"Ha! Of course you did. But go on, what about Mr. Sergeant Campbell?"

"Well, you told me that that's why you taught us to use guns. 'Cause they make it not important who's bigger."

Sakura felt her eyebrows raise, but Campbell simply chuckled again. "Well, you're right about that, Hitomi. And you and Francisco've done pretty well learning. But using a gun in a fight, that's a lot different than plinking at a target, you understand, Hitomi?"

Her image nodded in the omni's view. Then Franky's viewpoint slewed around and they saw another raylamp, slowly climbing up the hull of *Emerald Maui*. Franky picked it off with a single shot that sent the scavenger plummeting back into the water.

"I know. But I've been watching Francisco. I can do this and I don't want to stay inside all the time!"

Sakura looked up to her mother, who had just entered the room. "Mom?"

"I'm thinking, Saki." It didn't take any special effort to see the frown on Mom's face, or guess what she was thinking. But finally Laura Kimei drew in a huge breath, and nodded. "You're right, Hitomi. We're trusting both you and Franky—Francisco, sorry—to get the job done. It's going to take both of you, maybe at some point both of you *at once* in the water, much as that terrifies me, to get *Emerald Maui* running in time to save Whips. Francisco, you belay her *good*."

"I will. Promise."

Fortunately, along with the cheap omnis they had a few view extenders—simple descendants of the "selfie stick" of the early smartphone era. The extenders had some other useful features, but the important one now was the original function: allowing the user to put the camera somewhere they, personally, couldn't reach. Hitomi put one of the spares onto an extender and tested it; the unit easily linked in and showed the little blonde girl standing next to a worried-looking Francisco. *Well, good. I want him worrying about my little sister!*

To her credit, Hitomi didn't look like she was all smiles; her expression was sober. *She's done a lot of growing up. Not the wandering distracted girl she was when we first landed.*

"Good pics there," the sergeant said. "Tav, can you highlight where she's going to have to put the stick?"

"*Oui*, I can do that easily. Hitomi, when you get outside, the engine area will be highlighted. Your omni will show you where to put the extender into the water, and it'll guide you to holding it just in the right place." He hesitated a moment. "You're going to have to go over the support so you can get a rear view of the engine, too. Both you and Francisco keep an eye out when you're doing this, right?"

"Right," agreed Hitomi, and Franky echoed her.

"Well, then, no time like the present," Sergeant Campbell said. "Once you're on belay and the rope's secured, get to it."

Sakura watched as the two youngest members of their group got ready for their latest expedition. Francisco was conscientious, seeming to be checking off parts of the preparation from a mental checklist. He insisted on verifying for himself that Hitomi's weapon was properly charged and loaded for use, and had her check his, before he fastened the rope onto the improvised harness they'd made out of cargo straps at Xander's instruction.

Hitomi made an efficient production of yanking and jumping hard against the knot to make sure it would hold, then nodded and stepped out cautiously, the view extender in folded configuration hooked to the harness, her weapon already out. "No raylamps toward the back."

She dropped gently down to the extended outrigger, then moved carefully along until she could reach the second exterior set of handholds and climbed up toward the top of the hull. Francisco paid out the line until she was standing atop *Emerald Maui*, then said "Wait." She halted and looked back, watching.

Francisco, keeping the rope loosely in his grasp, moved quickly to catch up with Hitomi. He then braced himself and let her move down the hull.

Hitomi moved hesitantly to the base of the shuttle's tail. From her omni's viewpoint, Sakura could see the drive jet, its upper housing just breaking the water's surface. Hitomi stood there, staring at the water and the blue-green tinted curve of the underwater housing. Then she took an audible breath and jumped.

It was a good jump; Hitomi cleared the gap and landed on the small patch of wet composite, skidding a bit but catching onto the support strut and keeping herself from falling into the water. Sakura loosened her own grip, feeling her heart hammering as fast as Hitomi's must be.

Hitomi swallowed hard, that sound also audible to everyone, then steadied herself. With the careful precision that Saki remembered well, she removed the view extender and omni from her harness, stretched it to a length of over two meters, and dipped it into the water.

A split-screen in the omni view showed the underwater imagery. Hitomi rotated the camera slowly, obviously checking to see where raylamps might be hiding. None seemed terribly close to the location. One of Tavana's highlights showed on Hitomi's view, directing her to stand almost directly above and lower the omni to face into the engine.

Saki heard Tavana's indrawn breath echo her own. *Something* was visible there, sticking half a meter out of the engine housing. Hitomi lowered the omni more, giving them a view of the entire forward jet opening. With Tavana's prompting, Hitomi scanned the camera across the jet three times, then climbed over to the other side and repeated the process from the rear.

As Hitomi was finishing up, Francisco called out, "Hitomi! A raylamp, coming up the support strut!"

The little girl retracted the view extender and turned to study the glistening black creature. It rotated in place, somehow adhering to the vertical side of the strut, and tendrils extended in Hitomi's direction.

Hitomi's hand was on her gun, but she hadn't drawn it, and Sakura could see why. Francisco was visible along a line very close to that of the raylamp; if she missed by even a small angle, she could hit Franky.

Even as the black, gelatinous stingray-shape began to ooze towards her, Hitomi very carefully unsnapped the omni from the extender, and then pointed the shaft at the approaching raylamp.

Without warning, the view extender shot out to its full length of three meters, the blunt tip ripping entirely through the body of the creature. It gurgled and plummeted into the water without a pause.

The impact also drove Hitomi backwards and she teetered on the edge, but Francisco yanked back hard, and Hitomi instead was drawn upward and half onto the support.

"That was close," Sergeant Campbell said after a moment. "But excellent thinking, Hitomi. You really made me proud, there."

"Made us all proud," Laura said, her voice perhaps a little shaky.

"All of us," Sakura echoed. "Now Hitomi, you get inside. Time for us to take a look at this data and figure out how to finally get you moving!"

Chapter 30

"We're going to start moving out of here now," Campbell said. "Just shot up one of those stinging-worm things, and the air here's gone way beyond foul, it's getting toxic."

"But we can't just stop work on getting *Emerald Maui* home!" Sakura said sharply.

"Calm down, Saki, ain't no one saying anything like that. But we gotta start packing and get out of here. It's not safe in any way. Move on down the coast, this side where it's nearer them anyway, while we keep giving them support."

"The sergeant is right," Laura said. "It's not like any of us are physically able to do anything for those kids." He could see her pain-filled wince at having, once more, to admit that Francisco and Hitomi were, in the end, on their own on Lincoln's seas. "All we can do is advise them, and we can do most of that while we're still working."

"I think the idea of rafting everything makes sense," Pearce Haley said. "The way the continent's moving and the water currents work, they'll help us move in the direction we want to go."

"Agreed, and like we noticed, lots of downed trees." Campbell surveyed the area, making sure there weren't any more opportunistic predators lurking about. "Xander, any progress?"

"It's a column shard, Sergeant. Got jammed right in there, probably during the tumbling."

"Can the kids get it out?" That was, of course, the only question that mattered. If they couldn't remove the shard, *Emerald Maui* was dead in the water—at least, unless they could figure out some new jury-rig trick. But at some point, you ran out of tricks.

"I think so. I hope so. There's no sign that it's seriously damaged the jet, so that should mean it's jammed but not held in by, say, splinters of the fans or anything. If they can get a line around it and hook the block-and tackle on, I'd bet that it could be pulled out, especially if the pull's pretty straight."

"Block and tackle?" Pearce asked, eyebrows high. "Why not just use the winch connection?"

"External connectors are totally fouled, maybe just scoured off like the antennas. And they can't open the cargo doors while they're floating, so the internal connector won't work unless they set up the tackle to relay through the ship—way too many ways for that to go bad." Xander gagged as a particularly foul gust of wind blew by. "Jesus!"

"Even with nanosuppression, this stuff is rich. We'll be burning our clothes after we move, you bet." Campbell nodded. "All right, sounds like we have a plan for the blockage. How long to get it set up?"

"Figure it all out and get Hitomi and Franky on the job? A day. Worst part's going to be getting the cable on the fragment. We'll try doing it without anyone going in the water, but I have a bad feeling that it just won't work."

Campbell saw Xander's face three shades paler than normal, and knew he was reliving his own near-death experiences. "We'll cross that bridge when we come to it," he said after a moment. "Get everything arranged. Tavana, you said you had Franky and Hitomi working outside already?"

"Yes, Sergeant. Once we saw that the comm channel connections looked to be clean, I thought maybe we could make new antennas. They would maybe not be efficient, but all we need is a nice long strip of conductor that is connected to the radios."

"And?"

"And so Hitomi, she found a roll of repair cable which has the all-weather tape built in. Models show it should work as a good dipole antenna. Hitomi just finished taping it down, and now she's painting it over with goop."

"Goop," in this context, meant a radio-transparent, hard-drying aerospace epoxy-like substance that was a standard across known space. Every ship carried some for general repairs, smoothing of nicks and dents, and so on. It hadn't changed much in anything but detail since the twenty-first century.

"Well, then it'd darn well better work, 'cause you ain't getting that goop *off* again."

"Pretty sure it will. Once it dries—about twenty minutes—Franky's going to go out and do the connections. Probably have to do soldering, there's no actual connectors left."

"And then?"

"Drop some goop on the connections to keep them safe from sea spray and such, and then we should be good to go. We'll know once he does the hookup whether it works; *Emerald Maui's* onboard systems will automatically try to connect to the network."

"Here's hoping. We'll all feel one hell of a lot better once we know they can always talk to us, even when the doors are closed."

"God, yes," Laura said.

"All right, then. I'll need all the strongest people here to move stuff—that means me, Xander, Tav, and Laura. The rest of you, start packing up everything we can bring. Making a raft shouldn't take too long, even with the tools we've got left; at least both groups kept a bunch of the smaller stuff above water level, and your long-suffering winch is still with us." He grinned. "Got more work out of *that* than the manufacturer ever guessed, I'll bet."

"That is for sure," Akira's voice said, transmitted from inside Sherwood Tower. The temporary stairs and platform over the nigh-endless pit below allowed them to go in and out, but Campbell had agreed with the engineer's evaluation. Eventually that tower was coming down, even if the kids hadn't wanted to admit it. Moving now was just getting a jump ahead of disaster.

"And everyone stay in their groups if you are not in one of the towers in a defensible position," he said. "Just takes one second for something hungry to get the drop on you."

"Got it, Sergeant," said Maddox.

"Pearce, you'll be in charge of the packing," Laura said. "Everyone else clear on that?"

There was a chorus of yeses from Sakura, Melody, Caroline, and Maddox. "Yes," Akira added with good humor.

"Good. We'll all leave our omnis on. First, let's get all the tools and stuff we'll need—rope's top of the list, but we'll want hammers, things like that."

It didn't take long to fill a pack for everyone—both with the tools and materials Campbell thought they'd need, and with food and water for the day. Turning away from the clearing, Campbell began to lead the way towards the shore. Here at ground level the going was incredibly hard, with still-soft mud, tumbled obstacles, most things still a uniform grey-brown of mud which made it difficult to tell where one thing left off and another began. It was particularly bad when you thought something was a rock and it turned out to be a partially-decayed corpse of some unfortunate animal. *What I wouldn't give for my Pathfinder boots now, a whole case of 'em.*

"So...uck...Sergeant, we're making a raft. You've done that before?"

"Oh, sure. Survival training's got that as one of the basics. There's all sorts of rafts you can make, but for this we'll want one that's pretty sturdy and carries a lot of weight. Several logs across, pretty long. Have to lay some kind of deck on it—think we might have some pieces left in storage that might do, we'll get those once we have the main raft assembled—then rig up a simple mast, sail, rudder—maybe just a steering board or steering oar—and some poles for near-shore work."

"Sounds like it could be a little complicated."

Campbell grinned, remembering. "Nah. Hard work, that I'll grant, and some of it gets a little fiddly if you want everything just right, but it's mostly getting it right the first time that matters. Don't want to have to go back and try to redo part of your raft; gets messy." He slipped and barely caught himself before taking a full faceplant into the muck. "Not that anyone here will notice 'messy.'"

Laura snickered, turning it into a cough. "No, I don't suppose we will. The logs will still float covered in this...stuff?"

"We'll roll 'em in the water, get 'em cleaned off first, but sure, they will. Takes time to get waterlogged. Depending on how the decay works here, we might end up with 'em stripping their bark as we roll 'em, which wouldn't be a bad thing."

Tavana came to a half-fallen tree blocking the way. Rather than go around, he shoved it up and over, sending it down with a resounding *thud-splat* that sent mud all over the party. "Whoops."

"Watch it, Tav. This stuff's bad enough to smell, ain't none of us want to eat it." *That boy is strong, though. Not sure I could have tossed that tree like that, and I've got thirty centimeters on the kid. He started out a little round, but he's turning into a regular brick.*

"Sorry, Sergeant, everyone."

"It's okay, Tav. Not like I'm really noticing another spot of this crud," Xander said. "I'd be more worried about people getting hurt, though. If that log turned out to be heavier than you thought, or fell the wrong way..."

"Yes, I know, it was stupid. I will not do that again." Tavana's voice was serious. *Good, he's taking it the right way.* With teenagers you were never sure whether they'd take a lesson to heart, or just take it badly instead.

The air was slightly less foul now as they approached the coast. Their floating continent was drifting through the ocean, leaving some of the wreckage behind and replacing it with cleaner water. The four of them stood on the shore for a moment, just taking the time to breathe less-tainted air.

"All right, that'll do. Let's get this going." He looked around. "We'll want...eight, ten logs that size," he said, pointing at one tree about thirty to forty centimeters in diameter. "Keep 'em as close to the same width as possible. At the same time, keep an eye out for smaller logs, maybe around ten centimeters; we'll use those for the crossmembers to secure 'em together."

"How long should the logs be?"

"Four meters or so. We'll trim the ends a bit to make a prow when we're done, so maybe go for five meters."

"You sure this thing will fit all of us and our gear?"

"This'll be a cargo carrier. A few of us on board at any time, the rest'll swim or walk and be ready to help pull her in if something goes wrong. It'll carry all the stuff we've got left in one, maybe two trips at most."

He paired with Laura, Tav with Xander. Between the four of them, it only took a few hours to locate and drag ten good-sized logs to the water's edge. Xander collapsed onto a cleaner section of shore. "Whoosh! Time for a break."

"Sure is. Everyone take ten. Maybe twenty. Eat something, get some water in you. This stuff takes it out of you quick."

"Sergeant? Sergeant Campbell, do you hear me?"

"Francisco? Sure, I hear you, son."

A whoop of triumph almost pierced his eardrums from one side to the other. "*¡Funciona!* It works!"

"Ow! Down about ten notches, son. Wait, you mean you're calling from *Emerald Maui*?"

"*Si!* Yes! We are inside with the lock shut tight!"

He felt a broad grin on his face. "Well, that's just great! You kids did fantastic! Xander, can you confirm a connection straight through to *Emerald Maui*?"

"Got it! Signal quality's so-so, but well within our ability to work with. If we can get any kind of decent eyes to work with there, and get that engine working, we can bring her home now!"

"That took longer than I thought it was going to," Laura said. "Did you have any problems?"

"Oh, you did not hear me talking to him on the private channel?" Tavana asked. "The solder, it would not stick at first, kept coming off. I did not know that Francisco *knew* words like those. Finally we figured out how to clean and prep the surface right, though, and the solder flowed on fine."

"So long as it worked, that's what matters. Now you kids can sleep safe inside and still reach us if you have to. Makes us all feel better. And we can run parts of things from here direct. Good work, you two."

"Thank you, Mr. Sergeant," Hitomi said with a giggle.

"I'll 'Mister Sergeant' you, young lady." He laughed with her. "Well, take it easy for a bit. Next big thing won't be 'til tomorrow. Meanwhile, we've still got work to do here."

"Be kind of ironic if we end up getting *Emerald Maui* back like right after we finish this raft," Xander said.

"Yeah, but I prefer that kind of irony to the kind where we end up without raft *or* shuttle."

"True enough. Now what, Sergeant?"

He looked around the shoreline. "Well, first what we do is see if we can drive some shorter poles into the seabed here, just to keep the logs in a sort of corral. Make it easier than trying to herd 'em all the time. Then we get all the big logs lined up, tie 'em together so they keep pretty much in position."

Laura nodded. "After that?"

"That's where the smaller ones come in. Lay those crosswise, top an' bottom, and tie 'em together, rope between each gap, so they clamp the logs in between 'em. Then we tie the front and back *tight*, wind a little rope around each gap, too. Then we'll put on our deck, mast and sail, and steering, and we'll be set. Figure we can finish the first part today, then come back in the morning with the deck plating and get her ready to go. First trip, maybe as early as tomorrow evening, but we won't move out with cargo until day after."

"Then tonight we pick out the spot to move to," Laura said. "Akira, hon?"

"Yes?"

"You and Caroline are probably the best to pick out our next home—I want you looking over all the satellite imagery of the coast and let us know where we'll be going."

"We will certainly do that," Akira answered. "I've already noted some promising spots nearby; as long as we've cleared the area of the impact flood by more than a kilometer or so we should be fine, but I'm recommending we move to a distance past the mountain ridge. It won't be a long distance by water, although obviously those walking or wading will have a harder time of it."

"That's quite a few kilometers of harder time, Akira," Campbell said after a moment. "What are you not telling us?"

A pause. "Let us say that I am not sanguine about the chances that this portion of our continent will be entirely intact. While there was no *immediate* obvious damage on the level of the impact damage we saw on your prior island, the inundation severely impacted a vast majority of the trees and, I believe, columns on this portion of the island. All the debris may also be choking off the living coral-like organisms that underlie much of the land we walk on.

"And while it was only at the very tip of this continent, we *had* sustained another impact in the not too distant past; that's where our circular harbor came from. So there may be lingering effects from that damage that would be exacerbated by the tsunami."

"You're saying that in your view it's possible that a large part of our continent might become *terra non grata* to the rest."

"It is possible. And we know what happens to those parts of our floating landmasses."

"That's . . . just peachy. When'd you come up with this theory? 'Cause I think we should've started moving earlier, if that was the case."

"Not much earlier than now; the more immediate survival issues rather outweighed it. I started thinking on this in detail at the point you started talking about us having to move, in fact."

"All right. In that case, just makes it even more imperative we complete the move. So we'll press on and you'll finish choosing our new home. Looking forward to seeing what you pick out. You know everything to look for."

"Sound columns, nearby water supply, signs of game, possibly higher ridges to serve as wave breaks just in case there is another occurrence, flat areas for farming, and so on, yes."

"Carry on then, Doctor." He rose up and futilely slapped away some of the omnipresent mud. "Well, then, let's get back to it; we have a raft to finish!"

Chapter 31

"No, it's just not going to work," Tavana said, reluctance clear in his voice, as Hitomi and Francisco hauled the line back in after the who-knew-how-many-th attempts to get a good secure attachment to the column shard that was stuck in *Emerald Maui*'s drive jet. "The currents, the angles, they just are not going to work."

"We're going to have to go in the water and tie the rope," Hitomi said. She was trying to sound matter-of-fact about it, but she heard her own voice waver uncertainly. Try as she might, she couldn't force away the memory of the raylamps, dozens of them, oozing their way up a hillside to consume Mommy and Caroline and Whips.

"No way around it. I don't think any of us like it, but we've spent the last three hours trying to do it from above the waterline."

"How about the rebreathers? Those working?" Campbell asked.

"They work," Hitomi said, "but we have to hold them on our faces and even then they leak."

Tavana grimaced in the VR-projected image of the raft he and the sergeant were on, piled high with all the food, weapons, and other equipment they'd salvaged from their homes. "As Hitomi says, the rebreathers, they are not made to fit children. To figure out adaptors for them, that will take quite a while. I do not think we want to take more days for that."

"Damn. No, they're drifting farther away every day, and Whips isn't getting any better. But working underwater just by holding your breath and diving, that's tough and dangerous stuff even for adults, you know."

"We only have to tie on one rope, Sergeant Campbell," Francisco said. "It's scary to go into the ocean, but that shouldn't be hard to do."

"If you're lucky, son, yes. You could get everything to go right, and do it all in one quick shot. Hold on!"

Campbell pulled out his sidearm and fired once; Hitomi thought she had seen an underwater shadow in the image, a shadow that had fled as soon as Campbell fired. "Damn thing was trying to sneak up on the wading party. Where was I? Oh, yeah. If everything's perfect, no problem, but if your rope snags or tangles, and you have to keep straightening it, and the currents move stuff as you try to put it on, and all that? You'll find out the sea ain't always helpful." He put the steering oar over a bit. "Show me the best projection you have on that blockage."

The VR-view split as Tavana displayed the model he had built from their images, showing the three-meter-long fragment projecting from the jet housing.

"Hm. Yeah, no wonder you're having trouble. Currents will be pretty chaotic around that thing, where it's sitting. How about the block and tackle? How're you getting the straight pull?"

"Here," Tavana said, highlighting the outrigger. "Reshaped the material to provide a good clamp mount on the lower edge, then secured one of the pulleys there. Still a small angle on the pull but it's about as straight as we can manage."

He could see Campbell's frown. "Not bad. But that little angle could still be an issue. Kids have any prybars?"

"Yes, Sergeant," Hitomi said. "We had some in storage. Shelf one, starboard."

She could see the sergeant's grin. "Damn good stroke of luck, you with that memory on board."

Hitomi felt a warmth through her at the compliment, but honesty forced her to say, "Thank you, sir, but now that we're communicating the omnis can do the job just as well."

"Maybe so, but having a catalog that also understands what we're looking for? That's priceless."

"I have an idea," Francisco said. "We have some tubing, *si*? So we put tube on the strut support and run it down to where we work under water. Then we can breathe!"

Tavana screwed up his face. "That won't work. Will it? I mean, my reaction is that it shouldn't work, but I can't say why."

"Pressure differential," Sakura said at the same time as Campbell.

The sergeant chuckled. "Go ahead, Saki."

"You have to pull the air down against the pressure of the water above you," Sakura said. "If you're snorkeling you can do it down ten centimeters or so, but even that's tiring after a while. I don't think even the strongest set of lungs on Earth could pull air down under two meters of water, which is about where the jet is."

Hitomi tried to figure out what that meant, but gave up. It wasn't important—she could get Mom or Dad or Whips (*if he got better... please let him get better!*) to explain how that worked later. The important thing was that it wouldn't work, which, as Saki would say, sucked.

"Good thinking, Franky, don't feel bad," Tav said, seeing the younger boy looking embarrassed. "It looks like a perfectly reasonable idea. Most people would've thought it made sense until they tried it." In fact, Tavana remembered seeing old movies where someone did do something like that.

"So we will have to do dives, then."

"Afraid so, son," Campbell said. "At least the supports give you something to hold to." He looked up, pulled the oar over again. "Ho, the shore! Pull us in a little ways!"

Hitomi saw the little images of Laura and Maddox start pulling inward; the others in the shorebound party took up the slack, drawing the raft in closer to the shore. "Okay, kids, your omnis now have the info for the best place to secure the rope. You'll see it as a red band around the shard, a little less than halfway down. There's a bulge just before it that should help keep the rope secure when we start pulling."

"Why did you ask about prybars, Sergeant?" Franky asked. "You think we might have to pry while it is under water?"

"Maybe not, but maybe so, son. And that'll probably have to be you; Hitomi's just too small to be able to pull hard enough to matter. She can crank the block and tackle, though, with the right attachment."

Hitomi saw the problem with that right away. "But if I'm doing that, Mr. Campbell, then I can't watch Francisco underwater!"

"That's the part I'm worried about, yeah, honey. You'll both be working and there'll be no one to help either of you. But there doesn't seem to be any way around it. Once you get tied on, we'll sure try just pulling it out, but if it won't move, someone'll have to be down there to pry it loose."

"Then I will have to do that," Francisco said simply. "Hitomi, I will have my lifeline."

"But I won't be able to *hear* you underwater!"

"Without a full-face mask, I won't be able to *talk* underwater, either," Francisco said. "We only have the omnis. Dive goggles should have been on board but we did not find any."

"Someone slipped up," Campbell agreed. "If you've got rebreathers, obviously you're assuming someone's going for long swims and ought to have the other equipment around."

"There is no point in waiting," Francisco said after a moment. "Hitomi, we have to get the cable hooked on."

We're going to have to go into the water. Hitomi swallowed hard, then forced herself to focus again. *Forget the raylamps. Focus on the work. Focus.*

Slowly she felt the frantic jig of her mind smoothing out, as she went over the steps—prepare the cable, evaluate the situation, make sure everything is clear, prepare for dive. Finally she turned and picked up the cable and started detaching the extender sticks they had been using to try to move it remotely.

"Check for raylamps," she said, trying hard to make her high-pitched voice sound as calm and controlled as Mommy's.

"On it," Franky said, and in his voice she heard the same determined imitation—this time of both Xander and the sergeant, as Francisco Coronel began a careful sweep of *Emerald Maui* and the water surrounding her.

Hitomi thought that the number of raylamps had been going down, maybe because all the free food from the flood had started to run out, drifting away or being eaten. Even so, they were still around; not a day had gone by without seeing at least one.

"Time to swap out crews," she heard Campbell say. "Tav, you stay onboard with your oversight on the kids. Rest of us, let's go."

Hitomi could vaguely see the trading of crews in her omni view, but focused on her job. She made sure the rope was ready, then set it down over the rear support; it looked kind of like a hangman's noose, which was creepy, but she tried to ignore that.

Francisco appeared atop *Emerald Maui* from the other side. "No raylamps on board. I do not see any around *Emerald Maui*, either."

Hitomi swallowed, loud enough that she knew Francisco had heard. "Then... Then we do this now, right?"

"Right. Check safety lines."

The two checked each other's lines, tugging hard to make sure they were secure. Hitomi pulled on Francisco's a second time, just to be certain. She checked that the knife on her hip was secure but able to be pulled out easy. If something bad happened, she'd need that.

Francisco was looking into the water, shifting uneasily. "Remember, take lots of breaths first—"

"I know, Francisco, I swim better than you!"

"Sorry," he said, looking guilty. "Just making sure."

"It's okay," she said. "I'm scared too."

Francisco bit his lip, then nodded. "But we go, right?"

"Right."

"Be careful, both of you." Mom's voice was calm but firm, a reminder that even if she couldn't help, somehow she was still there.

After a few hyperventilating breaths, Hitomi and Francisco dove into Lincoln's sea.

Everything was suddenly immersed in green-blue, shimmering shafts of sunlight dancing through the faint mist of the sea. Her implanted omni optics adjusted the view, focusing what would otherwise be blurred. Goggles would have been better—they had no idea exactly what might be suspended in Lincoln's water here—but at least she could see.

She looked down, following the rays of light into the vanishing, unguessable depths, and gulped, looking up again. She didn't want to think of how far, far down the ocean floor was. She remembered hearing Caroline talking to Mom, and saying she thought that somewhere below them the water turned to some kind of special ice that could only exist kilometers and kilometers underwater. *I'm swimming in water almost like a bathtub, and below me are kilometers of water and then kilometers of ice...*

She gripped the cable in her hands tighter and kicked hard, pushing forward towards the shard of a column projecting from the engine, Francisco next to her.

The wobbling, soft loop of cable nudged the jagged front point of the column fragment, then stuck; Hitomi yanked it off impatiently, then she and Franky tried to slide it over the front.

A wave above passed over, shoving her forward and then back, just enough to make the loop miss. Francisco's mouth tightened, but he didn't change the approach. They shook out the loop, made it open up again, and then started up.

Hitomi paused, feeling the motion of the water, remembering the rhythm. She gestured for Francisco to hesitate, then turned up, watching the mirror-shimmering surface, the waves...

She raised her hand and pointed as another wave approached, then made a sort of looping up-and-over gesture, and by his widened eyes knew Francisco understood. If they timed their attempt correctly, the wave-motion could help rather than hinder.

The wave lifted the two forward, and they pulled the loop with them. It nudged up and over, with the lower portion now caught by the front of the fragment. But Hitomi somehow got a grip on the piece of column, feeling it rough and sharp-edged under her hands, and held on, ignoring the minor pain, as Franky drifted back and under, pulling the loop back.

It's on! All we have to do is just move it back to the right place! She could see that location, a meter or so farther back on the column fragment.

But her chest and throat were starting to ache from holding in her breath, even as they tried to drag the loop farther back. Francisco shook his head, then waved for her to go up.

Hitomi hesitated, but really, there wasn't much choice now, was there? She sprang off the fragment for the surface, two meters up, and broke through with a gasp. She took several quick breaths, dove back down; as she reached the rope, Francisco went up. She tried pulling the rope back more, but she couldn't stay with it; the few moments at the surface just hadn't been enough.

After two more tries, Hitomi found herself just barely reaching the surface, gasping for breath.

"Stop pushing it, you two!" Tavana said. "You'll drown yourselves if you don't take a break!"

"But...the rope," Francisco said, trying to breathe and look down at the same time.

"It's on, but not the right place," Hitomi said breathlessly.

"We saw," Campbell said. "Good work, both of you. Just take your time. Weather's good, sea's pretty smooth, it's warm. You have time. That column's plenty rough; it's caught onto your rope pretty good. I don't think it's going to drift away in just a couple of minutes. Take your time, get a breath, look around."

That made sense. The two of them clung to the support together, letting their breathing slow, occasionally glancing down to make sure the rope was still in place.

"Saw something moving by not far away," Francisco said. "Didn't look like a raylamp, though."

"That's not all that comforting. You kids get up and have a good look around before you go back in," Tavana said. "Looks like the loop should stay put for a few minutes at least."

Hitomi didn't like the idea of something swimming around that they didn't know. She and Francisco pulled themselves out of the water and balanced on the tail support. "You want to do the check-around?" Francisco asked Hitomi. "I'll watch everything here."

"Okay!" Hitomi carefully unhooked her lifeline and started a methodical round of *Emerald Maui*. After a few minutes, she paused, looking down from atop the shuttle-turned-ship. "There's *something* there, Tavana," she said, making sure her omni got the image clear.

Tav grunted. A darker shadow was definitely visible under the rippling water, a shape long and slender. "Definitely not a raylamp; wrong shape and too large. Could that be Finny?"

"Wow, I hadn't thought of that! You think it is?"

Campbell's voice cut in. "Lemme see. Huh. Sure is about the right shape. If it is, you might've lucked out. See if you can get an omni in the water there, but be careful. If it's *not* our old friend, something shaped like that might be hungry an' mean as hell."

"Francisco, throw me one of the extenders!"

The little pole flew through the air and Hitomi caught it, a casual gesture that surprised her. *We've all learned to do things we would never have done before.* She snapped her omni onto the end, extended the pole to its maximum reach, and slid the omni into the water.

"Good, now turn...too far! Back..."

The shape in the water was still somewhat dimmed by distance, but the long, contoured torpedo outline and the sharp points in front were very familiar. "Looks like one of Finny's people, that's for sure. Still, we'd want to be sure it's one of the ones that attached themselves to *Emerald Maui* before; they seemed to like us four-limbed types. But one that wasn't our friend, well, they're really badass hunters. Saw that up close."

Hitomi frowned. She knew they'd been able to identify Finny and the others of his...school? Pod? Group, anyway, from details of their markings. But they couldn't see the markings now, too blurred. "Sergeant? Do you think I could get it to come closer with some food?"

"Maybe. Worth a try. If it is Finny or one of his group, they'll remember us feeding them a time or two, and if it ain't, it still might come to see what's up. Then you'll be able to get a good look, anyway."

She went to the top of the shuttle. "You still okay, Francisco?"

"Okay. You are going to get food?"

"Yes. Wait there!"

She slid down to the base of the outrigger wing, then made her way inside. She had to step past Whips' nanosuspended body, and shivered a bit. *Whips, get better.* The rations were all in their place; she found some dried capy meat and brought it out, tearing the jerky into little strips.

Climbing back to the top, she quickly located the long, narrow shadow, toward the nose of the craft but now on the outrigger side. *Good, I can probably work a lot better from there.*

She got down to the outrigger and then snapped her lifeline to one of the loops on the winglike structure. She slung the extender pole over her back, then started tossing little pieces of the jerky into the water, toward the blurred shape.

After the third or fourth piece, she saw the silhouette change direction; it drifted cautiously forward, then gave a short lunge; she thought it must have caught one of the pieces. It seemed to approve, because it started looking for the other pieces.

Great! She tossed them now in a path that slowly drew the creature closer, then, as it began eating its way forward in a leisurely manner, Hitomi unslung the extender and put the omni back into the water.

The creature's image was much sharper now; there was no mistaking that it was, in fact, one of the same species as Finny. The question was whether it was actually Finny or one of his allies. "Tavana? Is that good enough?"

"Comparing...*Merde*, no, I don't think it—"

The torpedo-shaped thing suddenly lunged forward, exploding

from the water, shattering the extender and sending the omni flying away. The impact sent Hitomi sprawling—meaning that the thing's spined front just barely missed impaling her. A tentacular tongue lashed out, scooping up some of the jerky.

Oh no. I've, what was it Daddy said, I've made an association, made it think of me in connection with food!

She scrambled backwards—and found herself brought up short as the lifeline went taut, still locked tight to the outrigger. The creature slewed around, and she saw to her shock that its fourfold symmetry was distorting slightly, the fins being brought into alignment that made them usable for land-based movement. It rippled forward, the spined tongue whipped out again, and Hitomi heard herself scream as it twined around her left arm, burning and stabbing like red-hot barbed wire.

But she was still *focused*, and she remembered her preparations. Her right hand dove down, yanked the knife free, and slashed up, almost in a single smooth motion.

The carbonan-reinforced, razor-sharp blade sliced clean through the thing's tongue, and it recoiled with a bubbling hiss of pain. But instead of backing away, it simply slid sideways, and Hitomi could see it was still intent on her. *Maybe it can regrow the tongue? It wasn't hurt enough?*

She had no omni—even if the others were giving her advice, she couldn't hear it. But she remembered big sister Sakura's forest walk and her encounter. *I have to make it back off. If it thinks I'm scared, it will kill me.*

Of course, it might kill her anyway. Behind the focus she could feel terror clawing at her mind, trying to turn her thoughts to screams, and her hand shook; she knew if she did lose that focus, she would be dead.

Instead, she lunged at it, jabbing with her knife at one of the eyes set at the corner of the mouth.

Startled by her motion, it slid back, barely evading the lunge. She wanted to continue the chase, maybe force it off, but she knew she was close to the end of her lifeline. *Can't take the time to unhook it, and even if I did, would that be good? I might slip and fall into the water, and then...*

The creature humped itself up, clearly being more cautious but still not giving up. It approached as she backed up, to give herself more slack in the line, then circled to the left. She turned to face it, mouth dry. *I'm going to have to charge it before it tries again. I'll never survive if* it *does the charge first, it's too big!*

And then the creature whipped around as another figure leapt on it with a scream of terrified fury. Francisco's machete came down with a meaty *chunk!* noise like Caroline cutting up a capy carcass, and the creature gave an ear-torturing shriek of pain and anger.

Hitomi charged and buried her knife in the thing's side to its hilt. Then it tried to spin on her.

The rotation ripped the knife down the creature's side, and Hitomi staggered, barely holding on, her lifeline going taut with the impact of the thing's massive strength. But the surgically-sharp blade carved a perfect, deadly path along the thing's flank, and blood fountained from the thing. With a cough of agony, the long, slender creature reversed course again and managed a sort of eel-like lunge that sent it over the edge of the outrigger back into the water. A dark plume of blood followed it as it swam unsteadily down, and Hitomi thought she saw other shadows moving in the water below.

"Hitomi! Hitomi, ¿estás herido? Are you okay?" Francisco was up to her, eyes so wide the white showed around them. "Hitomi?"

She gritted her teeth as a fresh wash of pain came up her arm, but she remembered how the adults did things, and forced a smile on her face. "Better than *it* is."

"Doctor Kimei, her arm, it looks bad!" He looked around. "No, her omni...I think it fell into the water. I can get another of the ones...no, of course, I will give her mine." He touched his omni twice and then handed it to Hitomi; she felt the new omni connecting with her implants. "Mommy?"

"It's okay, baby, now that you're connected I can see," her mother's voice said. Hitomi could hear the worry behind her calm words, but despite the pain, she relaxed. Mommy would know what to do.

After a few moments, she spoke, and the worry was far reduced. "There was a mild venom in the wound, but your nanos have it under control. Same with potential infectious organisms. I've tweaked the protocols to make sure they get everything."

Hitomi could see that the bleeding had already stopped, and made herself stand. Her knees felt funny, like they weren't really hers, weak and wobbly like a doll's knees, but she made them steady. "Then we've got to get this finished."

"Hitomi, no, you need to—"

"Girl's got a point," Campbell said; she could hear he didn't like saying it. "They've just made a statement to the local predators. Scavengers have something wounded and dying to keep 'em distracted. It's gone a ways off, so not too near *Emerald Maui*. If they can get that loop fixed fast, the most dangerous part of the whole game's finished."

Mommy was quiet, and Hitomi unhooked the lifeline and made herself walk towards the rear of *Emerald Maui*. Her knees started to feel more normal.

Finally, Mommy spoke. "I suppose there's no time that it's going to be safe," she said quietly. "Then...all right, you two. First, you need to get one of the waterproof bandage wraps on your arm. Otherwise you'll be bleeding into the water."

"I will get one," Francisco said, and bounded towards the airlock door.

"I know this has to be done, Hitomi," her mother said, quietly. "And I want you to know I am so proud of you, and of Francisco. You handled that as well as any of us would have."

"One-hundred-per-cent, yes," the sergeant said, his gravelly voice emphatic. "Plenty of older people that wouldn't've come out of that alive. You've both learned a lot of good lessons."

Francisco came out and helped her apply the translucent, water-tight bandage wrap. Hitomi did her best not to show how much it hurt, but she felt a couple of tears go down her cheeks. *Doesn't matter. Whips was hurt worse, he kept moving.*

"All right, both of you. Get that rope on. Just..." Mommy's voice hesitated, then finished, "...just be careful."

Hitomi swallowed, and nodded. "We will, Mommy."

Chapter 32

Sakura sank down onto the amazingly clean, bright white sand of the beach. "I am so tired. Did we really have to go another five kilometers down?"

"The more I'm looking at the telemetry from the nanos we left behind," her father said, "the more I have to say 'yes.' That wave did massive damage to the entire ecostructure of that end of our continent. Not as much as it would have if it had hit the actual floating landmass, of course—"

"Then none of us would be here to argue about it," the sergeant said.

"Yes, that was certainly fortunate. Though if it had hit farther away, we would have been much more fortunate. In any event, I am now rather pessimistic about the survival of that section of our floating home. If all of us weren't about at the end of our endurance, I would in fact rather we kept going. If an island-eater or three come calling, I would like to have as many kilometers between me and them as I can get."

All of them had seen one of the monstrous creatures in action at least once; Sakura remembered the three titanic curved spines bursting through water and coral-based land like breaching mountains, rising so high that they cast a shadow that blotted out the sun, and she shivered. "How far away should we go? Maybe we should just camp here for a bit and wait for us to get *Emerald Maui* back, then we can use it to move?"

"That suggestion, I think I like it," Tavana said, sitting next to her and giving her a little one-armed hug.

"Actually...so do I," Laura said, with a speculative gaze out towards the ocean. "If the kids can get that piece out of the drive jet today."

Sakura nodded. After securing the cable—which had taken them about an hour—Hitomi had been almost completely exhausted, and after checking her vitals and those of Francisco, her mom had decreed that both of them needed to take a day or two to rest before trying any more strenuous work. "Francisco was suffering from mild shock," she'd heard Mom say to Campbell and Xander. "Emotional stress can do that, and the two of them have been in an emergency situation all along; this attack upset him more than he let on. And Hitomi...she took a lot of strain through her whole body, and she's so *tiny*..."

"You don't need to justify anything to us," Sergeant Campbell had said. "They need to rest, they need to rest, that's all there is to it."

But with the improved healing nanos provided and the quick recovery that kids usually had anyway, both Hitomi and Francisco were fully recovered today—and they didn't want to wait any more. Not that Sakura could blame them; it had to be creepy and lonely, sitting in *Emerald Maui*, floating along with no one else but the unconscious-and-nearly-dead Whips.

That thought made Sakura shudder again; she felt Tav's arm tighten on her. "What is it, Saki?"

"Just...just thinking about Whips. Time's going by and...and I just..." she shook her head. "You know, we grew up together. This is the longest I've ever been away from him, really."

"So, it is like he is your brother."

"Yeah, the only brother I had." She tried to smile. "Though I guess I've sort of got some more now."

"Well, I am not exactly feeling like your brother, you know."

That got her to laugh, a little. "Well, I guess not. But Maddox and Franky, definitely."

"Yes, they are like my little brothers too." Tavana looked out at the ocean. "How far away are they now?"

"Satellite positioning says they're about two hundred seventy-five kilometers from our current position, and their drift's speeding up."

"That's about ten hours or so away if they get the engines running."

Sakura tried to ignore the "if" in there.

"What do you think, Captain?" Sergeant Campbell was addressing Xander Bird, continuing the earlier conversation.

"We could," Xander said after a minute. "Satellites don't show any significant weather for this area over the next few days. We ought to know one way or the other about *Emerald Maui* by then. If everyone else is on board with this, I say we camp—move inland a hundred meters or so just to stay away from the worst of the beachside predators, go hunting and see if we can get some fresh meat and maybe berries and such."

"All in favor?" Laura asked. "Well, it looks like it's unanimous. Hitomi, Francisco, we're going to wait for you here. It's marked now on your maps."

"I see it, Mommy! That little bay on the side."

"That's right, honey. How are you two coming along?"

"Francisco's tied the prybars so they hang right near the shard, and he's ready to go. I've got the manual controls for the winch."

"How will they know when to pry and when to pull?" Laura asked to the group at large.

"Tav and I linked the right libraries to track the behavior. If they're lucky, it'll just pull right out with a straight pull. If not, well, we track the tension on the rope, the outrigger the winch is connected to, and the jet engine. We don't want to damage anything else while we do this. If it looks like it can't be just pulled straight out, we should have data from the strain sensors that tells us where it's hanging up; that's where Francisco will have to pry. Hopefully that can be done without tension on the cable, but if not, all we can do is advise Franky where the safest place to pry from is."

Sakura bit her lip. Francisco was going to be in the most dangerous position if that happened; with tension on the cable while prying, the massive shard could suddenly pop loose, and if he was in the wrong position when that happened . . .

"We have to do this," Francisco said, and she could tell he was trying to sound like the sergeant, or maybe Xander. "So how dangerous it is doesn't matter. If we do not get *Emerald Maui* running, Whips will die. Maybe we won't—there is a lot of food and water here, and before that runs out maybe you could make a boat to get us back—but Whips won't live that long. So we have to do this."

"Right," said Hitomi. "And we're ready."

"We may not even need to camp," observed Maddox. "If this works...we can get them home soon, I think."

"Even best-case, we'll be camping," the sergeant said. "But maybe only one day. Let's see how the kids do." He raised his voice. "Okay, Francisco, Hitomi—go to it, and good luck!"

Chapter 33

"Thank you, Sergeant!" Hitomi said. She looked across the water to Francisco, who was sitting on the tail above the jet. "Cross your fingers, like my dad says."

She saw Francisco hold up his hands; he'd crossed all four fingers of each hand and hooked the thumbs together so they were crossed, too. "Let's go!"

Hitomi activated the winch. "Taking up the slack... getting tighter..."

The cable, which had been somewhat loosely wavering below, became straighter and straighter. Now it was tense, going in a ruler-straight line from the front of the winch into the water at a shallow angle, up from the floatcoral fragment embedded in the engine. "Tension rising. You see this, Tavana, Xander?"

"We see it. All looking good so far. Keep going, Hitomi."

She slid the control up slowly. A faint hum transmitted itself through the outrigger to her boots as the winch's motor applied more and more force to the line. "Could this break the cable?"

Tavana chuckled. "No, Hitomi. The cable, it could hold up all of *Emerald Maui* without any problem. The winch's anchor might pull loose, but the cable, it will be fine."

The winch hummed louder, the cable thrummed from the vibration; little ripples emanated from the cable where it entered the water.

"All right, that's enough, it's not coming out with a simple pull," Xander said finally.

Hitomi hit the cutoff as soon as she heard "that's enough." The hum faded away and the cable relaxed a few centimeters.

"Hmm. Analysis coming...Okay, Francisco, we're highlighting two points in your omni. Try prying at those a few times, then come up and we'll try again."

Francisco nodded. First he stood up and looked around the water carefully. Hitomi went onto the top of *Emerald Maui* and also made sure there were no suspicious shadows in the water nearby. "Clear!" she shouted down.

"Okay! I am going down!"

She saw Francisco's thin form dive into the clear water of Lincoln's ocean. Distorted by ripples, she could still see him grab one of the dangling prybars and insert it somewhere at the base of the shard.

It took about ten minutes of Francisco prying, coming to the surface to rest, then diving back down to try levering against the shard from a different direction. Finally the boy pulled himself out of the water. "Did a lot of prying on both points," he said, his voice somewhat breathless. "Try again?"

"Okay. Are you clear, Francisco?"

"All the way out of the water and out of the way, yes, Tav."

"Okay, Hitomi, try it again."

Once more the winch returned to its humming and the cable stretched out, straight as a steel bar. Hitomi carefully increased the power, a little bit at a time.

"Keep going...keep going...I'm seeing a little variation in strain, maybe it's going to—"

Without warning, the cable sprang back with a deep *thung!* that made Hitomi jump. She hit the *emergency stop* control; the cable sank from nearly horizontal to vertical, bouncing slightly from the weight of something on the other end.

"Did it work? Is it out?" she asked, feeling excitement and hope bubbling up through her. "Something's still on the cable, is it out?"

"Checking the cable...there's definitely something heavy tied to it! Francisco, what do you see?"

"The shard, it is gone! I don't see anything sticking out of the engine now!"

"Excellent!" Sergeant Campbell said. "Now, you've got to reel in that piece and then get it loose, so you can put the winch away and we can test the engine."

"Maybe not," Xander said; Hitomi tensed at the tone of his

voice. "Well, yes, get that piece off the winch, but I don't think we're ready to test the engine."

"What? Why?" demanded Francisco. "The piece is out, isn't it?"

"That's what I don't know. Oh, I'm sure you've got most of it, but I didn't see the shifts in strains that I expected in the engine."

Francisco said something in Spanish that Hitomi was sure was a bad thing to say, especially since her new omni's auto-translator blocked it out. Since it was one of the cheap omnis they'd found a small case of, it didn't have any of the custom apps in it, but she was pretty sure even her old one wouldn't have translated *that*. "You mean it *broke off*."

"That's what I'm afraid of." Xander's voice sounded both unhappy and apologetic, as though the bad news was somehow his fault.

"Well, I will just go down and look." Francisco jumped off and swam to the engine intake.

He was back up in a minute. "You are right. There is a little piece of it stuck in; it looks like it broke off near one of the pry points."

"No way to tie onto it again?"

"No. Here, I took a picture."

Hitomi saw the image pop up in her omni; the piece of float-coral didn't stick out more than about five or ten centimeters, nowhere near enough to tie the cable onto.

"Damnation." Sergeant Campbell sighed. "Well, then, no help for it; you're going to have to start prying and chipping at it somehow to get it out."

"Hold on," came the voice of Pearce Haley. "Sam, do they have any Bond-All on board?"

"The universal adhesive? I dunno. Hitomi?"

As the question was asked, she could see a little box, set on the wall halfway back in the cargo hold. "There's a box with tubes in it marked as Vaneman's UA #3. I think it's a kind of glue. Is that close enough?"

"Universal Adhesive Three? Yeah, that's Vaneman's version of Elmin's Bond-All. What's the idea, Pearce?"

"Bond-All works underwater, I know that. If Vaneman's does the same, they could bond the end of the cable to that piece and pull. If it sets properly it will be about as strong as the cable."

"Damn good thinking, Pearce. Francisco, Hitomi, you got that?"

"*Si*, Sergeant! We untie the big chunk, then use this Vaneman material on the end of the cable to hook it to the piece that's stuck in the engine. How do I do it, exactly?"

"I could do it!" Hitomi pointed out.

"You are right. How do we do it?"

"First, check the batteries on the tube—you'll want to be sure the nanocatalysts are still active."

"Be right back!" Hitomi ran across the outrigger and vaulted into *Emerald Maui*, heading for the back. *We are* not *going to be stopped now!*

The adhesive tubes were a little larger than she remembered; she couldn't quite close her hand around one. Still, she didn't know how many they would need, so she detached the whole case and ran back out. "There's no indicators on the tubes," she said after a minute, "but I'm getting a green status ping from the carrying case."

"Makes sense," Campbell said. "Okay, me and Pearce have it down." He sent a little animation. "You slather a bunch of it on the cable end, like you see here. Then you use that box and tell it to activate 'Bond Phase I'; that'll make it sticky but keep it from flowing away. Bring it down and stick it on the chunk of floatcoral. This is gonna take two of you, because one of you, probably Francisco, will have to drag the cable and hold it in place, and Hitomi will have to bring the case down with it. The controller's signal won't go more than about half a meter or so underwater, so you've got to get the box *close* when you trigger 'Bond Phase II.' Takes about ten seconds to set, so make sure you've both got the breath it's gonna take. Right?"

Hitomi reviewed the images and instructions. It seemed pretty simple even to her, though she knew from their previous underwater work that it might not be easy. She looked at Francisco, who nodded. "Got it, sir."

"All right. Get to it, crew."

Bringing up and releasing the big chunk of floatcoral took a little bit; it was easy to winch up, but the cable was deeply dug into the material of the coral and the knots were half-sunk beneath the surface. After about five minutes, her mom spoke up. "Just cut it loose, kids. You have lots and lots of cable. No need to wear yourselves out on this. Right, everyone?"

"Well, I hate losing anything...but yeah, you're right, Laura.

Four, five meters of cable's no big deal. Use the cutter control on the front of the winch."

The floatcoral shard dropped away into the depths, then slowly rose back into sight, drifting gradually farther away. "Okay!"

"Okay, you've got the sergeant and lieutenant's instructions. You know what to do."

"Right."

First Hitomi made the winch pay out the right length of cable; Francisco made a test dive to make sure it would reach easily. He came back, had her retract about half a meter of cable, then checked again. "Perfect," Francisco said.

"Okay, then we're going to do it, right?" She reached out and pulled out one of the tubes of adhesive.

"Guess so." Francisco held up the slightly splayed end of the cable as she carefully covered it with a heavy layering of the thick but still easily spread, glittering silvery gel. "Triggering Bond Phase I," she said, and had her omni engage that signal.

The gel shimmered, the silvery sparkle seeming to form into layered streaks. It also stopped flowing around.

"Looks like it's working the way you said, sir," Francisco said. "So now we go under and stick it on."

"Hold on!" Hitomi jumped up and did another survey around the ship. She spotted a raylamp crawling up the other side of the tail, but nothing else; a careful approach and quick shot and the creature was gone. "Okay."

They made their way over to the tail and stood, hyperventilating until Hitomi felt really lightheaded, then dove into the water.

As they approached, she could see the fragment—pure, bright white where it had broken off. It was slightly rough, like cement, with some internal structure she didn't understand. Francisco dragged the cable down and shoved the end against the fragment's surface. The adhesive belled out and then seemed to tighten, covering the entire area and some small part around the edge.

That fit the animation. She swam a little closer and held out the box, triggering the second bond phase.

Francisco held the cable in place with grim determination, his legs hooked over part of the engine support, his hands keeping the cable and fragment pressed together.

Ten seconds could seem like an eternity underwater, but she kept her eyes shifting between the cable and the timer in her omni display. The silver color began to mist over, the translucency of the gel started to thicken, as the adhesive became more and more a pure white color little different from that of the floatcoral.

Francisco's face was darker and jaw clenched, but he did not move until the counter dropped to zero; the two of them leapt for the surface. Francisco gave a huge gasp. "Almost . . . ran out," he said after a moment. "But wasn't . . . going to stop now."

"Is the bond strong now, Lieutenant Haley?"

"It should be. Nanocatalyzed adhesives work very fast."

"We'll give it a few minutes anyway," Hitomi said. She didn't want to take chances. Besides, that would give her a little time to rest and get the remaining adhesive and its box back to their proper places.

By the time she returned, Francisco was up by the winch. "Want to try it now?"

"Sure." She touched the controls.

The cable drew taut once more, the winch hummed its song of power—and with almost no pause, the cable suddenly sprung back and hung limp again.

"Oh, no! Did it come off?"

Xander laughed. "No, it didn't. Just saw the strain gauges shift the way we were hoping. Kids, you'll have to take one more dive to check, but I think—I *think*—you've just cleared the engine!"

Chapter 34

"By God, those kids are hard workers," Campbell said to Pearce as they cleared away brush and stones and other debris from the chosen camping area.

"They are that," she said. "Of course, their families were chosen for early settlers, so you'd expect them to be pretty adaptable." She looked to where the sea could be glimpsed, glittering in the very-slowly dropping rays of Lincoln's setting sun. "But stranded on that ship alone...yes, it's impressive."

"Hopefully we can get everyone together soon," Campbell said, then raised his voice slightly. "Tavana, what's the status on *Emerald Maui*?"

"The jet *was* damaged," Tavana said, "but not too badly. The nanomaterial can repair itself with the right direction, which we are giving it now. That will be...oh, six to eight hours, I think. Then we can test it and make sure there's nothing else wrong."

"How about navigation? Clearing up their window, maybe?"

"The extra nanodust could do it, and we'll get that started," Pearce said. "But that's going to take more time than we want to take. Since that quick-and-dirty fix of the antenna worked, though, there's an easier way."

"Omnis, you mean?"

"Exactly!" Sakura said, dragging one of the smaller tents that had been in storage up from their cargo. "The Vaneman adhesive will be perfect to bond a couple of those omnis to the front of *Emerald Maui* and their cameras are more than good enough to navigate with. Once we're sure everything's mechanically functional, it'll take Hitomi and Francisco maybe an hour to get that set up. Then me and Tav can remote-drive them home."

"Excellent news. Doc—Laura—sounds like you'd better get everything prepped to take care of Whips."

"Yes, I'm already working on that." Campbell noticed that neither she nor Akira were visible. "We've found a nice flat exposed surface, probably the base of that broken column you noticed. It was one of the ones with a sealed-off base. That will be good for an operating surface once I get it cleaned off."

"How you figure to sterilize it?"

"*Emerald Maui* has what I need; there's a UV sterilizer light that will do the job. Worst comes to worst we could douse it with alcohol and set it on fire; Akira doesn't think that would do too much damage to the underlying structure but it would certainly kill anything on the surface. We'll also be able to put a shelter up over it to serve as an operating theater."

"Sounds good. Let us know if you need anything."

"*Ow!*" Sakura was hopping around holding her foot.

"What happened, Saki? You get stung by something?" Tavana was immediately next to her.

"No, no . . . ow, that hurts . . . it was just that rock there, I went to kick it out of the way and it *stayed* there, must be stuck or something."

Melody and Caroline had just arrived, carrying a bunch of gathered deadwood for a fire. Melody dumped her load and went to look at the offending object.

Campbell saw the little girl—*well, not so little anymore, she's started to shoot up*—freeze. That immediately put his senses on alert. "What is it, Mel?"

Melody grunted, a surprisingly deep sound from such a slender girl, and hefted the irregular object in both hands. Campbell could see the muscles on her arms standing out with the effort of holding it. "This isn't an island rock," she said, and her soprano voice was grim.

"I can see that. What's the problem?" He knew there was a problem. Melody tended to be quiet—sometimes sulky, sometimes just private—unless she was either showing off, which had according to her parents gotten a lot rarer over the time they'd been marooned, or if there was something really important to say.

"It's a meteorite," she said flatly, flipping her straight black hair back. When he just raised his eyebrow, she went on—with only a hint of self-satisfaction—"We've only tried clearing, what, a few hundred square meters of Lincoln? And now I, well, no, *Sakura* finds a meteorite, and one in pretty good shape? Either we've just done what Dad would call hitting the jackpot, or meteorites are pretty common here." She let it drop with a *thud* to the ground. "That lagoon at the end of our island? Round hole, like it was punched through. Always figured *that* was a meteor. Your old island? *Big* round lake, probably meteor. And a big meteor just almost killed us all. Both landmasses we've been on, hit by at least one big meteor, and a third big one hit just a few kilometers away."

Campbell was getting the picture and he didn't like it. "You're saying it's *common* that things like this happen."

Mel seesawed her hand. "Well...lot more common than it is on Earth or most other inhabited worlds."

"Melody, do you have any idea *how* often?" Caroline asked.

Melody's black eyes looked distant; Campbell recognized the look of someone reviewing things on a retinal display. "Well... only a guess, really, but if you remember, we're always seeing comets and meteors. Comet orbits intersecting planetary orbits, you get a meteor shower. Bigger comets can break up and give you bigger chunks, I'd think."

Campbell looked up and to the left; sure enough, he could make out one of the bigger comets in the sky, even in daylight.

"Well, come *on* Mel," Sakura said, having sat down and let Tavana take a look at her toe.

"Best guess...um, there's quite a few bigger-sized meteors, like the one we just survived, coming down every year, I think. Of course, Lincoln's huge and most of it's going to be in ocean far from any of the islands, and if you're far enough away it won't cause much damage. Still...a hit like that one probably will come close enough for us to notice every few years. Maybe every ten? I don't know. Not enough data. But definitely it's a real threat, it could happen again, and not like a hundred years from now. Maybe even a bigger strike."

"Damnation." He wanted to argue the points, but his gut agreed with Melody. They'd had a major meteor strike within a year or so of landing, and there were lots of other meteor signs. Lincoln wasn't done with them yet; it had now revealed that it was a cosmic shooting gallery. "And no way to predict when or where."

Melody bit her lip, then shook her head. "I can *sort of* see some patterns from the year or so we've been here—like when we had heavy meteor showers—but with that many comets on so many different periods, there's probably always a chance of something big dropping."

Caroline had been looking up, a thoughtful expression on her face. "Xander, Sergeant, the satellites have cameras that look down; can they be made to look *up*?"

Campbell blinked, then grinned. "That's a damn good question, Caroline. My first thought is 'probably'; anyone got a better answer?"

"Oh, sure they can, Sergeant!" Maddox looked excited. "I was looking at their specs and they can rotate around their axes pretty easily. You're thinking of making them a sort of skywatch for meteors, Caroline?"

"That *is* the idea, Maddox," she said with a smile; Maddox smiled back eagerly. "Could they do it? Detect a big meteor in time to warn us?"

"I...think so? They've got pretty good telescopic capability and high resolution, and nothing to blur things in space."

"Well, that's something to look into. Maddox, why don't you and Melody get on that? I think it's something the two of you can do while the rest of us are doing our other work," Xander suggested, with a glance at Campbell, who nodded, and at a vague nothingness that Campbell was sure was an omni-projection of Laura Kimei. She had evidently also agreed, because Xander nodded to thin air and grinned.

"Okay! Want to do that, Mel?"

"Now? Um..." Melody looked a bit flustered, but then nodded sharply. "Yes. Yes, let's. The faster we get something watching, the safer we'll be."

Campbell smiled. "Okay, we'll keep setting up camp, then. Hitomi, Francisco, you guys okay out there?"

"We're fine, Sergeant!" Hitomi answered promptly. "Francisco is making dinner and then we're going to play some Jewelbug together!"

"A good end to a day. By the time you get up tomorrow, it'll be dark, but the engine should be ready and with luck we'll start bringing you home then."

"Oh, I hope so!"

Laura's warm laugh came over the omnis. "So do we, honey. Now you have a good night, and call us if there's any problems."

"We will!"

Tavana started building a fire. "Then it is time for us to start getting dinner, too!"

"Sure is," Campbell agreed. He looked up at the sky, where the hidden stars were watching.

He just hoped none of them were getting set to fall.

Chapter 35

"All right," Tavana's voice came over the omni, "Are we all ready?"

"Ready!" said Hitomi, checking her straps to make sure she was fastened into her seat properly.

"Ready," agreed Francisco, in the seat next to her.

"Okay, testing engines in three, two, one..."

A deep hum rose, resonating from the rear of *Emerald Maui*, a new sound for Hitomi, but she saw a brilliant white smile on Francisco's face as a gentle pressure pushed her back in her seat. "*It works!*" Francisco shouted.

"*Oui*, it definitely is working," Tavana said, and she could hear the smile in his voice. "Xander, Pearce, everyone—does it all look good to you?"

"Looks good to me," Xander said.

"It's just a little rougher than spec," Pearce said, "but nowhere near a problem. Running it for a while will probably show us where the issue is, and then nanorepair can deal with it."

Sakura and Maddox both agreed that everything looked good. "Okay," Tavana said, "then you guys can unstrap now. Time to put eyes on *Emerald Maui* so we can bring her home."

"Where do we put them?" Hitomi asked.

"Been modeling that," Sakura said, "with Tav's help. You're going to want to put two of them up front, one just on either side of the front port—we'll mark the coordinates in your omnis so you can get them right where they should go. One in the back, just so we have coverage back there."

"We'll only have four spare omnis left after that," Hitomi said, remembering the box. "You sure?"

217

"A good question, Hitomi," said Mommy. "But yes, we're sure. *Emerald Maui* might be working for us for many years, and she needs good eyes."

"Okay, Mommy. We'll put those on now!"

"It's *dark* out there," Xander said. "Are we sure we want them doing it now?"

"We can turn on the lights outside," Hitomi said. "And I know the omnis can, um..." she searched for the word, found it, "...enhance the view, so we should be able to see just fine."

"That's not what the captain's worried about, I think," Sergeant Campbell said. "If I guess right, anyway."

"You usually do, Sergeant." Xander's voice was deadly serious, and Hitomi could tell he was worried. "I remember talking about fishing—with Tav and some of the others—and Tav mentioned there were fish that got attracted by light—"

Hitomi felt like something icy-cold had just draped itself around her. Her mind showed her the brightly-lit *Emerald Maui* with two little kids working on her, and something looking up from the black water below...something that she couldn't see coming..."Ugh."

"*Ugh* is right," Daddy said. "You're completely correct, Xander. A number of predators on at least six or seven worlds would be attracted to lights on the surface, and of course with them working in the illumination the children wouldn't be able to keep an eye out. And it'll be harder to see raylamps coming out of the water, too. Laura, can we wait until the sun rises?"

Hitomi saw her mother's face looking thoughtful. "I don't know, Akira. That's another ten hours, and Whips' suspension is really...experimental. The telemetry from him isn't exactly what I hoped. I don't *know* if anything's going wrong...but it might be. And remember that it will take them at least ten hours more to get home, if there's no problems on the way."

"Which we probably shouldn't bet on," Pearce Haley said.

Xander sighed. "Sounds like we have to go forward, then."

"*Have* to...no," said Mommy. "But...I really want Whips back as soon as possible." Hitomi heard her swallow. "But I don't want to risk the other children, either."

"I don't want Whips to die, Mommy!" Hitomi said loudly.

"Honey, none of us do. But if you get hurt..."

"It shouldn't be too much of a problem, Mom," Melody said.

"Mel? Thought you were working on the meteor-watch."

"We are," she said. "Still heard the argument. Look at the way *Emerald Maui*'s built. If they work sitting on the inside—toward the center—they'll be well on top of the ship. Nothing's going to be able to just grab them with a jump, unless it somehow knows the edible parts are up on top, which would be weird."

"Mel has a point," Tavana said, voice more relaxed. "An island-eater's not coming after something that small, and so far nothing big seems interested in *Emerald Maui*. More normal predators, like the finny-types? They won't be able to grab our kids without warning."

"I see," Daddy said; his head was nodding the way it did when someone gave him the right answer. "And since we have the exact design of the *Emerald Maui*, we should be able to program their omnis to recognize if anything's crawling towards them, even if their eyes don't immediately spot it."

"Easy to do. Take me ten minutes, max," Maddox said. "Leave it to me."

"Go to it, little bro," Xander said with a grin. "Okay, so we're doing this, right?"

"Right!" Hitomi said, unstrapping. "We'll keep the lights off until we're on top of the ship, okay?"

"Works for me. Be careful, kids."

"We will!" She thought of the dark water and the monsters that might wait beneath it, and shivered. "We will."

It didn't take more than a few minutes to get up top; the fact that there were two brilliant comets lighting the night helped a lot. One of them looked about as bright as the Moon back home. Still wasn't really enough light to work with, so they *were* going to have to turn on the lights.

Hitomi looked up at the stars as Francisco clambered up next to her. "What are you looking at?" he asked.

"Just...the stars. We came from there. I wonder what Lincoln thinks about us, coming here from so far away."

"I don't know. Lincoln doesn't think, does it?"

"Maybe. Tav and Saki and the others still haven't figured out where those weird radio waves come from. Maybe it's the planet, thinking."

Francisco looked nervous. "That is creepy, Hitomi."

"Why?" She thought the idea of the planet having thoughts,

maybe long, slow thoughts like the Ents in one of Saki's favorite books, was kind of cute.

"Because..." Francisco's face wrinkled, then he gave a low laugh. "I...will think about it. It is creepy, but I find...I don't know how to explain why." He turned towards the front. "Okay, *Emerald Maui*, turn on interior and exterior lights."

Instantly white radiance filled the area; at the same time, Hitomi felt that was kind of creepy, because it made the stars fade and the night around them looked even darker. It was as though *Emerald Maui* had to suck the light out of the rest of the universe to make itself bright.

Stop it. Focus. Focus. She saw her omni marking two small bright red squares at the edges of the forward port. The ridge below the port that contained the cleaning equipment and protective shield would make it easy to stand there, so they should be able to place them safely. As she brought her brain slowly under control, she could see the exact position she'd have to stand in, and the way that Francisco would..."Tavana, can we put them a few centimeters lower? I don't know if I can reach the right place where you've put them; we can't really stand on the forward port, we'll slide off."

"Oh, *baka*," Sakura said. "Of course they can't. Tav?"

"We can drop them a decimeter without interfering in the view too much. Is that enough?"

"Show us?" Hitomi asked.

The red rectangles drifted down the sides of the port. Hitomi, having slid to the ridge at the bottom of the port, was now able to walk over and reach up. "Yes, I can reach there now!"

"Great!"

Her omni pinged, showing an app update from Maddox labeled "Raylamp Detector." "Got your update, Maddox. What do we do to use it?"

"It's automatic right now. All you guys have to do is take a look around every few minutes so it can update its scan and let you know if anything's changed."

"We can do that," Francisco said. "Ready, Hitomi?"

"Ready!"

"Okay. The first thing we do here is strip the protective coating off. Found this out when I was trying to put on our new antenna, the bonded coating really doesn't want to let anything stick to it. *Maybe* Vaneman UA would anyway, but I don't want to go getting that angry at something again, so we do it right the first time."

He handed her a small can and gloves. "Put the gloves on and only open the can after you have them on. The debonder is not nice stuff."

She remembered his hands having white burns on them that day and nodded. "How do I put it on?"

"Paintbrush—I'll give it to you once you're ready. Then I'll go do the other one."

A few minutes later she was armed with a paintbrush and the can of sharp-smelling debonder. Her medical nanos alerted her not to breathe the fumes if possible. *That's funny! We've done so many more dangerous things than that!*

Still, there was no reason to make anything more dangerous, so she carefully kept the can as far from her as she could. Focusing, her world narrowed to the projected red rectangle on the hull of *Emerald Maui*, Hitomi carefully painted the debonder precisely onto that rectangle, covering every square millimeter with a thick coating of the chemical. She then closed the can and backed away, as faintly-visible fumes began to rise from the hull. Her nanos reported that that stuff would be even more dangerous, and even the tiny whiff she got of it made her very sure she didn't want to smell any more.

Francisco joined her near the center of the forward port. Her omni and his pinged at nearly the same time, and they saw, outlined in blue, a familiar near-amorphous *something* drawing itself slowly out of the water. "Stupid things," Francisco murmured. "You want to get that one?"

Hitomi nodded. Drawing her little pistol, she sighted carefully with the help of her omni and fired three times. The little coughing sound of the SurvivalShot Mini echoed loudly in the near-silence of Lincoln's ocean, and the raylamp slid limply from the hull, blown nearly in half.

"Let's just hope that doesn't attract more," Mommy said.

"It might, but the kids don't have much choice," the sergeant said. "Can't let those things get near them."

After a few more minutes, they were able to go back and check the debonded areas. There was just a film of whitish material left, which scraped off easily with the help of her Shapetool. That left a clean, white surface with just a hint of linear structure in it—the carbonan composite that made up a lot of the hull. "It's ready, I think!"

"Good. Let me look." Francisco came over, took a quick glance, and nodded. "*Si*, exactly what it should look like. You put the debonder on really good; I had to do it twice the first few times I did it."

"Thanks!" She smiled at him. "So now we can bond the omnis on?"

"Should work fine now. And since we're above water the control box will work for both of us."

Since they'd used the universal adhesive in far more difficult circumstances, it wasn't more than a few minutes before Hitomi triggered the second bonding phase for both. A short time later, the bonds were as hard and rigid as the composite below them. "Tavana, the omnis are in place! Test them?"

A moment later, an image of the water before *Emerald Maui*—with maybe a tiny piece of her head visible—flashed onto their omni retinal displays. "They work perfect! We have good binocular vision and side peripheral imaging, too. The vision app is calibrating now. Just put one on the tail and we'll be set!"

"Right!"

They had to pause on the way to the rear to let the Raylamp Detector get a good look around the other parts of the ship, and again when it found one toward the rear. That dealt with (by Francisco, this time), Hitomi found that she and Francisco could easily place the third omni; it took even less time than the ones in front. "All set!"

"Hold on . . . yes, yes, the rear camera, it is also working! *Emerald Maui* has eyes again!"

There was a low cheer from everyone.

"All right, kids," Sergeant Campbell's voice, deep and rough and reassuring, spoke. "Everything's finally ready. Hitomi, Francisco, you've done absolutely professional work, kids, handled every problem you ran into, and we're all as proud as can be. You give each other a big hug and a high-five, right?"

She laughed and embraced Francisco, who squeezed her so hard she gasped, and then the two of them slapped hands.

"Damn right. Now get yourselves inside and strapped in."

Just like an hour or so before, Hitomi slid into her seat and fastened the harness, making sure it was tight as it should be. She saw Francisco check hers as she took a look at his.

The display on the inside of the port suddenly lit up, and it was as though the port was now crystal clear; a full-3D image of the water ahead, illuminated by the full brightness of *Emerald Maui*'s forward lights, sparkled darkly before them. "Display working, kids?"

"Working perfectly, sir!"

"Good. Tavana?"

"Cross fingers, everyone."

The pilot's board lit up—many yellows and reds from the areas that were damaged, but a core of bright green was there was well. The deep drone of the jet rose up, and she felt movement. *Emerald Maui* was moving!

"We're moving!" she shouted, and heard Francisco echoing her at the same time.

"You *are*, Hitomi, Franky!" Tavana said, his voice as excited as theirs; Francisco didn't complain about the use of his nickname, which showed how excited *he* was. The water rumbled beneath the hull, and she felt the *bump-bump-bump* as *Emerald Maui* began to really cruise, hammering smoothly through the waves. "Up to ... twenty kilometers per hour!"

"Probably as fast as we want to go right now," Xander said. "Any faster and even the automated anti-collision apps won't be able to react fast enough; the headlights can only reach so far ahead. Plus we need to go easy on her for a bit to make sure everything's okay."

"But it all looks good now," Pearce said. "No sign of significant strain from the engine or hull or the outrigger or tail. Hitomi, Francisco—you're coming home!"

Chapter 36

Light flowed slowly into him like water softening an *annitil* core, and with it came coolness... and the return of pain, sharp, dull, throbbing, grating, every form of agony he had ever imagined.

But Whips grabbed onto that pain, let it sharpen his awareness. *I hurt. That means I'm* awake. *It means I'm* alive, *and they woke me up for something.*

He didn't try to open his eyes yet; his mind was still sluggish, wrapped in murk and muck, clouding his thoughts and comprehension. *I... I think I'm still bad hurt. It doesn't feel like after an operation.*

Okay, that made sense. He felt he'd gotten that right. But he also remembered Laura putting him to sleep. So there were only two reasons he'd be awake.

For a moment his brain stalled on that. He knew there were two reasons, but it was several seconds before he managed to remember them. The first would be if they'd made it home. The second... the second would be if there was something badly wrong that needed him to help the kids, hurt or not.

With a tremendous effort he deliberately moved his worst-injured arm, making the cracked plates within grate against each other. The electric-hot jolt of protest from his body sharpened his wits and perceptions. He forced his uninjured eye open.

Even hurt as he ways, the well-loved faces in front of him sent a warm wave of relief and triumph through Whips. Deep chestnut hair glinting with red highlights above worried brown eyes, and to the right worried blue eyes below a cascade of pure abyssal black. "L... Laura," he managed, hearing his voice buzzing and weak. "Saki... we made it."

"Whips, oh, thank God yes, yes, you did," Laura said, her voice near to breaking. Sakura just blinked hard, two tears falling, and nodded;

"Why...am I...awake?"

"I'm about to operate on you, Harratrer," Laura said, her voice back under control. "And...and I honestly don't know if you'll survive."

He had known that for a while. If he thought about it, his nanos would tell him just how badly he was hurt and give him dispassionate projections for how likely he was to survive. The percentages...were not good. Very bad.

"So," Sakura said, her voice forced-steady and not fooling anyone, "We wanted you to know everything else was okay, before..."

He flicked his upper arm in understanding, let the chromatophores flicker the pattern of gratitude. "You mean, know that Hitomi and Francisco would be all right, that...that all of you were..."

She nodded.

Hitomi and Francisco appeared; from their positions, he realized he must be lying on some kind of smooth surface that was at ground level, because they were taller than him right now. Saki and Laura stood, towering over him, and stepped back.

Hitomi reached out and hugged him. That didn't hurt too much, because the little girl was being careful to touch him in the least-injured areas. "We're all right!" she said, and Francisco added his own, slightly-more-painful, hug. "*Si*, we are. All together. All safe. Thanks to you making sure *Emerald Maui* would work for us."

Relief flooded through him, finally, erasing for a few moments some of the agony. "Good. Good. That makes me very happy, Hitomi...Francisco."

The other Kimeis came forward and touched him gently. "We're all here, Whips," Akira said. "Laura's going to take care of you now."

"Yes, I am, with the help of Pearce, who's the closest I've got to a medical assistant. Now everyone's going to have to clear the area. I have to sterilize everything as much as I can, and that means no one tramping around in the operating theater."

Whips looked around as much as he could. He was one some kind of smooth flat surface...*base of a column? Has to be. It's like the bottom of Campbell's column.* But the light was diffuse, coming through...*a shelter. They put a shelter up. Cover this area, keep it clean. I guess that* is *the best you could do for this.*

He couldn't let Laura put him to sleep, not yet. "Wait. Need to talk...to Saki. Alone."

"Whips, we don't have..." Laura stopped, probably seeing the sharp black-green-white of determination rippling across his back. "Make it quick, Saki. The longer we wait..."

"I know."

In a few moments, the shelter was empty. Sakura took some of his good fingers into her hand, twined her so-stubby human fingers around them. He looked at her, so different from his people—so thin that she ought to break at the smallest current, a ridiculous fringe of useless fluff on her head (*why, it can't even strain out food from a current*), a mere two manipulative arms with only five fingers, and that strange skeleton, divided in huge, non-flexing chunks. And inside he felt a wistful burning ache that had nothing to do with his injuries.

"What is it, Whips?"

"We...haven't had much time...lately," he said, and it was harder to speak now. But the tension and pain that made it so wasn't in his body.

"No...I'm sorry, Whips, I...I mean...me and Tavana...I shouldn't have..."

"Don't apologize. I just..." He drew in a deep breath, ignoring the sparks of tearing fire throughout the length of his body as he did. "...just wanted to...say I wished I was human. Or you were Bemmie."

Her eyes widened.

"Stupid, isn't it? But...you were always there. We lived with you. I guess I just never...thought there'd be a day you weren't there, dragging me wherever you went, Saki."

"*Stop it!*" Her whisper had the force of an angry shout. "You're *not* giving me this...this...bullcrap deathbed confession stuff from one of Caroline's romance chips!" But her eyes were so full of tears he didn't think she could see him.

"Said it was stupid. I know." He pulled in another breath. "But...I realized I was *jealous* of Tav. And I...just couldn't die without telling you...how important you are. Everything about you, Saki. Just...that. Always were. Always will be."

"*Dammit.* Dammit." She repeated the word three more times. "I ought to kick you, Whips, you...Doing this to me now." She wiped her eyes roughly on the back of her arm. "I feel the same way, and you damn well know it." She leaned over and planted a kiss right next to his eye. "And...I should've thought about that. Just because me and Tavana are...well...dating, doesn't mean I should be forgetting about you, especially when...well...you've only got us. I'll try to do better."

A great warmth spread through him, and he saw her smile as a momentary pattern of peace and joy flashed across his body. "Then...it's all fine. I love you, Saki."

A tender, exquisitely gentle hug. "I love you too, Whips. Now...get better so I can give you that kick later."

Despite the pain he gave a hooting laugh. "I'll try."

Sakura stepped outside. A few moments later, Laura came back in, carrying her medical case, followed by Pearce. Both of them were wearing masks.

"Here," Laura said, "we tinkered this filter up for you. Breathe only through this for the next few minutes."

The two women swabbed the area thoroughly with something—he thought it was alcohol or some similar material—and sprayed something across him that stung, but not as badly as he had feared. *Or maybe I'm fading out again.*

Vaguely, he heard the built-in shelter ventilation running at high. *That'll drain the batteries fairly fast...but if there's enough sunlight...* his brain took a momentary, distracted excursion into power calculations before his eyes refocused on Laura, sitting down in front of him.

"All right, Whips. Time to start."

"Mom...will I be all right?"

Her lips tightened, barely visible beneath the mask. "I...don't know. But I'll do my best."

"Okay. Love you all, Mom."

"Love you too, Harratrer. Now sleep. If everything goes well, you'll close your eye and wake up better."

The nanosleep rose up, warm and comforting, erasing pain and worry, and Whips let it wash up and obliterate his consciousness.

Chapter 37

Laura's hand shook. She stared at it in a sort of disbelieving fascination. *I've done a lot of operations over the years. Not as many as I would have had to do a couple centuries back, but quite a few. What's wrong with me?*

Even as she thought the question, Pearce's gloved hand covered hers. "It's all right, Doc. You've got this."

And she already knew the answer. "It's...he's my son. My only son. Does that sound ridiculous or what?"

Pearce Haley shook her head. "No, why should it? He calls you Mom, and not as a joke."

Please, whoever and whatever might be out there, help me do this. "A mother...a *doctor* should never have to operate on their own children. Pearce, I'm *terrified*. What if Whips *dies* while I'm working on him?"

She saw by Pearce's wide eyes that she had, at least, successfully hidden her doubts and fears until now. "Jesus, Laura, I..." She paused. "Laura, I guess it *has* to be frightening. But who else, Laura? Is there anyone else here who could even *try* this... gauntlet of operations?"

Laura closed her eyes. *Of course there isn't. There isn't anyone within ten light-years who could.* "No." She drew in her breath, let it out. Her hand steadied. "No, there isn't, and if I don't, he's going to die."

He might die even if she did do the very best she could. The thought of that—of having to face Sakura and the others after losing him—was horrifying. But it would be far more horrifying to lose him from doing nothing.

"All right. Pearce, you're my nurse and assistant. Most of what you do here will be to monitor vitals, adjust nanosleep and IV's, and support my work. Is there anything you need before we start? Bathroom break? Quick bite to eat? Once we start we're not stopping and this will take hours."

"Already did that. I'm ready, Doctor."

"All right. Sergeant, Akira, Xander, we are beginning. Unless another meteor hits, or something else that disastrous is on the way, *nothing* interrupts us, understand?"

"Yes, Ma'am," the sergeant said, and the others echoed their agreement. "We'll keep everyone away. Not like there isn't plenty to do to keep us busy."

"Thank you." Another deep breath. "Let's begin."

She looked again through her omni-enhanced vision at the HUD display it was generating that highlighted all the injuries on Harratrer's body. The Sutter Organ, oxygen-exchange manifold, and McCoy's Plexus were highlighted in red, by far the most critical injuries. In bright orange were all the other severe injuries—broken plates, ripped tendons, eyes, and two other significant circulatory leaks. *Dear Lord, it's absolutely incredible that he could move as much as he did. That much damage to the nodal plexus was probably interfering with nerve transmission.*

"What first, Doctor?"

"Sutter Organ," she said after a moment. "Circulation through it is damaged and nanorepair can't function with it torn as it is. If we fix that, we reduce internal bleeding and increase his body's ability to cope. Then...McCoy's Plexus. It's another internal bleeding site and is impeding his body's ability to adjust to conditions; he's not getting all the environmental feedback he should."

"I'd have thought the oxygen manifold would be first."

"I have to leave that one for last, honestly," she said with great reluctance. "It's by far the most delicate operation, given the way the manifold works, and the blood flow through it is so concentrated...I will have to cut that flow off during the operation, which means no oxygen for however long I'm operating and however long it takes me to restore the oxygen to him."

"Oh, no." Pearce paused. "Any way to introduce supplemental oxygen to his system beforehand?"

"That's what that IV bladder, the black-marked one, is for. I nanoadapted it from human blood oxygen supplements and I think it should work. If it does it gives him an additional hour, maybe. Which should be enough. We'll start dripping that in once I'm done with all the internal bleeding. With luck we'll have him effectively supercharged."

She nodded, looking down, seeing the overlay of the layers of skin, insulating fat, muscle, bone... "Scalpel."

With absolute focus, she began to cut into her son.

The Sutter Organ had split from multiple impacts, tearing slowly; its normal hourglass-shape was badly distorted, its brown-black interior exposed with deep fissures that ran more than halfway into it. She began her narration of the operation, a habit drilled into her years ago. "A stress laceration has torn open the primary inlet filtration artery. Secondaries above this point remain intact—which explains why he isn't quite dead. This has maintained about twenty percent of function in the organ, but it can't be sustained long. The artery laceration is at the deepest point of the main fissure. Subsidiary veins and arteries all severed to depth. Split areas must be rejoined as internals are restored or stress from split will reopen injuries. Beginning repair."

Laura bit her lip inside the mask. She couldn't just coat the entire interior of the split areas with fleshbond, tempting though that approach was. Fleshbond might not be cyanoacrylate, but it would still form a barrier and possibly even with nanorepair leave scarring along the entire seam, which would drastically reduce the operation of the Organ; it acted as a complex filter and secretion mechanism and relied on the free and active flow throughout its volume. "Best approach I can see given my limited equipment and knowledge is to use a combination of dissolving sutures with fleshbond at strategic locations."

"Concur," Pearce said, her voice strained; seeing the damage— and, probably, cutting into Whips this deeply—was putting her under pressure too. "Vitals still stable, blood circulation still at seventy-seven, circulation pulse fourteen per minute, internal temperature at thirty-eight point four."

Laura grimaced. Reducing Whips' internal temperature significantly—say, to about the current air temperature of twenty-nine Celsius—would have drastically reduced Whips' demand for oxygen, slowed his blood flow, and reduced possible operative bleeding. When he had just been suspended, that *had* been his body temperature. *But I can't devote so much nanosupport to keeping his metabolism shut down, not now.* They needed to be able to observe his responses to the operations, and such nanosuppression would interfere in those responses.

"Sheath around artery allows damaged edges to be brought into contact with minimal to no tension." Relief went through her; she didn't want to patch or splice if she could help it. "Commencing suturing of primary inlet filtration artery using nanoenhanced dissolving sutures." She carefully stitched the artery back together, then repaired the sheath, ensuring there was nanosupport to keep the sheath smooth around the artery as it healed.

Over the next hour she managed to repair all the other significant veins and arteries that had been damaged in the Sutter Organ, systematically working out from the deepest parts of the fissures, repairing the blood vessels and then pulling together the organ's tissues with both sutures and carefully spaced dots of fleshbond. Pearce had kept the pace going smoothly, handing her each tool or material as needed, controlling the flow of blood substitute, and monitoring the vitals.

Finally Laura sat back and sighed, stretching up. "Repair of Sutter Organ complete. Nanomonitoring shows blood flow is beginning to return to previously-severed portions. Preliminary indications are therefore cautiously positive."

"So far so good," Pearce said.

"Next we do the plexus repair. God, I hate fiddling with nerves."

"Worse than blood vessels?"

"Much worse. A blood vessel actually doesn't care if you chop out part of it and replace it with a synthetic, but even today we don't have easy synthetic nerve splices for major nerve junctions. On the positive side, the medical kit includes neurospecific repair nanos, so if I can dissect out the main nerve fibers and their associated secondaries and bring them into proper general alignment, the nanos can probably handle the rest."

"Ready?"

"Yes." She leaned back down. "McCoy's Plexus is visible through the current incision, located a few centimeters ventrally and towards the central axis of the body from Sutter's Organ, beginning approximately seven centimeters posterior from the rearmost portion of that organ and extending...seventeen centimeters in length. Again we see significant compression and impact damage to the organ, resulting in significant neural trauma. The ventral portion of the Plexus appears intact and unharmed, and there is sufficient functionality seen that full repair may be possible. Beginning dissection of primary neural components..."

As she passed Laura another set of microsutures, Pearce said "Campbell's pinged me."

"Hello, Sergeant," she said, beginning the placement of the sutures.

"Didn't mean to interrupt—"

"Not a problem right now, at least if it's just talking. I'm doing a bunch of fiddly little repairs, but they're ones I know how to do. I can talk while I work, at least right now."

"So it's going all right?"

"Fingers crossed. I'm still a long, long way from getting done, but Whips was in great shape before he was hurt and he's still very young, so his body can handle it much better than someone older. So far, he's stable. The Sutter Organ's repaired as best I could manage it, and I'm making good progress on the Plexus. If those are both done, I'll be on to some simpler work for a while. The real moment of truth is going to be working on the manifold." To distract her from worrying about that, she went on, "How's the work with the satellites going?"

"Satellites?" Campbell repeated. "Oh, that. Lemme put Mel on. Melody? Your mom wants to know about the satellite work."

"Mom? Is Whips okay?"

"So far, honey. So tell me about the satellites."

"Oh. Well...it's working, I guess."

"You *guess*?"

"They're still settling in, but we're getting images of the starfield and it looks like we can get full, pretty good res, scans of the sky around Lincoln every twenty minutes or so."

"You don't sound happy about that."

"Oh, no, no, that's just fine," Melody said. "But...even with the best metamaterials enhancing things and the multi-imager base design that gets built into all of them, the effective aperture's about seventy-five centimeters. We'll be able to see *some* stuff coming, but..."

"But?"

She sighed. "A lot of stuff that could do us real damage is still going to be too small to see. We'll probably spot big things coming, but not ones only a few dozen meters across...which are still awfully big if you're asking what kind of an impact event we'd want to avoid. *Really* big things...I don't think we could do anything about them even if we wanted to. If something ten kilometers comes down anywhere on the planet we could be toast."

That was disappointing. But at the same time, did they really want to know if something completely lethal was on its way? "Is there any reason for us to keep the cameras looking outward, then?"

"Probably not," Campbell said after a moment. "We got our imagery for anyone who just wants to take a good, no-atmosphere look at the area around us, but if we can't spot the stuff we wanted to, no point in keeping them pointed out. We can always make use of the planetside images for forecasts, navigation, that kind of thing."

"Okay," Mel said. "I guess we'll start turning them back, then."

"It was worth a shot, Melody. Still good work."

The last of the nerve sutures were in place. *Thank God.* She filled in the entire area with the neurorepair nanogel, then began the much more straightforward work of closing up the incision. "Repair of McCoy's Organ complete," she said.

The day continued. Momentary breaks for water or a bite of food were interspersed with painstaking, sometimes arm-strainingly difficult work. Pulling muscles and ligaments together that belonged to a creature six times your own size was challenging work, to say the least. Her narrations continued, dryly describing the horrific damage—a main skeletal plate broken in half, ligaments torn from their anchors, split muscle tissue, damaged interior veins leaking blood within the abdominal cavity, a mangled eye that had to be repaired, sealed, then injected with sterile fluid to re-inflate it—as she tried to stay detached and work to fix each of them.

Finally there was only one thing left. "Doc—Doctor Kimei. Do you really want to do this now? He seems able to breathe all right in air. Couldn't we just keep him out of the water until he finishes healing everything else, then fix this when he's as strong as can be?"

"I really wish we could, Pearce. I've been trying to convince myself to do that as I've been working. But...no. It's one organ, not two separate ones, though it does have separate working surfaces. That means, though, that the damaged surface is still connected to the other, and if he even accidentally tries opening the other—which they sometimes do, the equivalent of a human yawning—it'll start hemorrhaging everywhere, and the damage might even start propagating across the whole surface. Also, damaged the way it was, we might have some kind of infection set in; some of the nanoreports from the area aren't encouraging."

"So what's the plan?"

"We'll have to clamp off the respiratory vessels, here, here, and here." She indicated the points on the displayed virtual model in both her and Pearce's omnis. "Once that's done, Whips is getting no oxygen intake. Start the oxygen supplement drip now, I want his body as saturated with it as possible before we start."

"Got it." Laura backed away from Whips' still form, reached to a nearby table and poured herself a cup of water, drained it in a swallow, poured and drank another while Pearce hooked up the bag and made sure the infusion was working properly. Taking a deep breath after drinking, Laura could smell her own sweat, the sharp tang of Bemmie blood, the earthier undertones from the organs still hanging in the air despite the efforts of the air filters in the shelter. She grabbed a few hedrals from the bowl on the table, chewed and swallowed the tangy fruit, then pulled her mask back on.

"Without the blood pressure and flow, I'll be able to separate the layers of manifold, clean them, suture the major damage, and place a coating of nanorepair on each layer." What she didn't say—because there wasn't much point in saying it—was that there were twenty-one separate layers of manifold. In the hour that black-marked bag would give her, Laura would have just slightly less than three minutes to locate and suture any injury to each layer, or she'd be running into Whips' own reserves. And not too long after that, Whips wouldn't have enough reserve left for the repairs to make any difference.

But Pearce had apparently looked carefully at the anatomy of a Bemmie—as might have been expected. She took a breath, then glanced between Whips and Laura. "Laura, there's so much work to do in that time . . . why do we have to do it all so *fast*? Couldn't you repair a couple sections of the manifold, release the clamps and let him breathe a bit, and then repeat? This is going to be such a touch-and-go thing . . . I know there's probably a reason, but I'd feel stupid if I didn't ask."

Laura smiled, or tried to; she suspected the result wasn't very convincing. "You're right to ask the question. The reason? If the manifold isn't properly installed inside its enclosing membrane and the fascia that keep it tight and stable, it will swell up like a balloon once blood pressure comes back up. That would of course strain or tear out any repairs I've made and would damage the manifold itself directly. That's actually one of the more common life-threatening conditions that Bemmies get as they age, a 'manifold aneurysm'; a weakening or tear in the membrane allowing part of the membrane to escape, swell up, and burst."

"That's . . . frightening."

"It is. A potentially very painful way to die. The problem is complicated by the fact that the membrane, while very tough with respect to confining stretching, is not terribly strong if cut, so any damage I do to the membrane I will have to repair very carefully, and the membrane is fairly complicated in structure. The manifold itself is very delicate; it is a soft, complex structure of blood vessels, mostly at the capillary level, and very convoluted soft tissue structures for gas exchange. *Any* handling of the manifold has a strong potential to damage it.

"If I tried to do this in stages, I would have to—each time we wished to give Whips a break to breathe—carefully restore the manifold to the membrane, handling it in the process, then carefully seal the membrane, then seal the fascia, then remove the clamps, let Whips breathe, then rip out the seal or sutures on the fascia, do the same to the membrane, then pull out the manifold again and, effectively, page through the layers to reach the next one I was going to work on."

Pearce nodded, face sober. "Each repetition would make it more likely you would do more damage than you'd repaired."

"Exactly." She sighed. "So this is the way it *has* to be done."

She checked her own vitals, tweaked her nanos to improve alertness. A little stimulant wouldn't hurt for a few hours, and she needed to be at the absolute top of her game for this. "Are you ready, Pearce?"

"Hold on." The redheaded woman copied Laura's own little break, getting water and some fruit sugars into her to give her body the resources needed for this final run.

Finally the mask was back in place and the green eyes met hers. "Let's do it."

"Move the cradle up." The cradle was a structure that fit over the top, or dorsal, ridge of Whips' body, conforming well to the ridge outline and with long, strong leather straps connecting the wooden portions and lying flat on Whips' surface. Laura thought that it looked rather like the inverted skeleton of a boat, the keel at the top of Whips' dorsal ridge and the ribs that would hold the hull curving to hold Whips' body snugly.

Attached to the "keel" were flat, T-shaped braces that would allow the whole structure to be stable when Whips was upside-down; curved pieces like rockers projected from one side of the braces, to make it easy to roll the whole thing—Whips included—to that inverted position. Two of the rockers—the ones on the far ends—also had straight extensions that became handles, to aid in lifting and rolling the very heavy creature over. To make sure Whips didn't fall out when they rolled it, Laura and Pearce slid wide leather straps beneath him and fastened them to the ribs.

"Beginning procedure to repair oxygen exchange manifold," Laura said, then took another deep breath. "Subject must now be turned onto his dorsal ridge to allow access to the manifold through the ventral pad surface."

They first moved the IV as far as they could in the direction Whips would be rolled. Then both Laura and Pearce pushed and lifted in a single motion.

The curved sections of the cradle hit the floor as Whips' body rolled, and helped keep it rolling easily until it came to rest on the flat sections of the "T" shaped pieces. Whips' long, triangular-cross-section body was now cradled by the structure, kept stable and still even though he now hung with his dorsal ridge straight down.

"So far so good," Laura said, breathing somewhat harder with the effort. Whips weighed several times what either of the women did, but the cradle had worked.

"Vitals shifting! Pressure is down!"

God, no!

An immediate check didn't show any sudden change in his injuries, but then Laura suddenly understood. The body was try-ing to respond to the inversion, revising the flow of blood under these unusual circumstances, but under nanoanesthesia wasn't able to perform properly.

"What do I *do*, Laura?" Pearce said, voice tense.

"We'll have to risk some other stress. Give me two CCs of emergenine."

The Bemmie stimulant caused the pressure to waver crazily for a moment, setting off alarms on the monitors and in Laura's gut. *If it stimulates the wrong parts, or triggers bleeding or spasms...*

But slowly Whips' vitals smoothed out. Pearce breathed a long, shaky sigh of relief; Laura did the same, then turned back to her patient.

She checked the Bemmie carefully. "All external sutures appear not to have been over-strained. Nanotelemetry does not show any damage to previous repairs. Vitals are now stable. Procedure will continue."

She looked down at the belly pad, scrubbed it carefully with more alcohol, and then nodded to Pearce. "Scalpel. Beginning dissection of anterior air/water intake, exterior to manifold."

She made a long incision to give her plenty of space to work. Clean, straight cuts were not going to be a problem; working in cramped quarters that might slow her down would be. Pearce didn't need to be asked to apply suction to remove the upwelling blood. "The feeder veins and supply artery are now visible. Applying clamps to all three blood vessels." The clamps gripped well and nano data indicated that blood flow had been halted. "Begin one-hour countdown for oxygen supplement. Beginning dissection of the manifold."

She cut through the fascia that protected and assisted the breathing organ in smooth, flexible movement. Something like a squashed-together L-shaped accordion, the oxygen exchange manifold became visible as she pulled the manifold fascia aside.

"Air-water shunt is severely damaged and will require repair," she began. "This will be performed after current procedure as it can be done without clamping the blood supply. Trauma is immediately visible on the ventral lobe of the manifold," she said. Her dispassionate voice was belied by her wince at the sight. "A red-brown discoloration approximately thirty centimeters in length and ten in width is seen, roughly centered on the exterior surface of the lobe. No trauma appears to have extended to the vertical lateral lobe. Nanotelemetry indicates the insult to the lobe extends a considerable distance through the layers."

With trepidation she began the dissection of the lower lobe, considerably larger than the lateral lobe. "Damn," she said, before returning to the dispassionate narration. "Injury has produced tears through the layers of manifold. Each tear must be sutured. Beginning suturing of first layer."

It took her seven minutes to complete the suturing of the first layer. "There are indications of early stages of infection in the injured tissues. Treating with antibiotic nanospray and continuing."

The tears were slightly smaller on the second layer, and she was getting the hang of the precise motions needed to sew the thin, delicate, capillary-heavy tissue together; even so, it was nearly six more minutes. *Thirteen minutes...fifteen, really, counting the dissection time. A quarter of the time used and I've got one-tenth the work done!*

She shoved the intrusive worry from her mind. Rushing would do Whips no good either; the repair work had to be done right or it would be disastrous. "Applying antibiotic nanospray, beginning third layer."

Another nearly six minutes, and the thoughts were harder to banish. She caught Pearce's worried glance, shook her head, then moved on. "Fourth layer. Damage appears to cover a somewhat smaller extent..."

That one took only four minutes, but she was still falling behind. Approaching half the time gone, and only about a fifth of the way to finishing.

But the damage was becoming less with each layer, forming a broad, narrowing cone driven into the manifold, probably from an impact with a seatback. The next two also took four minutes, but the next was three, and then two, and suddenly as she peeled back the next layer she realized there was only a small tear and the one following showed no marks at all on its surface. Heart beating faster, she carefully sutured that one shut, applied the nanospray, and then paged carefully through the other layers, verifying what she thought and applying the antibiotic to the remainder.

"Damage appears to have been limited to layers one through ten of the manifold. Remainder appears reasonably healthy and intact. Preventive antibiotic has been applied. Now applying lubricant with nanorepair infusion to ensure flexibility is retained."

It took a few minutes to carefully fold the manifold back into its enclosing membrane. There wasn't any hope of manually getting the membrane to adhere to each separate layer, but she did her best; the nanos, guided from the outside, would have to do the job, millimeter by millimeter, before Whips would be able to enter the water again. "Now suturing the fascia."

She glanced up at the countdown. Five minutes, thirty seconds left of the estimated hour. But the estimate could easily be off; she checked the blood oxygen indicator; it still showed good levels. "Moment of truth," she said to Pearce. She couldn't keep from holding her breath as she slowly opened and then removed the clamps. "Clamps are now removed from the feeder and supply vessels. Nanoreports... nanoreports indicate only minor bleeding which will be addressed by standard medical nanos."

"Oh, thank goodness."

Finally allowing a real trickle of hope to flow into her own heart, Laura began the final repair on the air-water shunt. That was somewhat tricky—the shunt was a muscle-cartilage affair with three associated anchor-plates—but it wasn't by itself life-threatening, and Whips' vitals remained steady throughout.

Finally the two carefully turned Whips back onto one side—the side that didn't have any sutures. This time there was no major shift to his vitals from the change. "Are we really done, Laura?"

"All we can do for now, yes," she said, feeling exhaustion dragging at her. "If Harratrer wakes up from this... he's got a good chance at a full recovery.

"We just have to wait."

PART 5

ESCAPES

Chapter 38

Captain Ayrton looked up as she entered and smiled, which took something of the edge off of Sue's nervousness. The captain could be quite intimidating in appearance through a combination of his height and his sharp-featured face whose fierce gaze and beaky nose put Sue in mind of an eagle.

"Good to see you, Lieutenant Fisher," Ayrton said. "Please, sit down. Grab a cup of tea if you want, I've got a pot there." He indicated the table at the side of the room.

"Thank you, sir." Sue decided a cup of tea was just what she wanted, and poured herself one, mindful of the slightly slower motion. Orado Scientific Vessel, or OSV, *Sherlock*'s hab ring, was only rotating fast enough to give effective gravity of about four-fifths Earth's. She stirred in some lemon flavor and sweetener, then sat down in front of Ayrton's desk.

"Now, Lieutenant, are you going to finally enlighten me?"

The question was still in a friendly tone of voice, so Sue let herself smile. "So you know there's something more to the expedition already."

"Couldn't help guessing, anyway. Oh, a star that doesn't show on the charts, that's certainly worth looking into, but we could've taken a few years to build the ship, do more long-range surveys, maybe sent some long-range survey probes in. Instead, they got *Sherlock* built in months. That tells me that something is urgent about the whole business." He leaned forward. "What is it? Evidence of an actual alien civilization?"

That *was* the obvious guess. It had been exactly that kind of thing that had led to humanity's great leap into the solar system after years of simple automated probes.

"Not that exciting—or, maybe I should say, probably not. You've seen my file, I would assume, so you know what my job was before I got assigned to *Sherlock*."

"Emergency Watch Officer for Orado Station—five years duty. Hot pilot, too, I saw the records of your jump to *Outward Initiative* when the wreck came in-system." His eyebrows came together. "And you were also on-watch when that lifeboat came out of nowhere. There's a connection?"

Now she grinned. Ayrton was *sharp*. There was nothing better than having a commanding officer who could put the pieces together like that. "There is, sir. Until *LS-42* came in, we'd assumed that the lifeboats had to be total losses—maybe they seemed to come off in one piece, but were shredded as they entered normal space, or all their systems were ruined beyond repair, or the Trapdoor radiation pulse was lethal to everyone. After all those months went by, we simply gave up on the possibility that anyone could have survived, knowing what was available from their loading manifests."

Ayrton rubbed his chin. "And then *LS-42* comes in and changes everything."

"In two ways, yes, sir. First by the fact that they had made it back at all, so it *was* possible for enough of the ship systems to have survived, and second by drawing our attention to that unknown star system."

"Which has a habitable world in-system, yes. So we're not just survey and investigation—this is a search-and-rescue operation?"

"Well, we're *possibly* a search and rescue. If there's anything to rescue."

"Right." Ayrton took a sip of his own tea and pursed his lips in obvious thought before speaking. "But my limited understanding of *LS-42*'s return makes it sound like it was a pretty unique set of circumstances that let them survive and come home. What makes you think that either of the other two could have survived, and why in the name of Earth would they have gone to this completely unknown world instead of Orado?"

"A lot of it depends on exactly how the two shuttles were damaged." Sue projected a diagram of a typical LS unit. "What we learned from the *Outward Initiative* and then from the survivors of *LS-42* was that just how badly the systems were affected, and which systems were affected, was not entirely predictable because too many factors come into play. For instance, depending on the lensing effect of the decaying Trapdoor field, the radiation could end up inducing currents that would cause spot-welding through some of the LS Trapdoor coils... or it might not. *LS-42* had a few instances of this, but at least two or three of the shuttles that came back with *Outward Initiative* didn't."

Quick summaries of the crews of each shuttle appeared. "On paper, I'd give the best odds of survival to *LS-88*. Sergeant Campbell was an experienced pilot of just about everything, military experience of a couple of decades, and that included a lot of alien world experience and a lot of practical technical knowledge. He'd even been first-on-world at least once, so he knew the procedures cold. On board he had one engineer and a couple of students who'd gotten quite a ways along in their studies, and the cargo they were carrying would help them in a lot of ways.

"On the other hand, *LS-5* had an actual medical doctor on board, Dr. Laura Kimei, which certainly would make sure everyone stayed in the best condition. Her husband was a top biologist, and their oldest daughter was a planetologist. None of them were technical specialists, however, except for the Bemmie passenger who had some engineering training, and the second daughter had come some ways in her pilot training. Their cargo would also have been very useful for survival if they could access it."

"Right. But if they'd survived, why not come here?"

"It would have to be related to distance. If our determination of the breakout point for the shuttles is in any way correct, they were roughly a quarter light-year from this mystery system and about ten from Orado—forty times farther away. Lifeboat Trapdoor systems are limited to about a third of the maximum speed, which means that Orado was almost five months away. There were limited supplies on board the two vessels, with those on *LS-5* being the most limited. More importantly, their Bemmie passenger wouldn't have survived being out of water for that long, assuming they had enough to feed him. Looking at certain starvation for one and maybe several, it's possible they'd prefer to take a long shot for everyone surviving."

"And *LS-88*?"

She frowned. "I can't quite figure that one... unless their coils were damaged. In that case, they might be stuck, starving slowly to death because even their Nebula Drive wouldn't be able to get them anywhere in time...but they might also manage to wind themselves new coils."

"And new coils, not balanced, might drop their speed even more."

"Exactly. So they'd be forced into the same bet as the others."

Ayrton studied the ships and crews. "Damned long shots, aren't they?" he said. Then he grinned again. "But worth taking our best shot to find. So why keep it all quiet? I'd have thought it'd be great publicity, and might've made it even easier to ram through the funding."

"Neither I nor the portmaster wanted to raise any false hopes. If we find someone alive, wonderful, we can report that. But their surviving friends and relatives have already gone through their grief; let's not rip those wounds back open."

Ayrton nodded slowly. "Good call. Still, now that we're underway, I can tell the crew about our secondary mission, right?"

"I see no reason why not."

"Excellent. It'll add a different urgency and interest to this mission, and anything that engages my crew more with the work? That's a great thing."

Sue laughed. "I guess it is. And I'm glad you took it well. Some people really hate secrets, no matter what the reason for them."

"Oh, believe me, I understand. You saw my file, I'd bet? Well, I did S&R for eight years, and there's nothing worse than telling people their loved ones couldn't be found...and nothing better than being able to tell them they're alive.

"Except being the one that finds them alive."

Chapter 39

Nothingness gave way to an awareness of darkness, and darkness was a place of sensation, sensation of *existence* that included heaviness, pain...and surprise.

Surprise sparked awareness. *I'm...alive. I'm awake? Coming awake?*

A faint rippling pain coincided with a low sibilant sound of air. A sensation of tenseness and dull pain below. Aches and hot pangs reported in from his extremities, and a pulsing near-agony inside.

But it was less than he remembered. With difficulty, he forced his eyes open.

My eyes...eyes! All three of them are opening!

The place was dimly lit, the flat-light only bright enough to see by for humans, not bright enough to read with; something was odd about its placement, too. But Whips realized he could see it from all three eyes, though one of them still ached and there was an odd distortion across part of his field of view.

Pain warned him, again, to try any movements with great caution. Instead of moving yet, he moved his eyes to see what might be visible from here.

Immediately he realized he was lying on his right side, partially supported by some kind of leather-covered structure. Strapped into it, he revised, realizing that there was a wide, solid something strapped across his belly pad, holding him in place.

There was also a chair nearby, with a small figure slumped down in it. He pulled in a breath, feeling an ache through his breathing manifold but no problem with it working.

The breath and the sharp, small clarity of pain across his body focused him enough to trigger his nanos to report.

Wow. Even his memory of his prior condition hadn't quite let him admit to himself just how much work would have to be done. There were multiple repairs to skeletal plates, to injured muscles, torn ligaments...and even more in-depth work that touched on his internal organs. *I wonder how long Laura had to work on me.*

But the important point was that Laura had finished the work...and he was still alive to notice.

Whips focused on the chair nearby and felt his skin itch and spark pain as happiness manifested itself, involuntarily, in colorful patterns that were echoed in unwise movements. "S... Sakura..." he whispered.

The girl sat bolt upright. "Whips? *WHIPS!*"

She almost threw herself on him, but restrained herself with visible difficulty; instead she just reached out and squeezed the base of his least-damaged arm. "How do you feel?"

"Absolutely terrible," he answered, but flickered another smile. "But lots, *lots* better than I was before. I...I can *think.* I can feel my brain clearing up." He hesitated before asking. "Um...am I going to be okay? I can tell there was a lot wrong."

Saki's eyes were overflowing with tears. "Mom said if you woke up, she thought you would be, and so you woke up, and *God,* Whips, I'm so *happy!*"

She raised her voice. "Mom, Whips is up!"

"What? Thank goodness. I'll be right there. *No,* Mel, Hitomi, Franky, everyone else just stay back for now, we don't want to crowd him now. I want to take a look first."

"You need me?" That was Pearce Haley's voice, with, Whips thought, a slight trace of fogginess from sleep.

"I don't think so, Pearce. Go back to bed if you want."

The door of the portable shelter opened and the tall figure of Laura Kimei entered. She knelt down and began checking him over, starting at his belly pad; she did something that tightened the other restraints to let her get a look underneath the flat support. "How do you feel, Whips?"

"My brain's getting clear, no more murkiness. Some of the parts hurt more, but it's...*clean* pain. Does that make sense?"

"Yes, it does. Your brain can tell the difference between

possibly deadly trauma and the simple pain of cuts and splints and such." She readjusted the restraints and then began examining his left side. "Exterior looks good. Telemetry agrees. Can you move all three arms—I know they'll hurt, but can you try, carefully, to move them?"

If he'd had teeth he'd have gritted them; instead he tightened his mouth orifice in the closest approximation. "I'll try."

The pain was high...but still "clean," as he'd said. All three arms moved, up to the points where any serious work had been done. Even farther up, he could still feel his branches and fingers; the aches and pains were specific in their locations.

"Excellent," Laura said, and there might have been a hint of tears in her voice too. "And your eyes, are they all working?"

"Mostly. There's something funny in my lower left eye."

"There'll be distortion there for a bit; the incision and repair is still healing, and the nanos won't be able to fix it to optical levels until the gross damage is gone."

"And...the major damage?"

"All fixed. Oh, it's still healing—the Sutter Organ, McCoy's Plexus, your manifold—but all the indications are good. I'm seeing fine function out of all three and the manifold's no longer bleeding anywhere."

Whips drew in a whistling breath. "Then...I'm going to be all right, really all right?"

"As far as I can tell, yes, my overgrown son's going to be just fine."

"How long—"

"Your belly pad incision has to be fully healed before you're crawling anywhere. On the positive side, you've been doing so much on-land exercise that you shouldn't end up too weakened from it. About two, three weeks, I'd say—the nanos are doing a good job. Your mastication array and associated mouthparts should be almost healed now—you should be back to chewing... well, ripping and grinding normal food day after tomorrow. For now we've got some crushed food for you. If you start digesting that well, I can take out the IVs."

"But if I'm stuck here and I have to, um..."

"Your tail's over a big tub, just go when you have to. We'll empty it and clean everything off. Don't worry about it."

"Sorry about—"

"Whips, don't apologize!" Sakura said sharply. "You got hurt because you were so busy trying to save everything from an engine to my little sister. You've got nothing to be sorry for."

"And everyone's really all right?"

"Really all right. Soon as Mom lets them I'll guarantee both Francisco and Hitomi will be in the door."

He became aware of a vibration through the floor. "What . . . something *big* is moving outside!"

"Moving?" Laura looked startled, then suddenly she and Sakura laughed. "I keep forgetting how sensitive you are to things like that. That would be the sergeant and Tavana, who are working on building us a new home," Laura said. "Remember, you had two more of the excavators on board."

"Sensitive?"

"They're quite a ways inland, so we're high up, on the back side of the mountain ridge that runs across the continent. The wave couldn't get past that, and even if one like it came from the other direction it won't get as high as we're putting 'Chateau Lincoln,' as Tavana's called it."

"Can't wait to see it. But if it's that high up it's going to be hard for me—"

"We've thought of that," Sakura said with a grin. "It's next to one of the sources of the biggest river on this side of the continent, and so you'll be able to follow the stream up and down. The sergeant and Xander say they can make little loops to help you up the steeper parts, or you could just crawl up some walk-ramps."

"Wow. You guys have thought of everything."

"Everything?" came Campbell's voice. "Lincoln's laughing its pretty green head off over that. She's got a lot more curveballs to throw at us, bet on it. But we're covering all the bases we can think of for sure. Glad to hear your voice again, son."

"Thanks, Sergeant."

"All right, everyone," Laura said, "the rest of you can say hello to Whips, but then he's got to get some food in him and get back to resting."

Harratrer wanted to argue that at first, but soon he realized that despite just waking up a little bit ago, he was already worn out.

But it helped as most of the others came into the shelter and greeted him—an extremely gentle hug from both Hitomi and Francisco, an arm-shake from most of the others, and well-wishes from Campbell and Tavana who weren't nearby. The little parade of greetings left him both tired and energized, alert enough to eat the seafood puree that Sakura and Akira had prepared for him. It wasn't the best thing he'd tasted, and swallowing still hurt, but feeling food in his stomach brought a surprising sense of well-being.

And with well-being came a thundering wave of exhaustion. "Going...back to sleep, Saki," he said.

"No problem, Whips," she said. "I'll be here."

And that assurance followed him comfortably into a warmer and friendlier darkness.

Chapter 40

Campbell surveyed the work area, then glanced at Akira. "We're not digging too far into the rock, are we?"

The other man shook his head. "No, I worked with the boys on the design. We're filling much more than we're cutting, and with the acoustic signal processing Mel found and Caroline helped tweak, we've been able to verify that the thickness of the ... well, call it crust, I suppose ... of the crust here is something close to thirty meters. Given everything we've been able to learn about these floating islands, taking thirty centimeters or so off of it in a few patches tens of meters across should have minimal effect; there are natural processes that could do the same."

"Good. Just figured I should check; this island's had a hell of a shock just a bit ago, seems smart that we not give it any more." He watched the excavator back up, start another run.

"We are all in agreement on that." Akira glanced over, making sure that the smaller children remained visible and out of the way. "And I can't express how grateful I am that your *ad hoc* family found its way to ours. We would never have survived that event ourselves."

The thought had occurred to him, but Campbell grinned. "Don't sell yourselves short, Akira. Your Sherwood Column might've gotten too damaged to stay in, sure, but there's a good chance you people would've been inside, or gotten inside in time, and so long as you did, you'd have survived. Who knows, you might've ended up right where we are. Just ... not as comfortably."

"I am far more appreciative of 'comfort' or even 'not entirely backbreaking' than I was a few years ago."

"*So* true, Dad," Sakura said, dragging one of the tool cases past them, towards where some of the others were working on parts of their planned new home. "I guess I've learned stuff I'd have never learned even on Tantalus, if we'd gotten there."

"*Oui*, but many of those things, I would have been happy not to have learned," Tavana said; he was, predictably, following close behind Saki, two huge chunks of wood on his shoulders. "Still, I think we are just as lucky you were here. Without you, we would have been eaten by the island-eater, and if we weren't, that disease would probably have killed us all."

"We sure complement each other nicely," Campbell agreed, looking around. The day was clear, clouds drifting in fluffy whiteness across the very blue sky, and the brilliant green of the ocean was just visible from the ridge, through the tops of the trees and columns and giant land hydroids. "And we sure could've had a worse place to—*whoa!*"

A quiver had run through the entire clearing, making dust puff from the drier ground, leaves shake loose, and Saki, who'd been in mid-stride, lose her balance for an instant. "What the..."

WHOOM!

Campbell flung himself onto the ground; the great, deep booming sound was so like a massive artillery shell detonating that it triggered old reflexes. The others followed his lead, dropping their loads and falling flat, presenting as low a profile as possible.

Despite a twinge of embarrassment at letting reflexes trump thought, Samuel Campbell felt a glow of pride and warm gratification. These people weren't soldiers. They weren't warriors. But they were his friends and companions, and they trusted that old Sergeant Campbell probably knew what he was doing.

And who knew, maybe this was the right action. He still didn't know what that noise *was*, though now that his forebrain was processing instead of the backbrain, he could make out not-artillery aspects of the sound; it went on longer, and there was a background of grinding, splintering...

"Oh, crap," he murmured. "Keep down, everyone, just in case. Scrunch up a bit, make yourselves the smallest targets you can."

"What *is* it, Sergeant?" Saki asked tensely.

"I think I've heard that noise before, a lot closer up, and—*hold on!*"

Faint whistling noises were the only warning, before a scattered rain of *something* came smashing down through the forest and surroundings. Campbell saw something scythe straight through one of the trees and disappear towards the base of a column, which shuddered and then slowly, majestically tilted and fell, adding its own distant *boooom* to the sound of things falling and embedding themselves in the earth.

After a few moments, the deadly hail stopped. Campbell gave it a ten-count, then slowly stood; next to him, Akira did the same. "Think that's over. Everyone okay? Sound off!"

"Xander here, Sergeant; something bounced off the roof of the excavator but I'm fine."

"M . . . maddox. I'm okay, Sergeant."

"I am here, Sergeant," Tavana said. "No injury."

"Francisco here, Hitomi and I are all right, Sergeant!"

"Hi, I'm okay," said Sakura, waving shakily. "Almost got hit, but it missed me." Campbell could see something jagged and white protruding from the ground perhaps two meters from Sakura.

"Laura here," came Dr. Kimei's voice, as calm and controlled as ever. "Whips and Pearce are with me, and everyone's okay."

"Me and Caroline are okay too," Melody said, her voice also somewhat shaky. "What *was* that?"

"Unless I miss my guess, that was an island-eater taking a big bite out of the island on the other side. You figured right on that, Akira."

"That's kilometers away," Akira said, looking stunned.

"Yeah, but those damned things are a kilometer or ten long. Figure out how much power's in something like that striking at even a real slow walk—and they're moving a lot faster than that." Campbell shook his head. "Just hope the rest of our continent's not gonna attract them."

"I wouldn't think so," Akira said after a moment. "This mountain ridge separates us well from the damaged area and everything here seems very healthy. The continent is vastly larger, anyway. Huge though it seemed to us, losing that whole area is about like trimming a toenail to it."

"Just so long as the clippers don't slip and clip this part, I'm okay with that." He looked towards the ridge of "mountains" that rose fifty meters or more above him. Maybe it was his imagination, but he thought he saw a faint, dark cloud of dust rising from where the island-eater must have struck. "Still, I'm guessing it'll take quite a few more strikes before that toenail's all trimmed off. Everyone be ready to take shelter whenever another one happens."

He was right; there were three more massive concussions in the next several hours, each one resulting in sometimes-putrid remains of their old home ground literally raining down. Luck, however, remained with them, and no one was hurt, nor was anything important and fragile struck by the debris. The excavator took another hit, but even falling rock was no match for the machine's advanced alloys.

By the end of the day, the excavator was ready to be brought back to *Emerald Maui*. The selected clearing was flat and smooth, the fill tamped down by multiple runs with the excavator's roller mode despite the occasional rains of stone and mud, and stakes marked out the locations of the three buildings to be constructed: the Kimei home, Campbell house, and a third building that would be part-warehouse, part common room, meeting hall, and whatever else seemed needed.

Campbell looked at the site with the phantom projections of the future buildings on it, and nodded. *That'll do fine*, he thought, as they headed a bit downhill to where the current camp was. *Oh, in a year or three we'll have to probably build some new houses, or add-ons to the old, when some of us go from dating to more formal attachment—me and Pearce first, probably.* He grinned to himself, savoring that thought. *Forced retirement via shipwreck does have some upsides. Still, it'll do just fine for now.*

Rough wooden tables had been put together a few days after they arrived, and had settled securely into the thin soil on the ridge; sections of sawn logs made good stools. There were some camping chairs remaining, but those were being saved. It didn't seem to bother people, though. All of them had now been through so much that the important thing was that they were all alive, healthy (except for Whips, and he was definitely improving), well-fed, and not uncomfortable. Okay, the shelters weren't the same as real houses, but a hell of a lot better than sleeping out where the crants could get in and pinch and nip.

"Pass me the kraken tail, I'd like another slice," he said. One of the predators had gotten too close the other day, and now was the centerpiece of this meal.

"Sure," Xander said, hefting the wooden platter and passing it to the sergeant. "It's not bad, but I think I like capy better."

"I dunno, I like the texture of kraken. Still, it's a top preda-tor, probably not something we want to eat often for a lot of reasons." He noticed Caroline, Sakura, and Melody talking quietly and gesturing at something invisible. "What are you girls up to?"

"Astronomy," Caroline said. "We're letting the satellites keep doing their periodic heaven-scan, not because we think we'll catch anything, but because there's lots to look at here."

"You mean the comets?"

"Well, those are fascinating, and there's a lot of them, but much more than that. Both our groups found the biggest gas giant in our system—I want to name it Iris, by the way, because it's like a rainbow of stripes—and the other rocky planet near the sun, but there are actually *six* other planets in the Emerald system. Another gas giant—looks more boringly brown and white than Iris—a couple of Neptune-like planets, one I'm pretty sure is mostly a giant iceball about five billion kilometers out, and two more rocky planets. One of them's pretty close to opposition and it's the next one out, and we got some really interesting images of it. It has terrain that looks like a checkerboard from this distance; I have no idea what that could be."

"You think someone *made* it that way?" Tavana asked.

Caroline shook her head, smiling "No, no. If there's anything we've learned so far, it's that planets are just plain *strange* and you don't need alien interference to explain it. There are just infinite ways for them to become weird all on their own."

"Absolutely true," Campbell said. "They teach us that in the explorers. Hell, intelligent life usually doesn't leave anything you *can* see, at least unless it's still there and has the lights on."

"The differences are always fascinating," Caroline went on. "Especially those within a solar system. Theory says they all came out of the same nebula, so why, for instance, do you have something like Iris, all that bright-colored candy-striping, and in the next orbit a planet that looks basically like Saturn without the rings?"

"Oh, and look at this," Sakura said, "it's a composite from images of Lincoln over the last year. Looks like you were at least partly right, Dad!"

The image flickered onto everyone's VRD—at least, everyone that was paying attention; the little kids were talking over their own thing and Mel seemed to be studying a separate set of images. The familiar globe hung in front of them, but this time with the faster time-scale the motion of the floating islands was actually visible, the huge living constructs drifting slowly but unmistakably across the face of the globe.

More interesting than that, though, was the ocean. Slight variations in color swirled across the surface, deepened, shifted in tint; green changed to aqua and then to a crystalline blue, sweeping over a large portion of the seas, and then slowly became teal and then shifting back to brilliant emerald green.

"That's fascinating. I wonder what causes the die-off and repopulation of the plankton—I assume that's what's happening there. Nutrient flow from the deep ocean? Or perhaps from the islands themselves? I'll have to see if there are patterns in this."

"Heh. Still plenty of research to do, in between survival panics," Campbell said.

He glanced around the table, and felt his gut tense. Melody was staring at the same invisible screen, saying nothing, as though she was unaware of the banter around the table. More, despite the tan even the palest of them had acquired, Melody Kimei looked *white*, and her body was tense, locked in place.

"Mel? Melody, what's wrong? You look like you've seen about a dozen ghosts."

At her name, Melody started, then turned. Everyone else fell silent as they saw her face, saw tears starting down it.

"My god, Melody, what *is* it?" Laura was up, touching her little girl's shoulder.

Melody didn't say anything, just glanced at Caroline, and made a gesture that transferred whatever she was seeing to Caroline's display.

"Hmm. I don't quite..." Caroline suddenly sucked in her breath. "Oh no."

"*What?*" Campbell demanded.

For answer, the image appeared on all the adults' screens: an image of a starfield. At first, Campbell couldn't see anything unusual. Then his highly-trained observation told him there was a tiny, subtle change—a single dot, no more than a single pixel, halfway to the lower edge. It was moving—shifting perhaps one pixel to the side, then going back. *Comparator. That means whatever it is is...moving? Or close? Or both.*

Then text appeared in the display and Campbell felt a cold fist of ice close about his heart:

Diameter: 9.82 km ± 0.5 km
ETA: 221 hours ± 5 hr

Chapter 41

"It's not *fair*!" Sakura heard herself half-scream the words and instantly berated herself for sounding like Hitomi—no, younger than Hitomi. None of what had happened to them was *fair*. The universe, and Lincoln in particular, clearly didn't give a damn about "fair." But that didn't keep her from feeling angry and somehow betrayed, atop the rising fear.

"No, it isn't," Campbell said, looking around at the others.

Sakura looked over to Hitomi and Francisco. They didn't look quite as shell shocked as the adults, probably because they didn't grasp the extent of the disaster. They'd survived one big rock falling, why couldn't they survive another?

"Those numbers," Xander began, trying to sound calm and rational and doing pretty well, from Sakura's point of view. "The size and approach numbers, are we really sure about them?"

"You saw the margins of error," Caroline said, still sounding stunned. "I'm confident that's right. We'll get more precise as it gets closer. Right now we don't even know where on the planet it's going to hit."

"Does it make a difference?" Pearce asked. "That's a dinosaur-killer."

"Dinosaur-killer didn't kill everything," Tavana said, getting a nod from Akira. "If it hits where we are, yes, we are all dead; but if we are far enough away, we may survive. We *can* survive. Lincoln must have been hit by these things many times, and life still thrives. We can survive . . . right?"

That last *right?* didn't quite inspire Sakura with the confidence that Tavana had probably hoped for.

"Right!" Francisco said. Finding everyone looking at him, he blinked, then looked to Hitomi, who stood up and repeated "Right! We will get on *Emerald Maui* and run away from the meteor."

"Where could we run *to*?" asked Akira slowly. "I mean, we saw what a much smaller impact did. Wouldn't a larger one produce waves across the entire reachable ocean? If it strikes on the other side of the planet, that's one thing, but..."

"It's actually not so bad," Caroline said, and there was a hint of optimism that made Sakura swallow and let go of the fear inside—just a little bit. "That giant wave that hit us would have dissipated to a ripple in a relatively few more kilometers. If we'd been fifty kilometers farther away, or a hundred, it wouldn't have been a disaster." She frowned. "Something like *that*, of course, is going to make one incredible splash, no doubt about it, but on the open sea that will pretty soon turn into a not-terribly-big wave. I hope. It's the shockwave we have to worry about. And anything from the splash coming back down, if it doesn't turn to vapor. A big blast of steam won't do us much good either, but it won't last *that* long."

"Climate's going to go to hell, though, isn't it?" Maddox asked bluntly.

"It...won't be good, no. I don't have the models to be sure which way it'll be not-good, though. Put enough water vapor into the air, that's a powerful greenhouse gas, it'll heat the planet up, but if you also throw up a ton of new clouds, that drops the insolation, so that cools it down..." Caroline spread her hands and shrugged. "At this point, all I'm sure of is that it'll be drastic. And it'll last a while, months to years.

"On the positive side, unless it happens to hit one of the floating continents, the only thing it's hitting is water. There's no way it's getting through a hundred kilometers of water and high-pressure ices. So minimal sulfate dispersal, debris ejecta, and so on." She glanced at Melody. "I'll give everything I have to you, Mel—you can work on the sims and get more detail out of them than I probably would."

Whips' voice spoke from within the medical tent, starting with a Bemmie curse that basically meant *stagnation*. "I just don't believe this. We just survived one hit, and here comes another? How long can we keep doing this?"

Saki heard the exhaustion and pain in her friend's voice and bit her lip. After everything he'd gone through, she couldn't blame him. "I know, Whips. It's like another punch in the gut."

"We keep doing this exactly as long as we have to," Laura said, and her voice was filled with certainty. "This is my family—*all* of you are, now," and Sakura could see her looking at Campbell and his people. "Francisco and Xander and Maddox and Tavana, and even you two, Pearce, Sergeant—we are *one* family, and I *will not let my family give up.*"

Sakura could not remember feeling more proud of her mother.

"Damn straight, Ma'am," Campbell said. "Ain't none of us giving up."

"The universe punched us when *Outward Initiative* came apart," Laura went on, "and we punched back. And when we knew we couldn't get Whips safely to Orado, we found Lincoln. When we landed, Lincoln punched us again, and dumped *LS-5*. So we got up and punched back."

"You did that," Xander said. "We got punched more than once on the way here, and we found a way to make *LS-88* work. Lincoln tried to *eat* us but you guys gave us just enough warning to duck that punch. Tried to kill me, and the sergeant punched it in the face."

"Tried to kill us all, more ways than we can count," Pearce said. "But we kept standing, ready for the next one."

"Exactly," Akira said, and Sakura felt not frightened, but uplifted. "*We survive.* We have survived our own despair. As long as life can survive on this world, we will survive."

Everyone looked brighter, even Melody rising out of her shock, and the sergeant was simply nodding.

"So what do we do?" Sakura asked.

"Well, by that timeline we've got a bit more than a week," Sergeant Campbell said. "This o' course takes priority over everything else. What we do is we start stocking up *Emerald Maui*, and get her set up to carry every last one of us in as much style as we can. Might be we'll be living on her for a bit before we find a place to land."

Caroline gave a quick nod, glancing at her mother. "We'll know more about what we have to do once we get a better prediction of impact. Worst-case it's targeted right on us—then we've got to get in *Emerald Maui* as soon as we're sure and start running as fast as she'll go. Best-case, impact's on the other side of the planet and then we'll probably just want to stay here and hunker down. We'll still want all the supplies we can get now, because there's no telling how hard it's going to be to get anything to eat afterward."

"All right. So we assume worst-case; we're going to have to run as fast and far as we can, and it will take a while to find a safe place to land afterward," Laura said. She made a map of Lincoln appear. "Caroline, can you and Mel work on which direction we should flee, and how far in advance we should depart, depending on where it hits? I presume we have to go a different direction if it lands out there," she pointed to the nearby ocean, "than if it hits just on the other side of our little continent, or more north or south."

"Probably. I'm sure we can get that kind of modeling done."

"Let Maddox help Mel," Xander said. "Caroline, you're one of our best hunters, and we'll need you doing that to stock up. I know, you're also the planetographer, but I think my brother and Mel can do something like that, what with the models we already have. Yes?"

"Good point," Campbell said. "Unless anyone has an objection, I say do it that way."

"No, he's right," Laura said. "Caroline, you will lead the hunting; we'll need to split efforts between hunting and preserving, as fast as we can." She glanced at the medical shelter. "Whips should be mobile a few days before impact. He's healing pretty well."

"I could move now—"

"You will *not* move until I say. You'll be taking your first attempts at a pull-and-drag tomorrow, *if* all indicators stay stable."

"...Yes, Mom."

"That's *Doctor* Mom right now." A little laughter ran through the clearing. "But on the bright side you're out of danger. In fact, I think you should work with Mel and the rest of us in any modeling. You can't move, but there's nothing wrong with your brain."

"I can do that!"

"What about me, Mom?" Sakura asked.

"You'll probably be doing something of everything, Saki. Work with Tavana on proper stocking and balancing of *Emerald Maui*. Hunt with Caroline, or do some fishing—Maddox seems to have a touch for it, but so do you. Gather as many edible plants as you can find. We'll need it all."

People were starting to rise, then Francisco said "Oy! Wait!"

Everyone turned to stare. He looked a little taken aback, then straightened. "My mama said you never start a new job hungry. We have time to finish dinner, ¿*si*?"

This was a wave of laughter that brought tears to Sakura's eyes. Her mother *did* laugh until she cried, and then went and hugged Francisco so tightly he went *oof!*

"Yes, Francisco," Laura said, still crying with a smile on her face. "Your mother is a wise, wise woman, and there is *always* time to finish dinner."

Chapter 42

"I make it fifteen hundred to eighteen hundred kilometers, depending on just how it hits, how massive it is, and so on," Caroline said.

Campbell nodded, studying the projection of the section of Lincoln they currently occupied. "Assuming *Emerald Maui* doesn't have any hiccups, we can do that pretty easy in about ninety hours. Add ten for loading, minor glitches, that'll leave us about a hundred, hundred fifteen hours before we have to leave. Call it about four, four and a half days, if we're going to be near the center of the strike zone. If it's more'n that away from us, we probably want to just sit tight; in between we'll have a few more hours to work in."

"Mel, have you been able to refine the orbit any? Get an idea of strike location?"

Melody had insisted she was too upset to go to bed at her usual time, so she was still working away, a projected keyboard in front of her. "Not yet, aside from verifying that it *is* going to hit Lincoln. I've got all the other satellites focusing on it, though, so by next morning I'm pretty sure we'll have enough data to refine the track." She looked over at Whips in her display.

"Right," Whips said. "Multiple observations, and some of them separated by up to seventy thousand kilometers? That'll give us some real data on its approach. As it gets closer we might get some detail on the impactor itself which will tell us a bit more about its mass and composition."

"Right," Campbell said. "So for now we have to go with worst-case: assume we're standing on the bullseye. How's it going, Captain?"

Xander's voice had the hint of amusement that it always carried when the more-experienced Sergeant addressed him as Captain. "Finished hosing off the excavator while it sat on the ramp. It's drying now. Then I'll bring it in and get it locked down."

"We've got more room in there since we lost the one, right?"

"Right. We can use that whole area for food or whatever else, as long as we can pack it tight and strap it down." A pause. "You know, if we reshuffle storage space, we can probably make more interior living space. It's not like we have to maintain a secure lock between cargo and personnel."

"I think that's a good idea, Captain," Campbell said. "There's gonna be thirteen of us in *Emerald Maui*, twelve humans and one Bemmie. We've got enough crash couches, but at least two or three've got to be removed or reconfigured for Whips. Check the data from Doc Kimei, she has the info on that design and reconfig from *LS-5*."

"Will do."

"I'm off to do some harvesting myself," Campbell said, standing and grabbing a couple collection baskets. "Hitomi, where was that patch of hedrals you said you found?"

"Right here, Sergeant!" The smallest Kimei called up the map and put a pink dot on a semi-clearing visible on the satellite images. "Hedrals all over the place, though they're mixed with what Mommy called false hedrals, so make sure you look careful!"

"I sure will."

The brilliant sunshine of Lincoln hit him right in the eyes as he stepped out of the shelter. Based on sleep cycles this was late night, but Lincoln's slower rotation didn't cooperate with human preferences. Still, it sure helped wake a guy up when he had work to do.

He set off at an easy stride, observing the route to the target. *Almost a kilometer off, through jungle. Even that little girl's got endurance and stick-toitiveness that some of my recruits never got.*

He still noted every sound and motion; they hadn't been on this part of the continent long, and there was still no telling what might be thinking that these funny bipeds would be good snacks, or might be threatening their territory.

He noted a pair of holes on what seemed to be a natural path ahead of him. *Looks like minimaw burrows.* He had no fond memories or feelings for the wormlike ambush predators; his leg still twinged some days from the damage one of them had done. Campbell gave the holes a wide berth.

Nothing else appeared to impede his progress, so it wasn't long before he pushed his way—using a walking stick—through a patch of land hydroids, avoiding their stinging tendrils, and found himself in a sunnier and more open area.

Glitters like gemstones reflected from beneath the deep blue-green, almost globular bushes. The hedrals were faceted fruits—why they grew that way Akira hadn't figured out yet—which were brightly colored and almost transparent as glass, the seeds showing as little dots inside the flesh of the fruit.

Hitomi's warning had been appropriate; there were a lot of false hedrals growing here and there. They could be distinguished from the real ones by the fact that they were slightly oval in overall shape, rather than being faceted spheres, their color tended to shade from top to bottom rather than being even, and the bushes were greener and looser in structure. He checked all three indicators before he picked from any bush.

An hour and a half passed as he quietly, systematically picked the hedrals from their bushes. Occasionally a quadbird would dart down, snatch one of the fruits from a bush, and flap up; fluffpigs—tiny relatives of the capy—scuttled around in the brush, probably scavenging whichever berries fell to the ground. Campbell occasionally popped one of the gemlike berries into his mouth; they were tangy, sweet, and filled with juice, which helped him to keep going.

He'd worked his way across a fair amount of the clearing when his omni pinged. "How's it going, Sergeant?" asked Laura.

"Pretty good, Lau—"

He cut off instantly. Something had moved, shifted as he spoke, when his words broke the sleepy afternoon silence of the clearing, and that "something" wasn't three meters from him.

"Sergeant?"

He used his hand to touch the omni, send a "Wait" ping. Otherwise he did not move.

Slowly the massive, streamlined form became clear, and Campbell had to focus all his discipline to keep his pulse from skyrocketing. It was a tree kraken, lurking amid the bushes, and well within striking distance.

So why didn't it strike?

There was a tiny sound, rustling leaves, and a motion that vibrated one of the bushes nearby. Slowly, one of the kraken's head-arms became visible, holding a number of berries and pressing them into the multipartite mouth.

Well, I'll be darned. We're here for the same thing. Guess it's not an obligate predator. Or maybe there's some kind of medicinal value in the berries for it, like how cats will sometimes eat grass.

The problem was how to disengage. The creature had jerked, shown nervousness or confusion, when he'd spoken. On the other hand, he had managed to get this close to it without being struck. Maybe the kraken just wasn't terribly interested in attacking anything right now.

Well, I've got a big bucket and a half of hedrals. Good enough and no need to push anything. He slowly began edging back the way he had come.

He saw a gleam in the lower brush; the kraken's eye was now focused on him. He could also see one of the attack tentacles quiver, rise slightly in readiness. *Don't hurry. Don't show fear. Just keep backing away slowly. Movement of a predator that would prefer not to fight today.* The thing had a reach of at least three or four meters, and with a lunge and grab it was probably a striking-snake fast menace within seven meters or more, and Campbell didn't like his odds against the thing in close quarters. As he eased backwards another short distance, his one hand drifted down and unsnapped the machete. If it came to a fight, he was going to have to be as fast as it was.

Another half meter. A meter. The eye was still tracking him, but the striking tentacle hadn't yet lifted up. Now the outline of the creature was starting to be obscured as he put a bush between himself and the kraken. Still no strike. *Three more meters and maybe I'll be out of quick strike range. Still have to be careful.*

One meter. Two. Three, and he couldn't see the animal at all now. *Most dangerous point. It can't see me now and it might get nervous, and I won't be sure where it's coming from.*

There was a faint sound of a heavy body shifting, and rustling of leaves... but quiet, slow. He thought he heard the squishing sounds of the kraken chewing berries.

Another two meters, and now he decided to risk taking longer steps. Three more, eight, ten more. *Think I'm in the clear—let's get home!*

Still with an ear cocked for sudden movement, and scanning the jungle around him, Sergeant Campbell continued on. But he didn't really breathe easy until he'd gone at least a hundred meters clear. "Okay, Ma'am, sorry about that. Had a little close encounter of the nervous-making kind." He described his meeting with the tree kraken.

It was, not surprisingly, Akira who broke in. "Really? That's fascinating! There are stories on Earth of people encountering bears in similar circumstances. And that *does* fit with my dissection of the kraken; they have digestive systems more extensive than generally seen with obligate predators, so they probably *do* consume some significant percentage of vegetable matter. And sweet berries would naturally be a strong attractant for any creature that wants highly concentrated energy."

"Well, he's welcome to all he wants right now, so long as he doesn't chase me. Got us enough for a while anyway."

"Xander finished securing the excavator," Laura said. "Mel finally went to bed. We're the only ones up right now."

"Well, I'll be ready for some shut-eye when I get back," Campbell said. "We've got a lot of work ahead of us—you should probably get rest too. Perimeter sensors will warn us if there's any problems."

"I'll feel better waiting until you're safely back," Akira said. "Just in case."

"Okay," he said, grinning to himself. "I guess I'd feel the same way. Now that I'm clear, shouldn't be more'n a few minutes."

He evaded the minimaw burrows again and picked up the pace. He was finally tired enough to sleep and tomorrow was going to be a new day.

The countdown had already started.

Chapter 43

Sakura held her breath as Whips reached out, gripped the shelter supports, and dragged himself forward. She could see his mouth contracting, as it usually did when he was focused or when he was in pain. *Which is it?*

"Well?" Laura asked.

"It...hurts a little," Whips admitted, "but I don't feel anything coming apart. No tearing or burning feelings."

"Telemetry agrees with you. Your body's mostly healed. I pushed the nanosupport as hard as I could on this—given the circumstances, it made sense."

"So can I move around now?"

"I'd rather you not do too much..." Laura began, then she sighed. "Yes. Just be very careful, and pay attention to your body. Remember all the other times I warned you? This time it's really important you remember. Don't tell us it doesn't hurt when it does, don't try to 'push past' the pain. It'll be a while before you're back to your old self, and what none of us need is you having a relapse because you refused to take it easy when you should have."

"Yes, Mom."

"All right, everyone," Melody's voice came, sounding somehow cheerfully grim. "Do we want the good news or the bad news first?"

"Well, that sounds encouraging," Campbell's voice answered. "What's the good news?"

"Between the satellites and the processing, we've nailed down our meteor's track," Melody said.

"*Merde*," Tavana said dryly. "Then the bad news, it is about where that track leads, yes?"

"It's not *quite* on our heads, but best guesses have it coming down about fifty or sixty kilometers west of us."

"Damnation," Campbell said. "That thing's coming right down onto our continent, then. Fifty kilometers west puts it right in the middle of the big forest we marked out on the satellite survey."

Sakura felt a chill in her gut. She'd seen the simulations; at fifty kilometers they'd be blown to bits, if they didn't get caught inside the fireball and vaporized. *Also means there'll be more debris involved.*

"Then we've got about three and a half days to get everything ready. Saki, Tav, you two, plus me, are our pilots. Plot us the best-time course out of here to get us at least eighteen hundred kilometers away from the blast."

"On it, Sergeant!" Saki said, and immediately hooked in Tavana. "We want to run east, right? If it's west of us?"

"*Oui*, that would make the most sense. We are on the southern edge and near the eastern edge, so we can go reasonably due east, like this," he projected a line across the map. It passed fairly close to two other islands.

"Seems simple—wait." Sakura narrowed her eyes. "What's the drift speed and course of those two? Project position forward, um...seven days, more or less."

"Ah, good catch! Even after all this time, we assume things like islands stay put!" A pause. "The first one would cross the optimal path. The second...probably won't."

"What speed are we assuming?"

"Twenty kilometers per hour."

"I thought you were cruising at *fifty* before, when you came to our continent!"

"We were, yes," Tavana said, "But we didn't push her at all bringing the kids back, and after everything she went through, I do not know how well she will do at higher speeds."

"That makes sense," Whips interjected. "But still, power needed to drive through the water is related to the cube of the velocity. I'd think if you could do fifty easy before, even thirty shouldn't be straining it now."

"I think so," Sakura said, "but Tav's probably right to lowball it. That means we have leeway in case something breaks down.

There's nothing wrong with finding out we can do it faster. Remember, too, we're going to be loading *Emerald Maui* down a lot more."

"Stuffing her to the gills, to be accurate," the sergeant said. "Since we don't know what the consequences of this strike will be, we have to be ready to live as long as we can on board *Emerald Maui*. Maybe we'll get lucky an' just be able to land on another continent safely, maybe not, but let's make the worst-case bet."

"No argument from me, Sergeant," Saki said. She frowned at the projected map. "You know, Tav, I think this might be a better course." She caused a line with several curves to appear.

"Why? That makes our course longer."

"Yes, but it also puts some islands in between us and anything that might be coming outward. Maybe not much protection, but wouldn't every little bit help?"

"Hm. Yes, you may be right. Flash ignition won't be a problem for us inside *Emerald Maui*, of course—our tail will be facing the blast, and no one will be looking at it—so what we mainly want to avoid is impact and damage from whatever the impact throws up. That could be giant waves—though the models are still really fuzzy on that—and debris thrown up and coming down."

"Some of that might take a while to come down, too," Caroline added. "That kind of impact can eject material into orbit, or near-orbit and drop back down after several hours."

"Still, not likely any of it will hit us straight on, and *Emerald Maui*'s proved she's tough," Tavana said, pride evident in his voice. "This old girl can take anything we ask her to go through."

"Let's hope that continues," Campbell said. "Still, I like the idea of putting as much of pretty much *anything* between us and a dinosaur-killer."

"Okay, then we will follow Saki's plan," Tav said. "It should not be difficult; we do not need to go to any precise place, just run fast and not run into anything."

"Remember to be careful when we first leave," Pearce interjected through the omnis. She was, Saki knew, down on the beach loading everything they wanted to carry into *Emerald Maui*—at least, everything that they didn't need right now. "Not only is there still debris left from the first strike, but now the island-eaters have made a bunch more. Zoom in from satellites shows a lot of junk in the water and some of it's drifting near us."

Saki grimaced. "Part of the problem of being a floating continent—you drift right along with all the junk."

"That will slow down our departure speed," Tavana said, studying the images Pearce had indicated. "We couldn't go fast at all bringing the kids back, and from those pictures it's even messier. We'll have to do the first five, ten kilometers pretty slow."

"And we have to assume there might be other things we'll run into to slow us up," Campbell said, "which brings us right back to those pessimistic speed assumptions. Keep 'em that way."

"Will do, Sergeant," Sakura said. "Pessimism is our middle name now!"

"Okay," said Tavana. "So if the engine gives out, what do we do then?"

"*Tavana!*"

Campbell started to chuckle, but then she heard him cut off. "We laugh, but it might be worthwhile to think out even that situation. Say we get out a few hundred kilometers and something happens—another piece of floating island gets stuck in the intake or something. What can we do? Is there anything we can do? Will we survive? Think about it, everyone. Sure, we hate to think of that kind of disaster...but—"

"—but," Sakura picked up, "Lincoln's been throwing disasters at us all along, so maybe looking forward wouldn't be a bad idea. The reactor we can rely on, though, right?"

"I'd think so. Anyone have a reason not?"

"Only if we ran out of fuel. It's not even close to its overhaul interval and we've mostly not been pushing it." Xander displayed the current statistics. "So yes, if you're doing disaster planning you can at least count on having power available. Just maybe not the engine, if something happens."

"Great. Well...I guess it's something to work on. Whips?"

She saw that Whips had made his way, slowly and painfully, to the stream nearby and was luxuriating in water flowing over him. "Ooooohhhh that's good. Um, yes, I can work on that, Saki. There might be something we could do, but the more of these problems we solve the more...what was that name? Roog Gold-something?"

"Rube Goldberg," the sergeant said. "You mean if we keep having to improvise pretty soon it'll get ridiculous."

"Something like that. But I'll think about it." The Bemmie

slowly waved his tentacle-arms through the water. "One thing I won't argue with is that it can't hurt to plan ahead."

"Darn right," Saki said. "Sure beats the heck out of having to figure it out after." She stood up and opened up one of the nearby equipment boxes. "Right now, though, I plan to go to some fishing. Want to come with me, Tav?"

Tavana smiled. "I would love to, Saki!"

"Just don't forget to actually do some fishing," Whips said, his skin patterning into a laugh.

Sakura stuck out her tongue, then laughed herself and, linking arms with Tavana, set out toward the shore.

Chapter 44

"This is going to be crowded, isn't it?" Xander said, looking around.

"With twice as many people and the extra supplies, no way around it," said a buzzing voice.

Xander managed not to jump, and turned to look at Whips without being too tense. *I'm getting better.*

He doubted that he'd ever be able to see a raylamp without his pulse skyrocketing, but his brain was finally letting the differences—and there were a lot of them—between the slimy predators and Bemmies come to the fore. Whips' mouth still creeped Xander out, but it was less instinctive a reaction than it had been. "Guess not," he said. "But it's actually...kinda nice. All the empty seats used to remind me how alone we were, and now, well, we aren't."

"And thank God for that," Campbell said, stepping in from the cargo area. "Neither group would've done half as well as both of us together." He turned toward a thumping noise in back. "Maddox, watch it! You gotta put all that back and secure it!"

"Yes, sir!"

"Speaking of securing," Xander said to Whips, "let's get you strapped in. You're not going to load any cargo and Laura'd rather you stayed still."

Whips gave a bubbling sigh, but rippled a pattern that Xander thought meant reluctant agreement. "Guess we might as well."

Xander laid out the harness with bracing plates and watched as Whips undulated himself onto the support structure. That motion was also a bit disquieting, as it did echo the rippling motion of the raylamps.

"That bothers you, huh?" Whips' voice wasn't annoyed, more dryly amused.

"Sorry. A little, but it's a lot better—a *lot* better—than it was."

"I can sense it. Smell, movement, all that—you're more just uncomfortable than terrified."

"A lot better. But," he tried not to look too embarrassed, "still not great."

"Don't worry about it. You had a good reason, unlike lots of people I met before who just didn't like us for no real reason at all."

"Being mobbed by completely different creatures isn't a good reason," Xander muttered, as he carefully secured the straps around Whips. In theory, Whips could do this himself—his three arms were extremely dexterous and had an astonishing range of motion—but he was still recovering and there was no need to force him to do the work.

Whips' retort was a sound that was a cross between a growl and a balloon losing air, utterly dismissive. "It's not a *logical* reason but it's a good reason. Friend of mine, Smokerunner, when he was young he got attacked in the smokes—the vents that cloud the water—and barely escaped. For about three years after that he freaked out whenever the water got cloudy, and, well, most of the time the water's at least a little cloudy. Took that long for the Elders and the therapists to get him back on level. So don't feel bad, you're doing great."

"Thanks, Whips. That means a lot coming from you." He pulled two more straps. "How's that feel? Loose? Too tight?"

"Pretty good—tighten the ones around my tail just a little bit, maybe two, three centimeters?...yeah, that's good. Now you can just hook everything in."

"Right." The Bemmie's crash webbing and support, the substitute for human crash couches, was secured to the floor and wall with self-tightening hooks that were locked onto restraining loops on both surfaces. It only took a few moments to get them all attached.

"Good job, Xander," Laura said as she came in. "Telemetry confirms you've got it secured right."

"Let's hope that was wasted effort," Whips said. "I don't want to actually *test* how well this secures me in a crash!"

"Ha!" Tavana laughed from in front. "The plan, it does not

include any crashing, but the meteor has to cooperate." The big Tahitian boy strapped himself into the pilot's position.

"I see Sakura lost the coin toss," Xander said with a grin.

"Unfortunately," said the girl in question, entering from the main hatch, carrying two rolls of bedding which she tossed to Campbell, who disappeared in back to secure them. "I wanted to take her out of port."

"But this is just as well," Tavana said. "You have not actually driven *Emerald Maui* before. You will take over later—we have about ninety hours of driving to do, after all!"

"Sure you don't want me to do it, Tavana?" Campbell asked.

"If you would rather do it, Sergeant, I will unstrap and move," Tavana said, but Xander could hear the reluctance in his tone.

"Naw, son, you did fine before, I'll let you keep the conn, unless the captain says otherwise."

"As you were, Tav," Xander said.

"That reminds me—everyone on board yet?" the sergeant asked.

"Almost," came Pearce Haley's voice. "We're on our way with the last of the cargo. Campsite's basically empty except for the table and wood chairs that we're not taking."

"Who's doing last walkaround?" the sergeant asked. "And it ain't gonna be me—last time I did that, I ended up damn near eaten."

Xander and the others of Campbell's crew laughed, even though the actual event—watching the sergeant slide down into blackness as *Emerald Maui* (or *LS-88* as she was then) took off into the sky—had been one of the most terrifying moments any of them had ever experienced.

"I am doing that as we speak," came Akira Kimei's voice. "I am also optimistic that I will return uneaten."

"Don't go tempting Murphy, now. I think Lincoln's got that old imp on speed-dial."

Xander took a quick tour around *Emerald Maui*, making sure everything was in readiness. There actually was still a fair amount of room in the one-time shuttle, but they'd need all of it since they were going to be living in her for a minimum of about four days and possibly for weeks, depending on exactly what happened when the dinosaur-killer hit Lincoln.

Satisfied that everything was under control, Xander went and used the tiny bathroom before going to his couch, directly behind

Tavana, and strapping in. Caroline began fastening herself down next to him. "All ready for our big move?" she asked.

"I hope so. We've got as much food as we could get and preserve some way, all the equipment we could salvage, the reactor's hot, drive shows green. Tav just checked out the control surfaces and they're all responding."

The forward port was slowly responding to the nanorepair instructions that Whips and the others had figured out, but it was still so fogged by scratches that only vague shapes could be made out.

Tavana, however, made a quick gesture and suddenly there was a clear, bright image of the early-morning sunlight slanting over the green water of Lincoln's ocean. "The repairs by our smallest crewmembers are holding fine," he said. "Both forward cameras generate this image, gives us good stereo capability. I can get rear images too, if I need them. Everything looks good."

Maddox came in from the back and strapped in on Xander's other side. The rest of the castaways followed, with Sergeant Campbell coming in and securing the cargo door behind him before taking his position to the far side.

Looking around, he saw only one missing member. "Mr. Kimei? Are you almost done?"

"Just arriving, Captain," Akira Kimei answered, his use of the title completely serious. "I found a few very small objects worth keeping; other than that there's nothing left behind. Shall I cast off the mooring ropes?"

Xander looked around, then nodded. "Do it and come on board."

"That reminds me," Campbell said. "On board a ship, there's only one captain. Laura, it's got to be either you or Xander; just the way it's worked out."

"Not you?" Sakura asked in surprise.

"I handed that job over to Xander, wouldn't be right for me to just grab it back. But your mom, seems to me she's been *your* captain."

"No doubt about it," Akira said as he entered.

Laura Kimei looked over at Xander. He felt suddenly very young and scared. "Ma'am," he said, "You're welcome to the position, if you want it."

She tilted her head as if considering it, then smiled. "Xander, this is *your* ship. You and the sergeant and Maddox, Tavana and Francisco, and Pearce Haley, that's how you came here. We kind of lost ours. Like the sergeant, I think it'd be kind of rude for me to take it away from you...Captain."

Wow. That feels...like she just lifted me up to the sky and then dropped a hundred tons on me.

Xander swallowed, then took a breath. "Thank you, Dr. Kimei. I'll try to live up to that trust. Okay, Sergeant?"

"Don't worry, I'm still here to advise when needed. As for the rest of you, you remember ship rules. Captain's the boss, the boss of everyone. Even me, even you. Hope it won't come to matter much, but if it does, we all listen to the captain. Got it?"

There was a chorus of "yes" from the others in the ship, and that weight seemed to settle on top of Xander like a suit of massive armor. *Authority and responsibility.* He agreed with the sergeant; he hoped he'd never have to use it.

But for now, there was a simple exercise of his power to make. "All right then, everyone. Let's get moving." He looked forward. "Tavana, take us out. Heading due east, follow the course as plotted."

"Aye, Captain," Tavana said cheerfully.

Emerald Maui grumbled, the water jets coming to life in the shallows, gulping a little air along with the water and spewing it out in a bubbling stream. A vibration passed through the ship, built into a constant awareness of motion as the trees visible to one side began to swing away, replaced by green sea and small, bright patches of floating debris.

Slowly, *Emerald Maui* began to gather speed, and headed towards the rising sun as her passengers cheered.

Chapter 45

"Trapdoor shutdown in five, four, three, two, one..."

Sue was on OSV *Sherlock*'s bridge as pilot Amberdon counted down to their return to normal space. It was, by ship standards, a spacious and comfortable room, with stations for pilot, communications, deployed operations command, and sensing and data analysis. "Spacious" naturally meant something different to a spaceship crew. The bridge was only about the size of a living room, meaning that only a meter or two separated each station from the next.

The darker-than-dark of Trapdoor space vanished, replaced by the vast star-sprinkled expanse of normal space, dominated by a brilliant sun dead ahead of *Sherlock*. "We've arrived in-system, Captain," Pavla Amberdon said cheerfully. "Transition was unremarkable, all systems show green."

Captain Ayrton nodded. "Communications? Anything?"

Everyone was quiet for a few moments as Commander Gariba the comm officer, observed and directed a survey of the various RF bands, his deep-brown face furrowed in concentration.

After a short time, he sat back. "Nothing definite, Captain. There's the usual hash of RF coming from a couple of the gas giants, some strange low-frequency signals that seem to originate from the habitable planet, but nothing I can definitely tag as human in origin."

Lieutenant Machado looked disappointed and dropped back into his seat at Deployed Operations. "So no one here, you think?"

"Well, it's not good," Gariba said. "If they'd landed and everything was in order, you'd think that sending out a beacon would be top priority. But then again, it's been well over a year; so they might've decided the resources used were better used elsewhere," Gariba said. "Or if their transmitter has limited power, it might only send a ping out every so often. Or if it's on the planetary surface, it's turned away from us at the moment. Well, *was* turned away from us at the point we entered."

That was always a key point to remember when operating on solar-system scale; even light and radio took time to get to you. "How far did we come out from the target?"

"We're about a billion kilometers out," Pavla answered promptly. "Figure about a one-hour signal delay in and out."

Sue looked at the screen, then back at the Captain. "Captain Ayrton, why don't we jump in closer?"

"Don't see any reason why not. For either of our missions, it'd seem likely that a habitable world will be a focus of investigation. Any hazards to navigation we should note?" He looked at the only person who hadn't spoken yet, sitting with the glaze-eyed look of someone watching omni retinal displays that completely blotted out the regular world. "Tip? You have anything for us?"

The slender person—who preferred to be neither called he nor she—started. "Sorry, Captain," Tip said, and brushed their slightly-nonregulation red hair out of their eyes. "It's quite a system we've got here. The quick survey from Orado pinpointed the main planets, but for whatever reason there's a *lot* of junk in this system. Several big comets and a bunch of smaller ones, two asteroid belts of note, and I'd assume a lot more little things we haven't pinpointed yet. So . . . no immediate navigation hazards, but I'd keep a really close eye on things. Trip a radar alarm for anything larger than a few centimeters in range, maybe."

Sue frowned. "That bad?"

"Hard to say," Tip said, gray-green eyes serious. "It's a lot of junk, but without a survey of cratering on the major bodies I won't be able to say how much worse it is than Earth-standard." They nodded to the captain. "If you'd like, sir, I can start a survey right away."

"Can't hurt. Go to it," Ayrton said. "But nothing keeping us from jumping in closer, right?"

"Not that I can see, sir," Tip said.

"Right, then. Lieutenant Amberdon, take us in."

"Aye, sir." Pavla glanced up. "Sir?"

"What is it, Lieutenant?"

"I haven't done many short-jump Trapdoor transitions. Maybe our advisor would like to take the board and I could watch?"

"Oh, I'm sure you'll do fine," Sue protested.

"I'm sure Pavla would, but we've both seen your record. If you'd like, you're welcome to take the board; both of us would love to watch."

"So would I," Tip put in.

"Well...all right, I'd like to be the one to bring us in close, I admit it."

Sue sat down in the seat vacated by Pavla and checked the board. She already knew the parameters for *Sherlock*—she never boarded a ship without finding out what its performance was like and what it would be like to fly—but that was different from actually being the pilot. "I assume we want orbital insertion if we come out close enough to target?"

"Yes. That seems unlikely, though."

"I'd have to get lucky, yes, but it's happened before."

Check coil performance profiles. Just because the specs said, for instance, that maximum jump error was one million kilometers was no reason to believe the specs. Coil imbalance, detuning, stress on the hull causing slight variations in the geometry, electromagnetic signals from internal systems, there were at least a dozen specific variables that could affect the performance.

The profiles looked mostly good, though there was sign that there had been some minor detuning, centered on one of the hab-ring coils. That might mean that it wasn't fastened down quite as tightly as it should have been. Still, it remained within spec for now, and she could adjust the output geometry to compensate. "Once we get to target, someone should go out and adjust coil fourteen. It's a little out of alignment, I think."

"Noted," the captain said. "You don't need that done now?"

"No, I think it's compensable." The distance was not quite one billion kilometers. That was less than one-minute jump, around forty-seven seconds or maybe forty-eight seconds. Center jump on planetary core. The nice thing about the Trapdoor Drive was that it wouldn't let you jump into a gravity well stronger than a certain amount, and if you attempted to do so, you'd emerge just outside said gravity well. There was no risk in targeting a planet dead-on.

No more than there was for any Trapdoor emergence, at least. If you were unfortunate enough to emerge back into real-space in front of an oncoming meteor, well, that would be pretty much it. Happily, those odds were low enough that, thus far, she hadn't heard of any ship actually having that happen to them.

"Trapdoor jump in ten seconds," she said. Sue could feel the ship—nothing as responsive as *Raijin*, but still a fine vessel—and as usual, her gut told her to nudge the timing, just the slightest amount. "Jump in three, two, one..."

Perfect darkness recaptured the screen, along with the indescribable sensation of dropping away or jumping up over an unseen wall.

"You changed jump duration at the last moment," Tip observed. "Why?"

"Wish I could tell you. There's all sorts of variables changing as you set it—relative angle, current electromagnetic field, coil resonance... they call it instinct, but it's probably just a subconscious calculation based on all these things I'm seeing."

"How many jumps have you done?" Pavla asked.

Sue laughed. "Honestly, I have no idea. I did my first one when I was five—my dad was a pilot, taught me from the time I was tiny."

"*Five?*"

"Well, I didn't do the calculations, but he let me lay them in and set her going. Which was enough to hook me for life." The countdown was almost done. "Emergence in four, three, two, one—"

A blaze of white and green and blue and brown filled almost half the screen, a perfect globe spanning over sixteen degrees, more than thirty-two times the size of the Moon in Earth's sky.

"...wow," Pavla said in a hushed voice after a long moment of dead silence.

Sue was too busy to bask in the appreciation of her skill—and ridiculous luck, being honest about it. The accuracy of the ship was measured around nine hundred thousand kilometers and here she'd arrived only forty thousand or so off. At this range it was easy to get a relative speed and that told her they needed a strong burn to make this an orbit and not a quick zoom past. "Everyone strap in *now*, we have an orbital insertion to make and it will be a heavy shot."

She touched the intercom. "All personnel, this is a five-minute acceleration warning, repeat, five minutes to acceleration. Strap in or get in your bunks in secure mode. Five minutes begins now."

"How heavy a burn are we looking at?" the Captain asked.

"Looks like about five and a half minutes at three G's," she answered.

Ayrton winced. "That's heavy, all right. Ten kps difference?"

"Ten point one. And we're lucky, at that; differential in a lot of systems is enough to require months with the Nebula Drive to match up."

She gave a one-minute warning, then a thirty second one. Then the drive cut in.

Abruptly it was as though she was lying down and there were two more Sues lying on top of her, perfectly aligned with every single part of her, adding pressure to everything from her gut to her eyeballs. Her vision blurred slightly before her eyes compensated for the pressure deformation, and she kept her attention on the running status data for *Sherlock*. Automatics would handle most things, but there was still no substitute for human ability to notice oddities in a *gestalt* of events.

But *Sherlock* was a good ship, and the flight out to the mysterious system had given them plenty of time to shake down any problems. After five minutes and thirty-three and one-half seconds had elapsed, the drive cut off, and the world was suddenly light as a feather—lighter, really, because the bridge was at the center axis of *Sherlock* and therefore in microgravity.

"Burn successful," Sue said with a grin. "We are now in orbit around our life-bearing mystery world."

"Excellent work, Lieutenant Fisher," the Captain said, with a matching smile. "It really was a pleasure to—"

"*Captain!*"

All heads snapped around to stare at Commander Gariba, whose eyes were wide and glinting with disbelief.

"What is it, Commander?"

"I've got it. I have a *signal!*"

Sue was frozen for an instant, unable to grasp it. She'd thought of the *possibility*, but she'd never allowed herself to really believe there could have been survivors. "Are you sure?"

"One hundred percent sure, Ma'am, Captain! It's a GPS signal from an SC-178, just like you said the *LS-88* was carrying on board!"

"I will be damned," Ayrton said in a hushed voice. "They made it here. And put up a satellite? Mr. Gariba, is that the only satellite?"

"Can't be, sir...no, definitely not. I'm getting multiple signals now. Can't see the other side of the planet, sir, but all indications are that they've got a thin but functional network up and running!"

"If they have that...can we transmit to the network? They must be using them as comm satellites, yes?"

"Must be, sir. I'll get on—"

"Ohhh, *that's* not good," came Tip's voice, tense with worry.

"What is it, Tip?"

"Radar picked up incoming, confirmed with telescope—*massive* incoming, kilometers across, and—"

"*Kilometers?*"

"Yes, can't get an exact read yet, something funny with the geometry—"

Sue snapped her head back around to Gariba. "Call! Call now!"

I refuse to be one day too late!

Chapter 46

"Time's getting short," Campbell murmured to himself, looking out the window at the overcast sky. "We have updates on impact?"

"Trying to get new images," Melody said absently. "By now it's dropped down below the GPS constellation, so we've had to rotate back to the ground-facing position, and that took time."

"It's also harder to acquire; shift in perspective and all. But knowing the track helps," Whips said. "We should be getting good data shortly."

Campbell nodded. "Well, we're all ears."

Their run for the horizon had gone well, all things considered. With their ninety hours just about run out, they'd averaged almost thirty kilometers per hour, so they were well out of the target zone, about twenty-eight hundred kilometers from their prior home. Having that kind of cushion made him feel better about the situation. *Lord knows we don't want to cut it close when we're facing a disaster like this.*

Not that it would completely shield them even if they were on the other side of the planet. Impact and flash wouldn't be a problem, but the weather over the whole planet would go insane, with "insane" including hurricanes that broke the normal measuring scales. Not to mention the small but definitely real chance of being hit by secondary impacts—debris thrown by the impact so hard, so high, that it basically came down as smaller meteors.

They'd tested *Emerald Maui*'s diving ability, just in case, and it seemed that despite everything the shuttle had gone through, the seals were still absolutely solid, so that was one good thing. Diving under trouble was a good option to have, as they'd found out when they ended up in a hurricane on their way to meet up with the Kimeis.

"There's a small floating continent—maybe four hundred kilometers long—about a hundred kilometers in front of us," Tavana said. "Should we think about landing, or stay out to sea?"

"Avoid for now," Xander said, after a quick glance at both Campbell and Laura. "Let's see what happens after Lincoln takes the hit before we decide what to do. *Emerald Maui* works best in the open."

"Aye, Captain," Tavana said, and adjusted their course. "We'll skirt by it to the south, it's open ocean past that for—"

"Pictures and tracking coming in now," Melody interrupted. "Processing as fast as we can."

Whips rippled colors and patterns of assent. "Almost there. I..." He paused. "Well, that's interesting."

"Something bad?"

"...probably not. But I guess what we were seeing was a fragment of a comet, and in its final approach—you know the term 'Roche limit,' right?"

"Point at which a natural body over some size will come apart around another object, yeah." Campbell felt himself do a double-take. "Wait, are you saying our impactor came apart?"

"Broke into three pieces, somewhere between our losing it and reacquiring it below the GPS constellation."

"None of them are coming near us, are they?" Sakura asked nervously.

"No, no—natural spread isn't nearly that fast. They're going to shotgun our old continent, though." Whips' patterns showed uncertainty. "Might mean more ejecta, I guess. Not much we can do about it."

Campbell thought about that. "Might be we'd like to dive before any of that mess *can* hit us. What do you think, Captain, Laura, Pearce?"

Xander frowned. "We can go down, what, thirty meters safely?"

"Based on our experience, that would be reasonable," Pearce said. "Research showed almost ninety was actually done."

Laura nodded. "So the question is whether thirty meters down is going to protect us from anything."

"Oh, it will protect us from *many* things," Tavana said emphatically, echoed by Caroline, who took up the conversation.

"Xander's group already showed that they can escape the effects of storms very well diving to twenty or thirty meters," she said. "And smaller impact debris will be stopped by a relatively few meters of water. Larger, well, obviously if it's large *enough* that won't matter, but it's sure far better than nothing."

Xander surveyed the others, glanced back at the sergeant. "Any other points I'm missing?"

Francisco put up his hand. "It may be silly, but breathing? There are two times as many of us now as there were last time, will the air be okay?"

"Not a silly question at all, Francisco," Xander said. "Anyone have an answer?"

"Environmental systems are working just fine," Maddox said emphatically. "There's no more people here than *Emerald Maui* was designed for, and we swapped out filters just before we left. We could stay down weeks without worrying about air. Probably months, since she's been recharging her oxygen storage all along."

"All right," Xander said after a moment. "We'll dive shortly after impact—which isn't far away now. Stay down until we're sure any debris will have fallen back down. Right?"

"Sounds like a—"

An alert tone—the sound of someone transmitting on the emergency override frequencies—cut Campbell off; the tone was followed by a booming voice:

"Calling anyone within range of this signal, this is the OSV *Sherlock* out of Orado. LS-5, LS-88, are you there? Calling anyone within range of this signal..."

For a long, long moment nobody moved. Everyone stared at each other, eyes wide, all asking the same soundless question: *Did you hear that? Is this real?*

Then Laura Kimei shook herself and answered, a fraction ahead of even Campbell. "This is Dr. Laura Kimei from LS-5, *Sherlock*. We read you. My God, we read you!"

There was a sound—a gasp, Campbell thought—before the voice returned. "Lieutenant Susan Fisher speaking—the prior voice was Commander Gariba. How many of you are there, and are you all in good health?"

Laura caught Campbell's eye and nodded; he grinned and answered. "Chief Master Sergeant Samuel Morgan Campbell speaking, Lieutenant, and in answer there's a lucky thirteen of us here—the entire complement of *LS-5*, *LS-88*, plus Lieutenant Pearce Greene Haley of *Outward Initiative* who happened to get stuck with us when everything went wrong. We're all healthy at the moment, running southeast in *Emerald Maui*, which used to be *LS-88*. GPS constellation should have our coordinates."

"Thirteen. My god, all of you ... even Lieutenant Haley? She was put down as killed in the accident."

"I'm right here, Lieutenant," Pearce said.

"And Harratrer—is he—"

"Right here!" Whips answered.

"I can't believe it," she said, her voice cracking.

A deeper man's voice said, "None of us can." That voice, too, was somewhat unsteady with shock. "Captain Ayrton here. I must say, though, it's incredibly good to have the chance to believe it. However, there's a more pressing problem."

"The oncoming impacts? Yes, we know. Don't suppose you're in a position to stop them," Campbell said.

"We're a survey vessel, not a Skywatch task force, unfortunately. Not that even a Skywatch could do much at this point."

"Can't you pick us up?" asked Francisco.

"We can, yes—that must be Francisco?" Lieutenant Fisher said. "But not in six minutes."

"How long until you can get down here?"

There was a silence—very long indeed to Campbell, who could see *Seconds to Impact* ticking remorselessly down in his omni view.

At last, Captain Ayrton spoke. "Probably at least two or three hours minimum. We didn't expect to have to launch this fast and the prep for flight on our S&R shuttles will take time—can't shortcut it in a situation like this. I'm afraid you're going to have to ride out the impacts and whatever follows for at least a bit. Plus I don't want any of my ships flying down there until whatever comes *up* finishes going down, if you get my meaning."

Campbell sure did. Piloting a shuttle through the rain of debris from a dinosaur-killer impact? No thanks, pass on that.

"Understood," Laura said. "We certainly don't want you cutting corners on prep or safety. Lincoln will take any opening you give it."

"Lincoln?"

"Planet's name. This is the Emerald system, habitable planet Lincoln."

"I..." buzzed Whips, "am becoming more cynical about that 'habitable' business every day."

"Official names recorded," Ayrton said. "We'll get to work, people—just hold on down there!"

"Lincoln hasn't been able to kill us yet," Campbell said. "I'm willing to bet we can hold it off for a few more hours. But don't take *too* long, because it's going to get a lot worse on this planet before it gets better."

"We'll be diving on impact," Xander added. "We don't plan to surface until we're sure it's safe enough, so you won't be able to contact us for a while afterward."

"Copy that. We'll wait for your signal, then, because prep should be finished by that point. *Sherlock* signing off for now."

The interior of *Emerald Maui* exploded in shouts and cheers and even tears, all at the last-minute realization that rescue was here, was *finally* here...

...maybe an hour or three too late. Red numerals began to flash in the corner of Campbell's vision, and he saw the shutters sliding over the port, leaving only the projected view from the cameras.

Something flashed, a flare of light that somehow *expanded* even though they couldn't see it, from far, far over the horizon.

IMPACT.

Chapter 47

Three masses of nickel-iron, none less than five kilometers in any dimension, *in toto* making a single body ten kilometers in diameter, plunged through the atmosphere on very slightly diverging courses, the heat vaporizing the remainder of the water and ammonia ices that had bound the three together until minutes before. Though the atmosphere around them blazed into incandescent plasma, the journey was far too short to heat that titanic mass—trillions of tons of metal moving at tens of kilometers per second.

In about one second the three impactors streaked from the high atmosphere to the immense floating continent below. Huge as it was—over sixteen hundred kilometers long and hundreds wide, with a maximum thickness over ten kilometers, made of natural carbonan-reinforced stone—it could in no way withstand the inconceivable force of that triple blow, equal in power to the simultaneous detonation of millions of the most powerful nuclear weapons ever created.

The continent bowed under the impact and then *rippled*, the shockwave pulverizing the stone near the impact and shattering the rest in a widening ring of devastation that spread through stone and sea at tremendous speed. At the center of the impacts a hole was bored ten, fifteen, twenty, thirty kilometers and more into the depths.

The incredible forces of impact deceleration did what the atmosphere could not; much of the mass of the impactors, and a huge volume of water, stone, and living things about them *vaporized*, creating a detonation of plasma many kilometers across, hotter than the surface of Lincoln's sun. Trees burst into flame hundreds of kilometers away as a new and baleful star ascended, a seething fireball larger than a mountain rising into the sky on a pillar of fire and smoke.

What did not vaporize still had to *move*, and move it did, opening an ephemeral yet monstrous crater well over two hundred kilometers in diameter in the surface of the ocean. Some of the mass was hammered down into the depths, a combined impact and pressure wave that shattered the foundation of ice sixty and more kilometers below, blasting a gargantuan crater that even reached the actual bedrock under more than twenty kilometers of exotic ice; more streaked outward in a trio of immense waves that began kilometers high, and would not subside to anything resembling normal waves for many, many kilometers to come.

The crater in the ice-seafloor could not support itself, nor could the water remain water at that depth once the sea returned to reclaim the void. Freed of the icy pressure above, doughy magma welled from within Lincoln, contesting with the collapsing icy walls of the crater and the returning, crystallizing ocean in a bizarre cataclysmic contest that there were, unfortunately, no eyes to see.

The rest of the impactor and its victim-continent was hurled into the sky with cosmic force, some pieces of the shattered continent flying into space, traveling with such velocity that they would never again return to Lincoln, or might, undisturbed, take incalculable years to do so. Most blew outward as well as up, flying hundreds of kilometers; some few flew free of the atmosphere on high sub-orbital arcs, to return as flaming impactors of their own, raining incandescent death far, far from the scene of primary impact.

Most of these, however, were relatively small things; they might kill what they fell upon, start fires, send spectacular splashes skyward, but most of them were not threats to anything deep within a floating continent, or cruising tens of meters below the ocean surface.

Most of them.

Chapter 48

"Do we dive now?" Xander's voice was deceptively calm, but Tavana had heard him enough to note the tension underlying it.

"Not quite. About sixteen minutes before debris really starts to arrive."

"What's the rest of the disaster schedule look like, Mel?" Campbell asked.

"Seismic wave pretty soon, but that'll be nothing for us up here. Tsunami—with the water-compression wave riding along... that's a little more than an hour. We *don't* want to be below water for that one, we'll have to surf." She winced. "That's *tsunamis*, plural. Frequency separation means there'll be several of them, and the model says... it's not going to be good."

"Right. So we dodge the shrapnel on the dive, come up in about half an hour or so, then ride the waves. Anything else?"

Mel's eyebrows rose. "Wow. Um, we really want to dive about two hours from now; the airblast's going to be intense."

"We're two thousand eight hundred kilometers from the impact and the airblast's still bad?" Pearce asked incredulously.

"That's what you get when your impact's measured in the hundreds of millions of megatons, yes," Melody said. "And the outward airblast'll be followed by an inward blast. And I think a couple lesser ones afterward. The whole planet, including the atmosphere, is ringing like a bell. Outward blasts will be hot, inward will be cold."

"Okay, so dive, resurface, dive, maybe another dive for the second airblast. That it?"

Melody looked at Whips and shrugged; Whips echoed the

297

gesture in his own way. "As far as the impact goes. We don't have the data or experience to model what the weather'll be like after this, but it's going to be bad, that I'm sure of. Just the hot-cold contrasts of the airblasts says the weather's going to be hideous. And of course near the impact site..."

"...there will be some kind of mega-hurricane like we've never imagined," Melody said, voice unsteady. "That'll affect every weather system on the planet. We're still way too close for comfort."

Tavana shook his head. "Well, we had best update our friends, yes?"

"Yes," Laura said. "*Sherlock*, this is *Emerald Maui*."

The reply was almost instant, with a hint of static. "*Sherlock* here. We read you, *Emerald Maui*. Go ahead." The voice was shaky, carrying with it the implication that Captain Ayrton was watching the results of a major meteoroid impact.

"Debris will be arriving in...about ten, twelve minutes now. We're getting ready to dive. We'll stay down about half an hour. Then we have to surface to ride multiple tsunamis, which doesn't sound like fun, then dive *again* to duck the airblast, which I'm informed may be as much as a significant fraction of one bar." Tavana knew that this meant a wind-impact greater than any hurricane ever, maybe *much* greater depending on how "significant" that fraction of a bar was. "After that it's weather we'll have to worry about."

"Understood, *Emerald Maui*. Thanks for the update. We will continue to prepare rescue vessels so they will be on standby as soon as practical." Ayrton's voice held a note of humor. "My pilots would also rather not fly through a major overpressure wave. So we'll talk to you in about three hours."

"I don't blame them, Captain. And yes, three hours. Thank you again. *Emerald Maui* out."

"Wait a moment, *Emerald Maui*." This voice was a calm tenor, but not one they'd heard before. "This is Tip—sorry, Lieutenant Tip Henderson, Sciences. Your models may be making some things worse than they will be. They likely assume an Earthlike world. True?"

"Yes," Melody answered after a moment. "I tried to change parameters but I don't think it was handling the shift well."

"Sixty-kilometer depths, which is what it appears you're

dealing with, are well beyond the standard models carried in even colonist omnis. If this impact happened on an Earthlike world, yes, the waves would be something to seriously concern you. In this case, with the depth of those oceans, the waves will be high, but also extremely broad, even the ones with the shortest wavelengths. You will see the horizon retreat and approach, but the effective vertical and horizontal accelerations will be no greater than those of the usual waves encountered. The airblast, unfortunately, will still be quite significant, and the minimal but still present risk of the debris also."

"So, to sum up," Xander said, "we don't need to worry about the waves. We should just stay submerged until after the major airblasts are done."

"That would be my recommendation."

"Thank you, *Sherlock*. That's at least one piece of good news!"

"Glad to help. Good luck."

"Thanks again. *Emerald Maui*, out."

There was a moment's silence, then Maddox burst out, "I can't *believe* we're actually about to be rescued!"

The whole group exploded into laughs and cheers, which only slowly died down. "No one reluctant to leave?" Campbell asked with a grin.

"I don't think so," Laura said instantly. "I suppose ... if everything we'd built hadn't just been wiped off the face of the planet ..."

"Actually," Akira said slowly, "I must confess I will rather miss this place—it's absolutely fascinating." He looked around with a raised eyebrow at the others who were staring at him, then smiled. "But I would *much* rather study it with all the resources of a proper expedition. No, Sergeant, I think we are all very happy to think of getting away from Lincoln."

Sakura looked out at the sparkling water, then caught Tavana's eye. "I'll have some good memories of Lincoln, though," she said, and Tavana felt warm all through.

"I ... guess," Mel said slowly. "Scattered in among the days of grinding work, moments of terror, and unending exhaustion, yeah."

"It wasn't *that* bad," Caroline said.

"Well ... not all the time, anyway. But yeah, it was, sometimes."

"Life's pretty much like that a lot of places," Campbell said. "And shouldn't we dive about now, Captain?"

Xander nodded. "Yes." He looked at Tavana. "Make it so, Tav!"

"All right. Everyone make sure you're strapped in?" Tavana waited to make sure everyone reported in, even Franky and Hitomi. Then he grasped the controls and took *Emerald Maui* down.

They'd done this before, so Tavana knew what to expect; the glitter of the sunshine faded into brilliant shards of flickering light, slowly dimming a bit as they descended, until they drove at speed through an emerald sea twenty-five meters below the surface. He studied the telltales for a few moments, then nodded. "Captain, we are steady at twenty-five meters submerged. No indications of leaks. All green."

"Lock it in, Tavana," Xander said.

As he complied, the light began to dim. Vaguely he could see that the sky was darkening. "This fast?"

"I don't think anyone's ever actually *witnessed* an impact anything like this magnitude," Caroline said in a hushed voice. "Maybe the impact flash and heating is triggering cloud formation along its intersection with the atmosphere; who knows? We'd have to go up surface to see."

"And we are *not* surfacing for a while," Laura said. "Everyone, relax. We've got hours yet before we have to do more than ride this out. We don't have any other work to do. Just stay in our seats, in case anything happens."

It was quiet for a moment, then Hitomi said, "What the sergeant said...I guess things might have been tough even where we *meant* to be going."

Tavana nodded. "We were going to a colony world. It would have had better equipment, but I bet there would have been a lot of work, and not all of it fun, on Tantalus. Maybe even moments of terror."

"Probably all of that," Pearce Haley said. "Heard enough tales from the old man here on that."

"*Old man?* I come by these gray hairs mostly from watching you young people doing stupid-ass things that nearly get you killed!"

"Then I," Laura said, "ought to be as white-haired as my grandmother."

"*Mom!* We're not that bad, are we?" Whips protested.

"Asks Mr. 'oh, I'll ignore my injuries and almost get eaten'?"

"Oh. Yeah. I guess maybe we are."

"What 'we' is that?" demanded Melody. "*I* try to stay out of all that stuff!"

The banter and laughter continued, and Tavana found himself marveling at it. A few hours before, they were running from a cosmic disaster, knowing they were entirely on their own. Now they were *found*, and the knowledge was buoying their spirits, even though in a few minutes they would be having to survive the aftereffects of that same disaster.

Without warning, something began dimpling the sea above them, and a *plipplopploploplopPLIP* sound came from the external microphones, drowning out the mysterious distant moans and grumbles from below. Laura squinted up. "Rain?"

"No," Mel said tensely. "This is it. The debris from the impact."

The light had dimmed more—Tavana guessed that some of the debris was little more than dust, helping to block the light. The rest seemed to be tiny pebbles, with a smattering of larger stones among them. Faint taps came from *Emerald Maui* as some of those, slowed to simple drifting by the ocean's mass, bounced gently off the hull before dropping away into the depths.

"Why are they sinking?" Sakura asked. "Most of Lincoln's stones float!"

"If they were ejected at that kind of speed, they probably melted. Pieces that didn't burn up would've gotten denser as they melted and congealed," Mel said absently. She was still staring up suspiciously at the surface. "Plus some of this isn't going to be Lincoln debris; it's the impactor, and *it* was nickel-iron."

A distant *boom* coincided with a tiny vibration of *Emerald Maui*. "Whoa. That wasn't small."

"Stands to reason some big pieces would get thrown up and come down," Campbell said. "Just hope that I . . ."

An impact slewed *Emerald Maui* around and rang her hull like a bell, tilting the ship sideways. If Tavana and the others hadn't been strapped in, it would have sent them all tumbling like dice in a gambler's cup. As it was there were curses and shrieks. Those died away to a watchful silence.

The controls were stubborn now. "*Merde,*" he muttered. Red lights blinked on the board.

"What is it, Tav! Talk to me!" Xander said.

"Have to surface! We just lost most of our remaining wing, dive plane sheared off. And . . . and I'm showing seal integrity compromised on the rear door."

"Take us up, then, fast."

"Hold on!" Tavana directed the remaining, mangled shape-able material to become as functional a waterfoil as possible, then kicked in the jet to maximum. *Emerald Maui* wallowed for a moment, then seemed to understand; it steadied and lunged upward, charging to the surface and breaking it like a breaching whale to fall back with a *thud* onto the water.

"How bad's the leak?" Campbell asked with a strangely casual intonation.

"Can't...be quite sure, but it's pretty bad."

"Can we stay up if the cargo compartment floods?"

"I...dunno. Maybe. Maybe if I can use the jet to keep us up some. Can we dump the cargo?"

"We're up for rescue. We don't need most of it. Worst comes to worst we just need data, which we've all got stored. Problem would be if we *can* dump the cargo."

Campbell unstrapped. "Tav, I'm going to take a quick squint aft. If the water ain't *pouring* in, me and Xander'll go see if it's patchable. If not, well...we'll start loosening all the big pieces, like the excavators. When the water really gets high, then we open the doors, you hit the jet and hopefully tilt us up fast enough that we can dump the weight. If you're *really* good with it, might could dump a bunch of the water and then be able to close the doors again. Buy us some time."

"Better hurry," Mel said. "Tsunami may not be a big deal, but the airblasts are coming in only a couple hours. Maybe a little less."

"Oh, I know it." Campbell took a breath and then suddenly *bellowed,* shouting at the lowering sky showing on the viewport. "*God-DAMN it, we're* LEAVING! Just give us one goddamn *break,* Lincoln!"

The cabin was dead silent, everyone staring at the sergeant, who looked down, embarrassed.

"Sorry, everyone," Campbell said finally.

"No," Akira said, and chuckled. The laugh spread, rippling around the room like the waves on a pond, until even Hitomi giggled. "No, Sergeant, you said what every single one of us feels. And you're right. We've survived everything Lincoln's thrown at us. We'll beat whatever it has left."

"Damn right we will." He turned to the rear door. "Now let's do that surviving thing *one more time.*"

Chapter 49

The door slid open, and immediately a thin wash of water spread out into the cabin area. Sakura could *hear* the splash and swish of the sea through the open door.

"I'm gonna need muscles in here! Tav, Whips, Xander, get in here *now!*" came Campbell's sharp command.

Tavana began unstrapping. "Sakura, you've got the board!"

"Got it!" she said, feeling her pulse rising again. *Once more I'm the pilot in an emergency.*

She grasped the controls, tested them. "We're already getting rear-heavy, Sergeant! I'm going to have to accelerate forward, try to dump some of the water!"

"Understood, Saki. Do what you gotta do. Gents, make sure you've got a good anchor somewhere in reach, 'cause she ain't gonna be able to warn us every time."

Sakura accelerated as slowly as she could. The idea was to push as much of the water *back* as she could by, effectively, driving out from under it. "Sergeant, I can't do this for too long. When I say *NOW*, you've *got* to close the cabin door."

"That'll stick the four of us back here, you know," Xander said. His tone wasn't reproving, just a reminder of an uncomfortable fact, but she still felt a pang of guilt.

"I know, but we don't want water up here too. I've got to have confidence you'll get it cut off somehow...or at least be able to tell me when you're sure you can't and then I can let you in quick."

"We'll get it done," Whips said. "Like the sergeant said, you do what you have to."

303

Emerald Maui began to bump a bit as its speed increased over the increasingly choppy waves, and there were still occasional *ting* and *whanggg* noises as small pieces of ejecta rapped her. She saw a huge plume of water spout up where another large piece had hit, a kilometer or more away, and shuddered. *One more hit on us like that and we've probably had it.*

Now the movement was really getting rough, and Sakura had to remember that the unstrapped people back there couldn't hold on like the rest of them. "*Now*, Sergeant!"

Instantly the door slid shut and locked; there was effectively no water in the cabin. "Door shut successfully, Sergeant. You still hear us back there?"

"Loud and clear, Saki. Looks like the cargo door here twisted out of its track, that's where the water's coming in."

She slowed their motion until it was as smooth as feasible; *Emerald Maui*'s size did allow it to steamroller the smaller waves pretty well.

But the control for diving and steering's bad now. About the only good thing you can say about losing the side wing is that it made her more symmetrical, but in these conditions that's not so good; the outrigger helped a lot *in stability.*

"I say we drop the ramp," Whips' voice said. "Give me a chance to look and see what the damage is inside the track and lock, and the rest of you can start dumping the big cargo. We don't need the earthmovers anymore, and that'll gain us a lot."

"You think the ramp'll survive that? It'll be bouncing along in the ocean and then we throw tons of machinery down it?"

"It ought to. They built these things tough. And if we're going to try to fix it, I need to see if the internal seal's damaged, and if it is, whether it can be fixed."

"Right. Saki, you hear? We're opening the rear door. Try to keep us going smooth and straight."

"I hear." She looked around at the others. "Mom, I think someone should get the rescue boats out, ready to deploy and inflate."

"Good idea, Sakura. Caroline, Maddox, Mel, would you get on that?"

"Yes, Mom," Caroline and Melody chorused, and Maddox said "Yes, Dr. Kimei."

"I'll help," Akira said. Pearce also unstrapped and went to assist with the check-out of the rafts.

Sakura watched the camera views closely. The ship jolted and she suddenly felt a shift in the drag and motion of *Emerald Maui*. A second, turbulent wake was now visible to the rear, within the broader wake left by the former *LS-88*; the ramp was now dragging its way through the ocean.

She adjusted speed, tried to slow as much as feasible, but that was going to require balancing, given the waves.

Waves reminded her of the next problem—not the tsunamis, but what was coming behind and maybe during them. "Mel, how long before the airblast gets here?"

"Now? About one hour and forty minutes. An hour forty-three, according to the calcs, but there's a bunch of unknowns, so it could be plus-or-minus fifteen minutes on that time."

That's not long for a major repair. "Sergeant, to be safe, you've *got* to get finished in no more than an hour or so, so you can get back and strap in."

"I hear you, Saki. We'll do what we can."

"Melody," Maddox said, as they began checking the two inflatable, carbonan-fabric lifeboats, "Why won't the airblast be weaker than we thought? The other impact wasn't that bad that way, and according to our friends above the waves aren't going to be as dangerous as we thought, so is the airblast...or blasts, are they going to really be that bad?"

"Short answer: yes," Mel said. The quick, clipped answer told Sakura just how scared her little sister was. *Mel really* understands *stuff through numbers, I think.* "Longer answer...this impact is... just not even comparable with the first. We couldn't measure the first one, but it was probably something like ten million times smaller, maybe less."

Sakura saw Maddox flinch at that number, and Mel run her fingers nervously through her hair. "Difference is that the tsunamis here are moving through water that's many times deeper than the oceans on earth. That means their energy's spread out more, to be simplistic about it. The airblast, though—Lincoln's atmosphere isn't really much different from Earth's, so *that* model holds just fine. And like the tsunami, it's driven by how much...*stuff* got moved, real fast, by the impact, plus the heat-driven expansion from the collision.

"This...thing hit the ocean and probably blew a hole two hundred kilometers in diameter, down to maybe sixty kilometers. I don't know the exact geometry of that hole, but if I guesstimate it to be equal to a cylinder half that diameter, that's close to half a million cubic kilometers of water that just got shoved aside, then there's the explosion and the collapse back of all that water— which means the same volume of *air* being shoved around... Anyway, what it means is that this shockwave didn't just come from what amounts to one *point* on the ocean and atmosphere, it's top-to-bottom of the water column and the atmosphere and moving as fast as the speed of sound."

There was silence in the cabin, broken only by the occasional *ping* of another piece of debris and heavier *thuds* from behind the sealed cargo door.

"Then what do we expect when it gets here?" Laura asked quietly.

"Best guess?" Melody was trying to sound detached, but her lighter voice vibrated with fear. "Worse than a Category 5 hurricane. Worse than an F3 tornado. Maybe a *lot* worse."

Sakura felt her hands twitch on the controls, and a coldness spread out from her chest, gooseflesh rising on her arms. She'd seen a tornado, once, and seen the absolute devastation it had left. Encountering that howling horror *here*...

"Any...advice on how we deal with it?" Sakura asked finally.

"Just be strapped down, if we can't dive," Campbell's voice answered. "Honestly, something like this wasn't in the cards even in all the places I've ever been to. There's no cyclone cellars for us to hide in, so *Emerald Maui* is just gonna have to do." His voice lightened. "*Ha!* Clamp let go! All right, everyone clear the door!"

There was a huge, confused splash, and Sakura felt *Emerald Maui* waver, then continue—but this time, she thought, a hair higher up in the water. "Excavator?"

"First one down. Second one in a minute. Whips?"

"Hold off on the second one." Sakura swallowed. She didn't like the edge she heard in Whips' voice "That's a pressure door. It took a heavy, heavy impact to do this. I don't think we can force it back into track with hand tools, now that I've looked it over."

"We really don't want to be on the surface when the airblasts hit," Campbell said grimly. "You have any options for us? You want to keep this one on for ballast, that it?"

"Partly, yeah, but the excavator might also be the only thing *strong* enough to yank the door back on-track."

"There's that. You might have something in that idea. We'll want to lock her back down so she can't move, in that case."

"But the door, it is fairly smooth. How do we pull on it?" Tavana asked. "And exactly *where*?"

"I'll do the calcs," Whips answered. "Captain, Mel, I'll want you to check the results. That'll tell us where. How...Sergeant?"

"It'll have to be some kind of heavy pull ring. Carbonan adhesive. Bonding something *that* tough takes time, though..."

"Hear that, Saki?" Whips asked.

"I do." She glanced at the clock. "You've got forty-five minutes."

"I know."

She saw motion out of the corner of her eye, looked over to see Caroline, Mel, and the others strapping in. The two lifeboats were in prelaunch positions, still secured but now easily released to be tossed out through the airlock or the rear door. "All set?"

"Seems to be," her father answered. "All of the indicators check out fine, and—after all—this is actually quite a new vessel, despite how badly we've been abusing her, so these lifeboats are about factory-new."

"And a good model—used one of the same design myself about ten years back," Campbell said.

"Was that in the story you told me about using one as a *toboggan*?" Pearce asked.

"The very same," Campbell answered with a chuckle. "Come on, you damn stubborn bas...bugger, *lock down!*"

"You will *have* to tell us that story sometime, Sergeant," said Tavana.

"I definitely want to hear it," Whips chimed in. "Here, let me try...*got it!*"

"Good. At least she won't move while we try pulling."

"Those holdfasts good enough?" Maddox asked. "I mean, if you have the excavator pull hard..."

"They're able to hold it still through multi-G maneuvers," Campbell said. "Pretty sure she can't pull four times her own weight, so yeah."

"Close the ramp door," Xander said. "Need to record motion and seal behavior."

A moment later there was a huge clanging *thud* from the rear. "That's...*dang*. Almost but not quite. Still a gap."

"Can't we lever it shut?" That was Tavana's voice. "It's just jamming along this line..."

"Can't," Whips said after a moment. "First, since it opens

outward you'd have to pry from the outside to force it in. Second, like I said, this is a pressure door. Hand tools just won't cut it. I'm not even sure the excavator can, but it's the only thing we've got to try."

"Then let's get to it," Campbell said. "Time ain't moving any slower."

Sakura looked out the port and realized something had *changed.* The horizon was receding, farther and farther, as a wave many, many kilometers long and almost two kilometers from trough to crest raced towards them. Even though she knew it wouldn't hurt them—that it was so immense that it would no more disturb them by its passage than a flea is disturbed by its host's walk—she felt another chill, seeing finally the true power of the impact.

"The tsunamis are here," she said quietly.

Chapter 50

Susan stared speechless at the screen; the rest of the bridge crew of *Sherlock* were likewise frozen, unable to tear their gazes from the view of Lincoln below.

A blazing sphere of fire was rising from a hole blasted in the very ocean itself, rising with an apparent grace and grandeur that belied the speed and violence of the event. Clouds had been dispelled for hundreds of kilometers about the impact site, wiped away by the pressure and thermal pulse; a skirt of fire streaks surrounded the base of the column of flame below. It was, indeed, more than mere fire, for still it burned as it reached altitudes where oxygen was no more, burned with the brilliance of a savage and dying sun.

"Tell me we're recording this," she said finally.

The words seemed to break the malign spell of Armageddon. "Um...yes, Lieutenant, all cameras, all sensor suites recording since before the impact," Tip said after a moment. "EMP from the impact was significant but will die down shortly; probably not a problem at the distance our castaways are at."

"Waves?"

Tip paused a moment. Then they spoke in a hushed tone. "Big. Can't even guess at this point. They'll get smaller as they move out from the center but right now...tens of kilometers or more."

"Tip, do we have any software to give us any kind of idea as to what to expect in the *moderate* run? We know about tsunamis, airblast, debris, but what about the weather?"

Tip glanced at Ayrton. "Captain? Computations may be highly demanding."

"Give her anything she wants, Tip. Turns out she was right; this is her show now."

Tip grinned. "Good! I have a detailed impact aftermath model, in fact—although I admit it's focused on smaller impacts, the kind more likely to be encountered. Still, it should scale up fairly well. What do you need to know, Lieutenant Fisher?"

"Specifically? I need to know when we can pick up the castaways. Obviously we have to wait at least a couple of hours because of the airblast, but what about weather?"

"I'll get right on it. Without even looking it will be...horrid, to say the least."

"Get me details as soon as you can. Captain, I'm going down to help supervise preparations for the rescue shuttle."

"Very good, Lieu—"

A sharp *ping* echoed through the bridge, and everyone stiffened.

"Multiple high-speed fragments!" Pavla Amberdon called out tensely.

Jesus, Susan thought, appalled. *It's ejected stuff this far? What's it going to be like down there on the surface?*

She forced herself to continue down to the launch bay. Despite some very tense moments, *Sherlock* came through the hail of fragments essentially unscathed; the one impact had just been enough to frighten, not damage.

Prepping the rescue shuttle took time. They were, naturally, not normally carried fully fueled—too much chance for leakage of reaction mass, and rocket fuel was even touchier. In the normal way of things they'd have taken several days to prep the vehicle—but Susan was pretty sure they didn't *have* a few days.

Tip confirmed that an hour or so later. "Once the first airblast passes, the storms are *really* going to get started, Lieutenant," they said, with a combination of grimness and glee that Susan found uncomfortably easy to understand; after all, no one else in human history had ever had this chance to observe a great impact.

"How bad? And how much of a window will we have to get down and up safely?"

"How bad? Lieutenant, we're talking hurricanes and tornadoes *both* at Category 5, maybe some that make those look like breezes. At the center? Transonic wind speeds, rain measured in multiple decimeters per hour, lightning, hail the size of... I dunno, basketballs, anything you can think of, and nowhere within five thousand kilometers isn't going to be going through hell. Temperature's going to go crazy for a while—the outgoing airblasts will be hot, the receding ones cold, which is going to play havoc even with whatever weather patterns we *think* we see. The ultimate outcome's going to make it colder for a few months, maybe a couple years, but there's a *lot* of heat coming from that impact that's going to drive insane weather patterns."

Tip took a breath. "As for a window... you've got to get down there and back up fast. Honestly, if you could, you should be already down there now. The tsunamis aren't a problem; from our point of view they're really really long and flat—thank sixty-kilometer-deep oceans for that.

"Since that's not an option, launch before the first airblast hits, if you can, then drop down between blasts. You'll have maybe an hour, three or four at the outside, before things get really, really bad, but by the time thirty minutes pass, it'll already be turning into a major storm. What the following blasts do to the storm? The model's not sure."

Susan muttered a curse, glancing at the time in her omni. "That leaves me about an hour or less. The tsunami must be close to hitting."

"Yes. We spotted *Emerald Maui* on the surface nearby." Tip's voice was tense.

"What's wrong, Tip?"

"They surfaced *before* we expected. Imagery... looks like they lost the outrigger they had before."

Susan froze in the midst of locking a cargo net down. "Something *hit* them."

"Looks like it, Lieutenant."

Damnation. "That means they'll be stuck on the surface for the airblast?"

Tip shrugged. "I can't be sure, but that's what I'd have to bet. If they were hit that hard, either they can't dive because they lost the remainder of the wing, or they've sprung leaks. Or both. We could try calling them...?" They trailed off, looking to Sue for advice.

She shook her head. "They'll be dealing with their own problems now. You heard Tip, everyone—doubletime! I want to be ready to launch in forty minutes!"

There were so many things to check—and many of them just

could not be skipped; a rescue mission that cut too many corners on prep would soon be the subject of its own ironic rescue. And in this case, there'd be no chance of rescue. Winches had to be tested, medical nano station run through diagnostic and self-test, load balancing...

Her omni crackled, and a distorted voice spoke. "*Sherlock*, come in, *Sherlock*, this is *Emerald Maui*, still barely alive."

She grinned broadly. "Thank God for that, *Emerald Maui*. Is everyone all right?"

"For now," Xander said. "We got hit by one hell of a piece of debris; took off most of our outrigger and sprung the rear door out of its track. We had to surface before the cargo hold filled with water."

Sue bit her lip. "So you're stuck on the surface, with the first airblast ETA in thirty-seven minutes."

"Don't jump the gun *quite* yet," came Sergeant Campbell's voice. "We're trying a trick to get that door back on track, so to speak. Diving ain't going to be easy without the wing, but if we can seal up, we can probably manage it. Even a few meters'd keep the blast from seriously messing with us."

"Still, I'm assuming the worst. We will be launching ASAP. Keep your radio open on the following frequencies." She listed off several that Tip had given her, least likely to be interfered with under these conditions. "We'll contact you when we are on approach. I would recommend you trigger a full-power SAR beacon now, and if external lights are still functional, drive them to maximum."

"Roger that. Anything to make us easier to spot in the middle of that mess. We'll see you all in a little bit. Enjoy the ride down."

"I'm sure I will," Sue said with a grin. "Good luck, *Emerald Maui*."

Chapter 51

"I don't know if we *can* dive," Whips muttered after the transmission to *Sherlock* had cut off.

"No more do I," Campbell admitted. "Seemed to be no point in discouraging our rescuers. Little late for hindsight now, but if we're going to try diving we probably shouldn't have dumped that other excavator."

"If this doesn't work, we might want to dump this one," Xander said. He was checking the condition of the large, conical blob of carbonan epoxy surrounding a giant eyelet now cemented near one edge of the door. "Because if we start leaking more, we'll need all the help we can get."

"How are things up there, Saki?" Whips asked, trying to distract himself; all they could do was wait while the anchor cured.

"Not bad. The waves have a period of several minutes—they're moving *fast*, but really the only effect is like Tip said, I see the horizon going in and out. It's really...strange." She took a nervous breath. "Twenty minutes, Sergeant."

"I hear you, Saki. Just about ready."

Really we should let it cure twice as long just to be on the safe side, Whips thought, *but we don't have another fifteen minutes to wait.* Although, in truth, if the stuff was even half as strong as it was supposed to get, it would be more than strong enough to take anything the excavator could throw at it.

"That'll have to do," Xander said finally. "We're out of time. Hook her up."

Whips lifted the heavy hook and slid over to the door, spray jetting through the narrow crack. He knew he was much more

313

stable in this situation than anyone else. He couldn't quite reach the eyelet, but he could hold the hook in easy reach for the sergeant and Tavana, who grasped it from either side and lifted it in one smooth motion to drop into the eyelet.

"Set! Everyone out of here, now!"

Technically that was an order, so Xander should have given it, but no one seemed inclined to argue about it. A piece of very heavy machinery was about to pull very hard on a really, really heavy and solid door. Any of the likely failure modes would involve big pieces of *something* flying around in an enclosed space.

Whips was out first, by previous agreement; he needed the longest to strap in. Despite the awareness of time ticking by, he didn't allow himself to hurry; making a mistake here, he already knew from painful experience, would not only endanger him but everyone else in the ship.

By the time he locked down the last strap, all three of the others were in place. "Whips, secured!" he said.

"Captain, you want to do the honors?"

"Here goes."

There wasn't, after all, much to it—just a go-code for a preprogrammed action by the excavator, in which it would pull on the door with steadily increasing pressure, and not stop once tension had passed five kilonewtons—roughly five hundred kilograms of force—unless and until one of a few conditions were met: first, if the arm had moved directly away from the rear of *Emerald Maui* by more than one decimeter, which was slightly more than the distance the pressure door needed to be moved to seal appropriately; secondly, if the tension suddenly dropped (indicating either a break or a quick reseat of the door); and thirdly, if there was any indication of movement or yielding on the restraints holding the excavator itself.

Whips watched the indicators, which showed the tension steadily increasing, and the cargo area monitors, which showed the cable running straight as a ruled line between the excavator and the eyelet. *Cable's woven carbonan; it's stronger than either the excavator or the eyelet. If anything breaks, it's going to be the eyelet or the epoxy failing.*

Emotional tension rose along with that in the cable; he knew he was almost holding his breath, and suspected some˘ of his human friends were.

"Pulling over two tons of force now . . ." Tavana whispered quietly.

By itself that wasn't even very impressive. At just ten meters or so below the surface, there would be another atmosphere of pressure, ten tons of pressure on every square meter of surface. But that would be pressure evenly applied over the surface, against a door built to hold pressure in either direction. This was tension focused on one small area, meant to drag the door back into alignment.

"Four tons."

Whips could hear the humming of the excavator's motors now, transmitted through the restraints into the hull. The noise built in amplitude and pitch.

"Seven tons. How much more can this thing take?"

"Excavator's built for heavy work. It's got lots more to give, son. Just hope the door—"

There was a cannon shot so loud it nearly deafened them, and the door at the end of the cabin was *dented inwards* by something striking it. Sakura jumped, and both Hitomi and Francisco cried out. The video was fogged by what looked like a cloud of dust.

"It's okay! It's okay, it shut down," Whips said. "What happened?" he asked Xander.

"Looks . . . like the eyelet either broke or popped out of the epoxy. Or the epoxy tore off the door."

"Damn—"

"*But*," Xander went on, overriding the sergeant's curse, "there was movement—sudden movement—*before* that happened. Take a look."

The dust or vapor was settling. And where there had been a dark line surrounding light, a gap to the outside, there was a smooth-looking seam.

"Someone will have to go check, but I *think* what happened is she popped back into position and before the automatics kicked in, the sudden stop caused a transient tension spike, breaking the eyelet."

"Board's green," Sakura said in a whisper, then "Board is *green*, people! It's reporting seal integrity restored!"

"Now, that's fantastic, Saki! Question is, can we make a dive?"

"I guess we'd better find out," she answered, "because it's about time we did. Everyone still secure? Sing out!"

Everyone reported that they were secure, and Laura and the sergeant confirmed the reports from their own telltales.

"All right, then—hold on, everyone!"

The remaining smart material on the sides of *Emerald Maui* was extended into the best diving planes possible; far stubbier than anyone would like, but not entirely useless. To make use of that, Sakura was going to have to time her acceleration so as to hit a wave hard enough to go under, and then keep driving down.

This might be a little rough.

Sakura judged the swells and troughs carefully. "Sergeant, you sure you don't want to switch with me?" she asked suddenly.

"Might could, if you want. Captain?"

Xander looked over to her, and Sakura could see the question in his eyes—questions, actually. The obvious one was "do you want the sergeant to do it?" and the second was "and how cool are you with being replaced right now?"

She smiled and nodded.

"Switch over, Sergeant. We all know Saki did a hell of a job before, but for something like this, let's have the guy who's driven everything ever made."

"Yessir." Campbell was out of his acceleration seat almost instantly; Sakura felt positively sluggish, even though she thought she'd unstrapped pretty fast.

But honestly, I do feel better, she thought as she secured herself in the seat just vacated by the sergeant. *If Sergeant Campbell can't do this, I'd never have been able to. And we can't waste time with me failing, then switching afterward.*

"Okay, everyone, brace yourselves. This is *Emerald Maui*, trying for one more dive. I'm going to do it from the crest of the third wave ahead ... second ... here we go!"

Emerald Maui's jet roared and the ship lunged down the slope, slamming into the base of the next wave. A wash of blue-green water surged up over the forward cameras, and Saki saw the dim depths extending endlessly before them, fading into a blackness sixty kilometers deep. She could sense the sway and balk of the big shuttle, as the buoyancy of her contested against inertia and the thrust of the jet.

The engine's sound became deeper, and vibrations ran through *Emerald Maui*, but Sakura could see the faint shimmer of the surface receding. *If the tail submerges ...*

"Come on, you poor battered old girl, once more, come on, dammit, *dive!*" Campbell growled. "Overriding limits, absolute maximum *now!*"

The jet's roar rose to a shriek—and suddenly Sakura felt *Emerald Maui* moving forward—forward and down, down into the depths, fully submerged. She gave a scream of triumph.

"She still had it in her, by God!" Campbell said, grinning. "Reducing thrust . . . looks like we can hold this level at about three-quarters. Cruising at twenty meters."

"How does the seal look, Sergeant?"

"So far, all green! Fingers crossed it stays that way."

"How much longer, Mel?"

"Airblast begins in . . . a minute? Five at the outside. Not sure of duration, though. The reverse blast will last longer."

A pinging noise caused Campbell to stiffen, and Sakura did as well; she saw Tavana mirroring both of them. *That's . . . a sonar alarm? From* what?

"Damn you, Lincoln," Campbell said wearily.

Chapter 52

"Oh, that's not good," Sue heard Tip murmur as Sue passed them, *en route* to the rescue shuttle.

That froze her in her tracks. "*What* isn't good?"

"Model just popped up one of the major secondary effects of the airblasts," Tip answered. "Basically you have a Mach-speed pressure differential streaking over the surface, right? Well, that means high winds moving in one direction for the outward blast, and then back the other way for the inward."

Sue nodded. "Right, I understand that. What's the problem?"

"The problem is that because of the pressure differential, those winds are around three hundred kilometers per hour, maybe more." When Sue just raised an eyebrow, Tip shook their head. "Three hundred kilometer-per-hour winds blowing unabated across thousands of kilometers of ocean mean waves. Very, *very* big storm waves, and ones that aren't stretched way out like the tsunami."

"Crap. Double crap. That means we can't do our rescue until these airblasts run down?" Sue was appalled. "Tell *Emerald Maui* right now."

"Can't," Tip said. "They dove a few minutes ago—somehow they must have sealed their rear door."

Sue closed her eyes. "Tip, check me on this. We can't practically do the rescue now for...hours, at least. The airblasts will keep organized storms from forming over them, but they'll be bringing king-sized waves that would make this like trying to do a pickup in the middle of a Cat 5 hurricane."

Tip looked like they *really* wanted to argue that, but they closed their eyes and nodded. "Can't see any way around it, Lieutenant."

"And the *Emerald Maui* doesn't know about the airblast waves."

"Not unless they rejiggered their own software to do the projections there, and I suspect they're way too busy to have done that, especially after *I* gave them the new data." Tip looked guilty. "They'll have assumed I told them everything they needed to know."

"Oh, that's bad. That's *very* bad."

"It's bad, yes," Tip agreed, looking at her apprehensively, "but I'm guessing you've seen something badder than the bad I was thinking about."

"They're caught between some dangerous choices. These waves are large enough that, at the depth they said they were planning on—twenty to thirty meters—there will still be a large effect from waves that may be twice that height. If they want to avoid that, they have to go deeper."

"And they can only go so deep. So either they're going to be pushed up and down by the waves, which will stress the ship, or they have to go deeper, which could also stress the ship in a different way."

"It gets better," Sue said, feeling her expression harden. "They managed to somehow force a pressure door back into alignment, yes, but that door isn't anything like it used to be. It bent or buckled somewhere. There's a weak spot, like a place where a piece of paper got folded.

"What do you think is going to happen when it's subjected to more increases and decreases of pressure?"

Tip's eyes shifted to the screen. "We'll find out. Because that white line there?" They pointed. "The airblast's hit."

Chapter 53

Laura saw the reactions of the other three and Campbell's tired curse. "What?"

"*Waves*, that's what. That much wind over that much ocean, stands to reason. And they'll be here soon. I'm guessing they're thirty meters high, top to bottom. Maybe bigger."

"But we're safe here, right? That's why we dove. And even if they pass over us, the emergency depth was, what, up to ninety meters?"

"When in good shape—but this poor girl's been beaten around a lot. And if a few of them crash, might get a rogue wave two, three times higher, and *that* will be past our known threshold."

"It's not *that* bad," Melody said.

"What? How you figure that, Mel?"

"I looked up wave action. Seems that the pressure changes should be tied mostly to the position changes—that is, we'll be bobbing up and down with the wave, staying at the same pressure level. Real problem is that with big waves we're going to be bouncing up and down a lot—at least as much as being in a small boat in heavy seas."

"What can we do?" Laura asked, as the others stared at them from their secured seats.

"Not a damn thing," Campbell said. "We don't want to surface, and my guess is we'd have to dive to twice this depth to really damp out the motion. Just sit tight...and pray."

"First waves going to pass over soon," Whips said. "We won't feel it much down here...I hope."

Laura gripped her armrests, thinking about her whole family, trapped inside this metal-and-composite bubble in the alien sea of Lincoln, and her gut tensed and churned. *We're so close. So very close to rescue. We just have to survive a few . . .*

As *Emerald Maui* gave a rolling lurch, she said, hearing her own voice unnaturally casual in her ears, "Sergeant, if the waves are that bad, will *Sherlock* be able to make pickup when scheduled?"

He was silent far too long, and Laura knew the answer before he spoke. "I . . . can't see that they could, Ma'am. I don't see that they could. It'd be way too dangerous."

Another up-and-down motion, and something creaked in *Emerald Maui*'s superstructure. "That one was thirty-five meters high," Mel reported, trying not to sound frightened. "Based on the motion, sonar, and our depth, anyway."

"How many of these will there be?"

"Probably several minutes of them," Mel answered. "The air-blast isn't instantaneous, so it'll pile up a lot of waves."

Emerald Maui rose and dropped again, with a faint twisting motion evident—and as the drop happened, there was a loud *SPANGGG!* from the cargo compartment.

Instantly alarms screamed and Campbell cursed violently. "Damn door popped! We're taking on water fast! Ain't got a choice now—hold on, we're going up!"

The waterjet screamed as Campbell pointed the nose of *Emerald Maui* straight up and accelerated towards the surface as fast as he could make her climb. Laura could feel, already, that she wasn't quite as responsive, and shuddered at the thought of how many tons of water must be coming onboard, how fast Lincoln's ocean must be filling the cargo compartment, and glanced back, wondering how long the cargo compartment door could keep *them* dry.

"*Hang on!*"

Emerald Maui breached like a whale, flying entirely free of the sea, water trailing from the damaged cargo door. The impact with the sea would be impressive even under ordinary circumstances, Laura knew.

But these were far from ordinary.

The shuttle blasted from the side of a wave into winds exceeding two hundred kilometers per hour, screaming white foam obscuring all vision. *Emerald Maui* heeled over on her side despite everything

Campbell could do, and Laura saw the ocean coming up to meet them—

WHAM!

The straps felt like they were cutting into her even with the padding as they struck the seething ocean. She heard grunts of pain and a low hoot from Whips. *I hope that doesn't tear anything open in him.*

But *Emerald Maui* wasn't giving up. She rolled back upright, clearing the viewscreen—somehow the cameras had stayed attached and operating—just in time to show a massive wall of wind-lashed green thundering towards them.

"Aw, crap... hold on again!"

Somehow Campbell forced *Emerald Maui* to turn to meet the wave bow-on, coaxing performance from the stubby wings and the nuclear jet that Laura thought should be impossible.

They rose to the crest, to see a chaotic mass of ocean, titanic breakers as far as the eye could see in the howling mists; the shuttle nearly went airborne again as the wind tried to claw her into the sky.

"*Emerald Maui* calling *Sherlock*," Campbell said, his voice as calm as though he weren't fighting hill-sized waves for survival, "please answer, *Sherlock*, over."

The response was as fast as they'd come to expect. "*Emerald Maui*, this is *Sherlock*, what's your status?"

"Not good, *Sherlock*. Seal popped again and we are... hold on..." another crest sent a shockwave of white spray across the viewscreen before they careened down the slope, "as I said, we are now on the surface and the waves are way too big for surfing, wind's trying to make a kite out of us, and we're taking on water. Advise as to pickup?"

There was no response for a few moments. "*Emerald Maui*," Sue's voice said finally, "We cannot safely attempt field pickup before 08:30 your local time tomorrow, according to calculations. Conditions will still be poor, but better than current."

That's... sixteen hours from now. Dear God.

"Kinda figured that, *Sherlock*. We'll try to keep in contact. *Emerald Maui*, out."

Laura heard a higher hum that had risen to prominence. "What's that?"

"Environmentals. It's *hot* out there now—forty Celsius, according to the readouts," Mel said, her voice squeaky with fear but still speaking with precision. "It'll get real cold when the backblast hits."

"Sergeant," Xander said, face deadly pale under his tan, "How's *Emerald Maui* holding up?"

Campbell was still wrestling with the controls as they skidded down the back of one wave, heading for the next. "Not... good, son. That door's popped way open now. We're gonna sink, sooner or later—whenever I can't manage to keep her up. No way to dump the rest of the cargo now, 'less it just breaks free and goes out on its own—and I'd have to open the door to let it out. Not sure it *will* open now. Might be jammed."

"*Sink?*"

The word silenced everyone for a moment, as Campbell continued his battle against wave and water. "What do we do?" whispered Pearce.

"The only thing we *can* do," Xander said hoarsely. "Prepare to abandon ship."

"We're still floating!" Francisco said, restraining panic in his voice. Laura couldn't blame him. "Shouldn't we wait? *Emerald Maui* is tough, maybe she can keep going long enough?"

Laura and the others all looked at Campbell, who shook his head. "The captain's got it right. See, I'm keeping us above water now. Maybe for a while. But if and when we pass the point of no return, *Emerald Maui* is going down *fast*. We won't have time to move, then, 'cause it ain't gonna be a picnic getting everyone safely off this ship."

Hitomi pointed a shaking finger at the screen. "We can't go into *that!*"

"It sure looks real bad," Campbell said, "But Hitomi, when this ship starts to go down, it'll take us all with it for damn sure."

Abandon ship... into hurricane winds and waves. Laura couldn't believe it... but on the other hand, she *could*. Lincoln just didn't want to let them go. This was its last, most vicious shot, to send them all out into the cataclysm without the armored steel of a shuttle to protect them.

Damn you, Lincoln. You're not getting any of us. "Then we abandon ship. What's the procedure?"

"I go first," Whips said, unstrapping even as he said it.

"No, Whips, you're—"

"—a hundred times better off than any of you out there,"

Whips said flatly. "I can dive a kilometer down without a problem, I can swim much faster than any human ever did, I don't have to worry about keeping my head and eyes out of water. I go out first, I can steady the boats, catch anyone who falls." He looked into Laura's eyes and she could see the determination. "With me, I promise we *won't lose anyone*. Mom, trust me."

She blinked hard against the sting in her eyes, but smiled. "Harratrer...I trust you. Just...be careful."

"I will."

Sakura looked at him as he slid past, somehow staying stable as the ship once more tilted violently. Laura saw her catch one of Whips' arms; it wrapped around her, and she saw Sakura kiss the base of the arm quickly.

Then Harratrer of Tallenal Pod reached up, hoisted himself up the ladder, and slid into the airlock, closing the door behind him.

Chapter 54

The green and white water boiled in front of Whips, through the small window in *Emerald Maui*'s airlock, alternating with views of the turbulent gray, black, and sometimes bruised green sky. *Weather's not going to work for us either.*

He knew he'd been telling nothing but the honest truth about his chances. A human doing what he was about to do probably wouldn't survive more than a few minutes—but that didn't mean *he'd* survive, necessarily.

The worst part was going to be getting *into* the water. The airlock came out on *top* of *Emerald Maui*, a design that made sense for its usual operations but not so much for this. There were the emergency doors over each wing that could be opened, but that wasn't something to do until they were all actually ready to bail out; it didn't have an airlock to keep water out as people were processed through.

Just have to keep a tight hold when I get out. He remembered exactly where the handholds were on top . . . and let the outer door swing open.

The wind screamed at him, the ocean roared, with gusts of hot air like an oven door opening making his eyes water. He damped down his sound sensitivity and stretched out, grasping all the handholds he could reach, the gale tearing at even his narrow fingers and making it difficult to find and reach his targets. But he managed it, and—taking a breath of the now salt-spray filled air—yanked himself up, triggering the door to close behind him.

Even prepared as he was, the wind struck him with such

force that he was nearly torn from *Emerald Maui* and hurled into space. He didn't dare let that happen; yes, he might be flung clear, or he might just strike the tail and drop down to be caught in the rear jet.

Despite the heat, coldness welled up within as he really *saw* the ocean, the heaving, titanic masses of gray-green that reared up before him. *Emerald Maui* finished plummeting into one trench and the next mighty comber was before them, lifting the ship into the sky. *I have to get off safely.*

The only halfway-sane direction to go was down—to the side of the ship and the stubby fins remaining to her. If he could dive into the water, or let himself be carried off into the water, from one of them, he *should* be able to avoid being battered or sucked into a jet intake. The water itself would be no threat.

Meter by meter he dragged his way down the side of *Emerald Maui*. Halfway down, he realized the wind had gone from tearing at him to merely pulling hard. The airblast was passing.

Of course, that meant the reverse would be coming. How long, he didn't know, but he suspected it would not be that long. And the waves would last much longer; the sea, once driven mad, did not calm swiftly.

But the reduction in wind did make it a bit easier. He was at the base of the wing now, the dive plane extending maybe three meters. He stretched his arms as widely as possible, curling tendrils across the entire width of the wing, and inched his way forward until he could feel the end of the wing in front of him, only a few centimeters away from his body.

One eye swiveled, watching ahead, while the other watched behind. *When that wave comes, the sergeant will have to adjust... the ship will turn and tilt just enough...*

Wait... wait... wait... NOW!

The dive-plane bit into the water and Whips released his grip in the same moment, letting the sheeting water slide him off and into the sea. Instantly he jetted away from *Emerald Maui* and then came about, pacing the ship.

"This is Whips—I'm in the sea, near you. I'm okay! The wind's dying down. If you're getting out, now's the time."

"Thank god you're okay," Laura said. "It must be terrible out there."

"It's not as bad as it was, but... it's bad. You'll see, I guess.

My big question is how we can keep the rafts from blowing away when the reverse airblast hits."

"Each will deploy a smart sea-anchor that can react to sudden movements," Campbell answered. "Think of an underwater parachute; if the wind tries to blow you somewhere, it opens and the drag under the water keeps you right there. It can tell the difference between that kind of thing and the up-and-down with the waves, even big ones."

"Hope you're right. Not like we have a choice."

"*Emerald Maui*, this is *Sherlock*. Do we understand correctly that you are abandoning ship?" Sue Fisher's voice was tense.

"*Sherlock*, that is an affirmative," Xander said. "The aft cargo hold is leaking and despite our best attempts it appears it will fill up. We can stay above water with the jet for a while, but eventually that will exceed operating tolerances. We are evacuating into the two liferaft shelters. Beacons have been tested and should be easily detectable."

"We'll be down as soon as we can. Just try to hold on until then."

"We will. Next contact when we have completed the operation."

"Understood. *Sherlock* out."

Whips heard a shaky intake of breath, then Xander spoke again. "Then let's do this. In orderly fashion, all hands, abandon ship. Whips, stand by on the starboard side. We will use that side for the evacuation. Can you keep the raft in position?"

"I hope so. You can't deploy the sea anchor until everyone's on board, though, or it's going to try to stay in one place while *Emerald Maui* keeps moving."

"Understood. Wind speed has dropped to only a hundred fifteen kilometers per hour, so that should be okay for now."

The emergency door popped open a moment later, and Whips saw the bright orange package drop over the wing and inflate to its full dimensions. Whips immediately dove and caught one of the holdfasts on its side with one arm, and anchored himself to *Emerald Maui* with the other two.

Ouch! It's a strain! The shelter-raft was relatively lightweight, but "relative" still meant it was almost as heavy as Whips, and inflated it was vastly larger—and catching a *lot* of wind.

Fortunately, there were also holdfast lines, and he could snap one of those onto the remaining secure ring at the base of the nearby wing. Now he just had to help steady it and watch for any mishaps. "Raft is secured. Board fast, please!"

"Dr. Kimei," Xander said, "You and your family will board the first raft."

"Understood, Captain," Whips heard Laura reply. "Akira, you first, then Hitomi, Mel, Sakura, and Caroline. I will board last."

A flickering in the light from the door told him Akira Kimei had exited; a moment later, he felt a *thump* through the fabric of the raft. "I am on board," Akira reported. "It is not easy, Laura. The motion of the ship and the shelter are not identical, and if the sergeant maneuvers at the wrong moment..."

"I have faith in your reflexes, Akira. Hitomi—"

"I can do it!"

Whips tensed, ready to lunge forward if the littlest Kimei missed her step, but in a moment he heard her say "It's kind of pretty in here, and bigger than I thought!"

Melody stumbled but caught herself as she exited, and made the transition. Sakura managed it in a single dive from the exit; Caroline was a bit more sedate.

"All the family's safe on board except you, Laura," Whips said.

"And you, but I know you're not coming on board until everyone else is set. Catch me, Akira!"

"And we are all on board." Bright flashing white, red, and blue lights were now showing on the top of the shelter raft. "Visible and radio beacons active. *Sherlock*, can you confirm beacon?"

A moment later, they heard Sue Fisher's voice. "Dr. Kimei, we confirm we have a strong emergency beacon signal from *LS-88 Raft One*."

"Good. *Raft One* now releasing from *Emerald Maui*."

Whips had to struggle to release the safety line; the water and constant shifting in tension made it difficult, but after a few moments the hook finally let go. Immediately he dove underneath and dragged hard on the raft, making sure it cleared the tail of *Emerald Maui* safely, and then swam back to the wallowing shuttle. "Whips back in position, ready for second raft," he said.

"Damn, I can feel that breeze inside. Like stepping into a hothouse. Captain, hate to say it, but you can't be the last man off. I gotta hold the controls until everyone else is ready."

"Can't argue, Sergeant," Xander said. "Lieutenant Haley, deploy the raft. You'll be first on, then Francisco, Maddox, Tavana, and me. Sergeant Campbell will be last—how do we work that, Sergeant?"

"We all got our suits on, and mine's better'n all yours. Just get the raft clear, an' I'll take a dive and let Whips get me home. Can do?"

"Can do, Sergeant," Whips answered, warmed by the casual trust.

"Make it so, as they say."

Having done it once before, Whips found it easier to catch the raft's line and secure it, and Pearce Haley made the transfer with no trouble, as did Francisco, Maddox, and Tavana.

But just as Xander began his move, one of the surging crests broke over *Emerald Maui*. A torrent of foaming white momentarily erased the shuttle and strained the mooring rope, almost tearing the ring from the raft. Whips suddenly sensed another form, whirling down the side of *Emerald Maui*.

No!

He pushed water through him, jetting at maximum towards Xander, who caught at one of the tiedown rings on the ship's side and almost held on.

But that did slow him down, kept him from continuing towards the half-sunken tail and the furiously churning water around the nuclear jet. Whips stretched out one arm before him, driving his own organic jet so hard he could feel the ache in every muscle of his mantle.

Xander saw him coming and kicked out, away from the side of *Emerald Maui*, arm outstretched.

Whips' multiple fingers twined around the hand and he jetted down, dragging Xander with him, pulling as hard as he could. A moment later a blast of near-scalding water washed over them both, and Whips felt his whole body trembling with the nearness of death. They'd missed being either sucked in or boiled by the jet by meters at most.

He broke the surface sixty meters astern of *Emerald Maui* and began towing Xander towards the raft.

"Thanks...thanks a lot, Whips," Xander said, his voice as shaky as Whips felt. "That was *close*. I don't think we could have even tried this without you."

"Almost got both of us killed even as it is," Whips admitted. "But almost only counts in hand grenades and horseshoes, as

Grandpa Harding once said. Always wondered what horseshoes had to do with it, but..."

"I didn't know you remembered Grandpa Harding!" Laura said with astonishment in her voice. "He died when you and Saki were very little."

"Not much, but that saying stuck in my head." He reached the raft and Xander got a good hold, hauled himself inside. "Okay, everyone but you and me are on board, Sergeant."

"And you got an impromptu practice at dragging someone to safety, so I know it'll work."

"Try to jump *way* clear, Sergeant—I don't want to come any-where near the jet again."

"You and me both, son. Hold on, I'm setting our jury-rigged automatics. Get the raft safely off, now."

He repeated the prior maneuver and soon Raft Two was on its way. "All clear, Sergeant."

"Then get ready." A moment later, a dark silhouette showed in the brightly-lit doorway, and took a long, flat dive into the tumultuous ocean.

The emergency door closed on its own as Whips located the sergeant and quickly caught onto him. "You signaled it to close?"

"Set it to close a few seconds after I left the board, yeah."

Whips towed the sergeant to the raft; he clambered smoothly aboard. Then he seated himself in the opening and raised his arm and hand in a salute; Whips could just make out at least two of the others following suit, and looked back.

Emerald Maui, lights still shining brightly, charged up the slope of another wave. There was no one aboard her, no hand to guide her, but still she fought, still she kept herself above the water, her jet driving to deny the depths below. Her former crew sat watching, ignoring the hot spray driving into their faces, salutes held as rigidly as at a funeral, as she soared from the crest of the wave into space, momentarily free of the sea, before she vanished into the deep trough below, and then reappeared, carving her way indomitably up the next wave, and then the next, until her lights faded, still undefeated, into the mist.

Chapter 55

"Welcome back, Whips," Laura said, hearing the others echo her as she, Akira, and Sakura helped drag the Bemmie all the way onto the raft. "Mel, seal the door now."

"Got it, Mom." Melody's voice was still shaky from their latest fright, but she efficiently triggered the seal and followed its progress to make sure it did its job, while hanging tight to a handhold as the boat rolled up and then over another huge wave. "Ugh, I hate that!"

"Good to be back, Mom," Whips said. "Not that it's so bad out there for *me*, but I don't have a lifeboat beacon on me."

"What has this lifeboat got to offer us, besides just floating?" Laura asked, watching to make sure that Whips secured himself as well as possible. "Not that that isn't a lot, right now."

"And the sea anchor, which we should deploy right away," Whips pointed out.

"Deployed," Caroline said; she was sitting near the small control console built into the lifeboat.

"I looked over the specifications while we prepared them for launch," Akira said. He paused as a blast of water inundated the shelter with white foam and rumbling noise. "They're actually well-equipped compared to what one might think. You'll notice that it isn't as hot in here as it is outside—there are environmental controls to moderate things like temperature and humidity. Runs off superconductor storage batteries which can be recharged by solar harvesters in the exterior fabric."

He glanced out the nearby window in the shelter, where the sky seemed to be getting even darker. "That may not be a consideration now. Still, the batteries are rated for seventy-two hours, so I don't imagine we'll need to worry about it."

"The beacons, of course," Whips said. "That's the other big feature for us. Lights and radio signals so our rescuers can find us."

"Built-in desalinator so that fresh water isn't a problem," Mel pointed to the squat device off to one side of the shelter. "Don't think any of us brought food, but there's a small case of emergency rations next to the desalinator if we get hungry." She grimaced. "I don't know about the rest of you, but as long as the sea keeps doing that up and down thing I'm not hungry."

"Raft toilet," Hitomi indicated a small booth opposite the main door. "Manual says it works in even pretty heavy seas."

"Probably not *this* heavy, though," Caroline added. "Survival kit," she went on, pointing to another small case.

Laura shook her head. "Pray to all that is that we don't need that. It'd mean we're here far too long."

"Amen to that," Campbell's voice said. "Whips, when you've rested, I was thinking that we might want to find a way to link the lifeboats, so we don't get too far separated."

Whips made a self-flagellating gesture that Laura knew was the equivalent of a facepalm. "Oh, *vents*, I didn't think of that. How far apart are we now?"

"Looks like about two hundred meters and change."

Laura didn't like the idea of Whips going back out... but the suggestion was a very good idea. "How long a line do we have?"

"I think we've got one a hundred meters long."

"How long *should* it be?" She looked over to Sakura, Whips and Melody in turn.

"Probably... longer than that," Whips said after a moment. "We don't want any chance that interactions between us and the waves would get dangerous. Period of the waves might change... probably does, as they get bigger or smaller."

Laura nodded. "Sorry, Sergeant, it was probably a good idea, but it sounds like it could be dangerous to use a too-short tether."

Campbell's sigh was audible over the comm. "Yeah, I guess you're right. Well, that just makes it *Sherlock*'s problem."

"Speaking of that, time to let them know our status," said Laura. "*Sherlock*, this is *Raft One*."

"*Raft One*, we read you. What is your status?"

"All personnel are safely onboard *Raft One* and *Raft Two*. Please confirm you can detect and track beacons for both craft?"

A pause, then Comm Officer Gariba replied, "*Sherlock* is detecting and tracking both beacons, *Raft One*. We're also tracking *Emerald Maui*, now two kilometers southwest of your current position."

"She's on autopilot," Campbell said. "As a service . . . just note when she goes down."

"Will do, Sergeant Campbell. Are your shelters all in good condition?"

"Ours appears to be operating perfectly," Laura answered. "Sergeant?"

"All fine here," Campbell said. "Aside from these damn waves."

"Winds have dropped down," Whips said. "They're actually not bad now. Waves will probably subside. Do we have an idea for when the backblast hits?"

Tip replied. "Looks like another hour or two. We'll be able to give you a heads-up a few minutes before that happens. Unfortunately, we're seeing heavy weather in your area for that whole time."

A brilliant flash lit the interior of *Raft One* and Laura jumped at the crash of thunder. Rain was now beating on the exterior of the shelter. "Roger that, *Sherlock*," she said. "We have lightning. Is this a danger?"

"Shouldn't be," Campbell replied. "There are conductive channels in the walls for just that kind of thing. It'll be loud as hell if you're hit, though. Scare the crap out of you. I remember that happening to us on Fortannis, some years back—wasn't a liferaft, but a special ops boat, same basic size and all."

Laura shook her head. "Sometimes, Sergeant, it seems like you've done pretty much *everything*."

"Well, now that I've been here on Lincoln, I probably *have*, Ma'am."

She laughed at that. "*Sherlock*, is your ETA still 08:30 local time?"

"*Raft One*, that's an affirmative. Be advised that even then the conditions will be extremely poor. This rescue will be hazardous and we cannot guarantee everyone's safety."

"*Sherlock*, that's understood. Given current conditions, I think we couldn't guarantee our own safety over the next week." It hurt to admit that, but really, they'd done the best they could. Cosmic catastrophes were out of even the sergeant's bailiwick. "All we can ask is that you try. The lifeforms of Lincoln have weathered this kind of thing in the past, probably many times, but we're not native."

"Understood. Rest assured we will do our best."

Despite the storm, the waves did seem to be reducing. A blast of wind caught at the liferaft from behind Laura, shoving it along; then another, this one from her left. Then one from ahead, and another from behind. "No wonder the waves are smaller; the wind's completely *random* now."

"Right now we're getting chaotic local storms. Hasn't had a chance to get organized," Caroline said. "By the time it starts, the next airblast will hit. Then we'll *really* get rain, probably, what with cooling all this area filled with hot, humid air, but who knows...we've never observed this before."

Sakura's smile was small but visible. "Well, 'never observed this before' is like Lincoln's motto, right?"

Laura laughed. "Ever since we first saw a star that wasn't there!"

"We'll keep in touch, *Raft One* and *Raft Two*. Our rescue shuttle is prepped and will depart on schedule, barring any new surprises from Lincoln. We're also readying cabins for all of you onboard."

Laura imagined sleeping on a real, modern bed in a real ship's cabin, and for a moment was struck by longing so intense it hurt. "That sounds...absolutely marvelous, *Sherlock*. We'll call if anything changes."

"*Sherlock* out."

Laura looked around. "Well, the waves aren't so bad, and we've got fifteen hours or so before rescue. Everyone who needs to use the bathroom, and get something to eat. This is going to be one more day of Lincoln trying to kill us!"

Chapter 56

The reverse-blast hit like a screaming storm of demons, and despite the smart sea anchor *Raft One* heeled half-over before dropping reluctantly back to the ocean. Winds over three hundred kilometers per hour returned the ocean to the white-gray of spray and foam, interspersed with the towering walls of new and monstrous waves.

Sakura had held on grimly throughout that assault, feeling the temperature drop acutely before the environmentals could counter the ludicrous drop—twenty degrees Celsius in a matter of seconds. The waves threw them skyward, sent the raft spinning and slewing about, hammered *Raft One* and *Raft Two* with thundering torrents of foam as crests broke upon them.

In the middle of that terrible chaos, *Sherlock* called. "*Raft One* and *Two*, so you know: *Emerald Maui* just went down for the last time."

There was a moment of relative silence within the storm. Then Campbell sighed. "One of the toughest ships I've ever had the honor of serving on. Survived more'n an hour by herself. Salute, all."

Sakura had no problem saluting *Emerald Maui*.

She was, somehow, unsurprised when the limited sonar of the advanced life raft began to give an alert. "What are we seeing?"

"Hold on, *Raft One*, that alarm, we're getting it too," Tavana's voice answered. "Sergeant, what *is* that?"

"Lemme see . . . huh."

"Sergeant, 'huh' isn't terribly informative," Akira said dryly.

"Well, it ain't so bad as it might be, but we'll have to keep a real eye out. Chunks of one of the islands, that's what it is. Sure don't want to hit any of *those* with a raft."

"How big?"

"Big enough; sonar's seeing them 'cause they stick far enough down into the water that even all the chaff on the surface ain't hiding them. That's pretty big. Still, they're a few klicks off, so no big worry yet."

"Can these rafts maneuver at all?"

"Some—shape-memory material on the outside plus the sea anchor lets them sail a bit. There's a built-in motor but it's nothing like able to make a difference in this mess—mostly meant to help you make landfall or station-keep when a rescue comes. Tav, can you, Saki, and the others whomp up an avoidance app that can be tied to the sonar?"

"What do you think, Saki?"

Sakura looked at the indicated interfaces and code. "Together? I think so. Something to work on, anyway."

It didn't, after all, prove to be too difficult, and the work helped distract her while the waves of the reverse airblast had been trying to turn the world upside down and the winds were doing their best to help. *Raft One* and *Two* wouldn't ever be sailing yachts, but they'd be able to guide themselves in broad courses past large objects, like pieces of floating island.

"Hey, Sergeant..." Sakura said.

"What's up, Saki?"

"I was thinking—if we tie this into our location, we should be able to keep us close to each other. Do you think that's a good idea?"

She could practically see his grin in his voice. "Pilot Sakura Kimei, I think that's a damned good idea. Who needs tethers when the ships can do the work?"

"Tavana, Whips, can you help me figure this out?"

"On it, Saki," said her oldest best friend, while her newest best friend said, "No problem."

And it wasn't in fact very hard to do. Within a relatively few minutes of implementing the change, their coordinates began to converge. "How much of a separation you looking to keep?" the sergeant asked.

"A few hundred meters," she said. "We don't want to be so close we might hit each other or get in the way during the rescue."

"Sounds good. I feel better already."

Another slow settling to merely ordinary storm, and then the second airblast—this one still vicious, but noticeably weaker than the first. Another lull, and sometime during that one, Sakura actually fell asleep, only slightly roused by the second reverse, a while later.

And then she snapped instantly awake at a new message.

"*Raft One* and *Raft Two*, this is Lieutenant Susan Fisher, on board research and rescue shuttle *John H. Watson*, departing *Sherlock*. We are on our way, ETA one hour, twenty-seven minutes from . . . *mark*."

The cheer that went up nearly deafened everyone in the shelters, but no one seemed to care. "*Watson*, this is *Raft Two*," Campbell answered. "As you can probably tell, we're all happy to hear that."

"Can't blame you," Susan said with her own laugh. "Just hang on a little longer. Weather's going to be rough, but if we time it right, it shouldn't be much worse than rough, which looking at what's likely to happen is the best we can hope for."

"Roger that, *Watson*. Just get down here safe; we'll find a way on board if I have to figure out how to climb a wave and stand on the top."

"Let's try conventional methods first, Sergeant," Laura said.

"Much preferred, Ma'am. But I'm getting off this rock one way or another, and I'm not doing *that* until all the rest of you are first."

"We'll get all of you," Susan said. "I don't accept failure as an option, either."

"Then we'll get along just fine. We'll let you get to your flying, then."

"*Watson* out."

Sakura checked her straps. *I pull* this *for quick release. All my equipment's tied on right.* She debated dumping it; after all, she wasn't going to need anything but her omni once she got on board. Why carry anything they didn't need?

But . . . each of those tools was either a precious remnant of one of the two shuttles, or something that they'd had to *make*, with hours of work and often dozens of failures. Her ankle-knife, made out of the only successful batch of bog-iron based steel, was Caroline's ultimate triumph. She couldn't throw that away.

Sure, the arrival of *Emerald Maui* had made working metal much easier, but that knife, and the few others made in the time before *Emerald Maui* completed the trip to their continent, had been their final proof that even without another group of castaways, the Kimei family was going to do more than survive; they were going to *live*. Its sheath was Lincoln-made leather. Her clothes, a patchwork of stuff from *Emerald Maui* and what they'd made from Lincoln's animals and plants. Other things—ornaments, gloves, a shell-opener, climbing spikes—all things someone had made.

No. That's all us. I'm keeping them.

She noticed, with a smile, that none of the others showed any sign of getting rid of the few things they'd kept in this last evacuation. "You know," she said, looking to her mother, "I'm actually going to miss a few things."

"Like *what*?" demanded Mel, staring at her like she had just grown a pair of new heads.

"Hedral jam, for one. Not getting *that* anywhere else."

Mel blinked. Sakura grinned, because she knew how much jam Melody ate. "Um...okay. I guess."

"I *won't* miss stinging flowers and trees," Tavana commented. "Though that capy roast your father makes, that I will miss a bit."

For the next little while, the conversation continued. Sakura found herself surprised to realize how *many* things she genuinely *would* miss. Not enough to make her regret rescue, no... but enough to tell her that life on Lincoln wouldn't have been bad—minus the giant meteor, anyway.

She didn't know how to feel about that at first; hadn't they all desperately wanted to be elsewhere? Hadn't they almost broken because of everything they'd lost, all the little and big things that were gone, that they had to re-create or do without? She remembered that day with an echo of the terrible feeling of utter hopelessness, of defeat and anger and despair.

But...

But they hadn't broken. They'd survived. They'd turned the alien world into...into *home*. It hadn't, maybe, been the home they'd imagined. Hadn't been the home they'd planned on originally. But the thought of Sherwood Tower and her snug room, far above the forest floor, and Whips visiting her as they talked and sometimes played games, made her smile. The family dinners, in the big room two floors down, with her father constantly trying new and, usually, amazing things in cooking the native food. Hearing Mother and Father laugh one night, just laugh, the way they used to on the ship, or back on Earth, and knowing that they were home, that everything was all right.

She remembered Tavana, and walking through the sunlight-touched forest with him, holding his hand and just feeling, not threatened, but at peace. There might have been dangers in the forest, but at the end, they were *known*. At least for that short time, they'd confronted Lincoln on its own terms, and Lincoln had accepted them.

Maybe that's the problem, a part of her thought whimsically. *Lincoln knew rescue was coming, and didn't want us to leave it alone.*

If so, Lincoln was that *really* crazy boyfriend from so many sims. The planet saw fit to punctuate that thought with a double bolt of lightning that almost dazzled and deafened them.

The radio came to life again. "*Raft One*, this is *Watson*," said Susan Fisher's voice again. "We have you on visual."

Chapter 57

"Those are sweet words to hear," Campbell said; Whips was pretty sure the sergeant was grinning ear-to-ear. "You have us, *Raft Two*, on beacon, I hope?"

"We do, *Raft Two*, and expect visual soon. You appear to be less than half a kilometer apart, which is, honestly, astonishing."

"Give credit to our team of engineers and app-hackers; they've encouraged our little boats to stick together."

"That makes things easier. Can you guide yourselves closer—minimum separation about a hundred fifty meters?"

"Tav? Saki? Whips?"

"Yes, we can start that happening," Tavana said. "But the rafts, they will not sail like liners. Probably we will not get that much closer."

"No problem, *Raft One*. We'll have to also keep an eye on the two local island fragments—one's fifty meters high, the other's about thirty-five, but spacing at the moment doesn't make them an immediate threat." A pause. "*Raft Two*, we now have you on visual as well, though sea-spray will make it difficult to maintain at distance."

"So long as you know where we are, that's good enough. Rescue *Raft One* first—they've been here longer, they get seniority."

A chuckle. "Will do. *Raft One*, prepare for rescue. We will be lowering a rescue harness. Do you require a rescue swimmer to aid anyone in boarding?"

"Negative," Whips said instantly, before anyone else could answer. "I will be rescue swimmer for both rafts."

"Understood," Susan replied. "I couldn't ask you to do it, but obviously I haven't got anyone a tenth as qualified." There was not a trace of hesitation or irony in her voice—a simple acknowledgement that he was right.

He couldn't hide the gratified patterns that danced over his skin. It was still a special event for humans other than the Kimeis to accept him so fully. "Thank you, Lieutenant!" he said earnestly.

"No, thank *you*. *Raft One*, we're matching vectors with you best we can. Rescue harness is...away."

Whips saw the brilliant orange harness, blinking all along its length with lights that further outlined it against the hundred-kilometer-per-hour spray, weighted ends plunging into the ocean to hold it at least somewhat steady. "Here I go!"

Saki opened the flap door for him, and as the raft tilted for the next wave, he slid straight out and down.

Lincoln's waters were still warm; how long that might last, or whether they might get *too* warm in a week, who knew? The important thing was that he was in the water now, near the harness. "Who's going first?"

"Children first," Laura said flatly. "Hitomi?"

He could see Hitomi looking, white-faced, at the ocean, and couldn't blame her. He knew how bad humans were at swimming, and even a really skilled human wouldn't be looking at this as a fun game. He jetted over nearer to the shelter. "You'll ride me, Hitomi. Trust me. It won't be fun, but I'll keep you safe."

Hitomi shivered, hand gripping one of the side straps. He could see her try to make a move forward, but her hand wouldn't let go.

"Hitomi, it's Whips. Listen to him. You've *got* to."

She closed her eyes, and Whips saw her face steady. She was still pale, but when the eyes opened, their gaze was not panicked; it was...not calm, but somehow *older*, and he remembered what she and Francisco had gone through. That hurt, somehow, deep inside, but at the same time he felt a spark of pride. His little sister wasn't going to let the fear beat her.

She nodded once. "I trust you," she said, and launched herself from the shelter.

The wind caught at her, pushed her sideways, but one of his arms fanned out, wrapped around the little girl and pulled her in. They plunged beneath the surface, but he felt her gripping hard, not letting go. Above the surface again, and he curled his arm back; a moment later, she was on his back, holding on with desperate strength. *And I'm keeping my arm there so she stays.*

As he reached the harness, another advantage of being a Bemmie became obvious. He could use one arm to hold Hitomi, and two others to open and steady the harness. The waves shoved them up and down, and a bolt of lightning made Hitomi jump, but in a few more minutes she was strapped securely into the harness. "She's in! Take her away!" he shouted.

Instantly the ladder began to lift into the belly of the big transport, hovering above them on nuclear-powered airjets. "Retrieving harness. Harness retracting... all indicators show secure. Halfway up." A few moments later, "*Raft One*, Hitomi Kimei is safe aboard. Dropping harness."

Whips allowed himself a Bemmie whoop of relief, echoing out into the storm-tossed water. But there was no more time, because here was the harness, and it was Melody's turn, also white-faced but methodically waiting and then diving almost neatly into the water, trusting Whips to retrieve her and get her to the harness. Then Sakura, who didn't hesitate at all but dove to meet him, his catch synchronized with her motion as they'd done it when they were so much younger.

Then Caroline and Akira, and finally Laura was there, standing in the almost-empty raft shelter. "Ready, Whips?"

"Whenever you are, Mom!"

Laura gathered herself to jump—

And the raft suddenly *whipped* sideways, the vicious motion hurling Laura Kimei far out into space. Whips was frozen in shock for a moment, seeing the raft continuing, *racing* off, tilted backwards against the force that was dragging it...

Dragging it?

Whips dove then. He needed clarity in his sonar, both to look *up* and see if he could spot Laura...

...and to look *down.*

He felt an electric tingle of horror go through him, but at the same moment his senses managed to extract the silhouette of a human form fifty meters off. He burst back to the surface and drove for Laura, who was barely keeping her head above water. "*Island-eater!*" he shouted into his omni. "Small one, I think, but caught the sea-anchor as it cruised by!"

He reached Laura and pulled her up onto his back, as Akira cursed. "Of course, broken island pieces *must* mean island-eaters nearby. And even hundred-meter waves would mean little to them."

"Did you say *island-eater*?" demanded Lieutenant Fisher.

"Yes, he did," Laura gasped. "First one we saw took out *LS-5*. First one the sergeant saw almost took out him and *LS-88*."

"How big *are* these things?"

"Unknown," Akira said, voice somewhat less tense after hearing Laura speak. While Whips helped Laura into the harness, he went on, "Fragmentary images we have gotten and so on showed us that they have three forward . . . jaws, ramming pincers, something of that nature—which measure perhaps up to a kilometer in length. The size of the body *behind* those . . . I can only hazard a guess."

"A *kilometer*?" Susan Fisher repeated. "That's almost—*JESUS!*"

One of the island fragments nearby shuddered and split, towering dark spines ripping through it like knives through a layer cake, monstrous chunks of the island and all remaining on it plummeting into a yawning abyss between the three Titan-sized daggers. The island-eater settled back majestically, unaffected and uncaring of the storm and waves about it.

"Laura Kimei is strapped in and I'm clear!" Whips said. "And that wasn't the one I just sensed—there's more than one of those things here!"

Whips heard one of the crew of *Watson* muttering in a different language, what he thought was a prayer. "Retracting harness now."

"I'm heading over to *Raft Two*. I also sensed another island fragment or two not far off." He extended his sonar senses more carefully. Where there were island-eaters . . .

Screaming vents, I hate *being right.* There were other, smaller shapes moving through the water—the scavengers and, perhaps, lesser predators, looking to take advantage of the scraps of the island-eater's meal. He could definitely make out several of the raylamps, and other shapes.

That's an island-eater . . . but so small. I mean, relatively. A baby? Is it with its mommy, learning how to wreck entire habitats, or do the big and small ones coexist as different species? Akira would love to study this.

Still, the "small" eater was probably three times the length of the largest whale Earth's oceans had spawned, several times larger than the *orekath* that dominated Europa. And there were other things moving in the depths . . .

He surfaced again. "*Watson*, *Raft Two*, be advised we've got a lot of predator and scavenger activity. I'm probably safe, but humans in the water will be in severe danger."

"Of course, Lincoln ain't letting us go easy, is she?" the sergeant said with a resigned air. "Then let's try to stay out of the water as much as possible."

"*Si*, I want to do that, sir," Francisco said, trying to sound funny and failing because his voice was shaking.

"Laura Kimei is safe on board," came Susan's voice. "*Raft Two*, I am now positioning myself as close as I can to you."

A few moments of careful maneuvering passed; Whips was awed by how steadily Lieutenant Fisher was able to hold *Watson* in the face of the winds that were now gusting to a hundred and fifty kilometers per hour. Even with automatics, that had to be tough. "Rescue harness away."

"Same order? Youngest to oldest?"

"You better believe it, son. If I could figure a way to work it, you'd go up before me, but I can't see that."

"No, you can't, and there isn't one. Francisco, come on!"

With the practice of the prior rescues, Whips caught Francisco perfectly and conveyed him to the harness. *One up, five to go. Plus me.*

Raylamps drifted in his direction, closing in on the mysterious floating object; Whips submerged and *bellowed* at them, full-power acoustic pulse tearing apart the nearest one and repulsing the others. "Maddox, make it fast!"

Two safely in, but the dead raylamp had attracted others, and his motion back-and-forth was clearly drawing attention. Through the hiss and growl and rumble of the storm came another booming, shuddering crash, and distantly living mountain-knives reared and settled back, consuming uncounted tons of literally living rock and whatever lay within and atop.

Tavana dove in to meet him, knife out; he had glimpsed dark shapes in the water nearby. But somehow Whips got him to the harness without any incident.

Now it was Xander's turn, and Whips realized Hitomi had been merely pale, not white. A raylamp broke the surface and scrabbled at the liferaft, barely failing to get a purchase, and Xander stepped back.

"Xander! You *have* to jump! I know what it's like, but there's no other way!"

"I . . . can't. I *can't!*" The older boy's voice was filled with a sickening combination of terror and self-loathing. "I'm *trying*, but my hand won't let *go!*"

Whips dove and bellowed again. "They've backed off for a minute—you have to go *now*, Xander!"

He could see Xander's eyes, so wide that white showed around them all the way around.

"Captain Xander Bird, god-*damn* you, *JUMP!*" bellowed the sergeant.

Maybe it was the reminder that the sergeant had given him that title and stood by it; maybe it was the drill-sergeant tone in the order; or maybe Xander had, himself, just finally found the self-control he needed. But whether it was one, two, or all three, at that shout Xander leapt from the shelter.

It was at the peak of a wave, and for a moment Xander Bird imitated his namesake, flying through the air, before landing directly atop Whips.

Whips grunted in pain at the impact, but at the same time he felt a grin flicker across his skin. That put Xander in the safest possible place.

The next one after Xander was Lieutenant Haley, which went smoothly and quickly. One more strapped in, and Whips turned, sensing the chaos about him—and sensed a strange motion below. *Diving, diving deep . . . turning . . .*

Oh, no.

"Sergeant! Sergeant, jump *now!*"

Whips was certain, even as he shouted, that it was too late; the rescue harness hadn't even been dropped back yet, predators or scavengers surrounded the shelter, and it would take *time*, time for anyone to understand the warning, gauge the situation, and decide that, even so, they had to move.

But Samuel Morgan Campbell didn't hesitate for the smallest fraction of a second; at Whips' desperate cry the sergeant sprinted and bounded from *Raft Two*, slamming his suit helmet shut even as he did.

A trio of red-streaked ebony knives rivaling small skyscrapers speared from the water, encircling *Raft Two* and sending it—along with raylamps and other creatures surrounding it—into the cavernous mouth between them. The wave that thundered outward from its passage caught the sergeant as he fell, washed him away, as the baby island-eater subsided into the depths.

"Holy Mother, that was *close*, son."

Whips caught the sergeant with one arm and jetted for the harness as it finally plunged into the sea nearby. "Close but he missed! Get *up* there, Sergeant!"

The passage of the island-eater had driven the other predators away for the moment; Whips watched as the sergeant disappeared into the rescue shuttle, and then waited, tensely scanning the waters.

Once more the immensity of the big island-eater moved, and this time Whips could see the entirety of the thing as it dove in preparation for another run, incomprehensibly huge flanks streaming by, a sense of ridges of scars along that mountain-wide body, a lobed tail moving with lazy, unstoppable power as it drove the thing downward.

Then a splash, and he reached out, twined all three arms around the harness. "I'm on!"

And with a hum and whine of motors, he was pulled from the sea of Lincoln, ascending towards the sky.

Chapter 58

In the rear view of her omni, Sue saw the three-armed, torpedo-shaped body of the Bemmie clear the door on the harness. Sergeant Almeida caught the harness, pulled hard, dragging Whips to the side and letting the door finally shut. "Last one in, Lieutenant!" she shouted.

"Get him secured! We're leaving as soon as everyone's strapped in!" she said, then turned her chair to face the cabin.

It was the strangest group she'd ever seen in one room, she had to admit. Sergeant Campbell's group didn't look *too* odd—they were wearing the suits they'd been issued, since they hadn't lost their shuttle until the end. But the Kimeis were dressed in a motley collection of clothes, some obviously reworked clothing from *LS-88*'s stores, some remnants of whatever they'd had when the disaster happened...and some completely different. Homemade leather, some kind of...cloth?...that was now coming apart after a severe soaking in the ocean, shining modern omnis next to hand-carved tools. And then, of course, there was Whips, the juvenile Bemmie wearing its own harness that was filled with tools that had never seen the inside of a factory.

"Welcome aboard *Watson*, all of you." She saw the glittering of tears in the eyes of most of the castaways, the half-joyous, half-unbelieving looks showing that they had given up on rescue and were still wondering if this was *real*. "And say goodbye to Lincoln, because we're about to depart."

Seeing her own crew now strapping back in, she spun around. Behind her, she heard whispered goodbyes to the world that was lashing them with storm—a storm still rising in intensity.

"*Sherlock*, this is *Watson*. All castaways are safe onboard. We are departing for orbit and should rendezvous in an hour or so, depending on just how we get through the first stage; conditions are worsening here."

"Great news, *Watson*," responded Captain Ayrton instantly. "Now get out of there and come home."

Sue touched the controls and began guiding them in a curve, looking on radar and satellite view for the best route.

There wasn't, honestly, a "best" route, only a number of routes that might be slightly less dangerous. The storms were organizing everywhere, intensifying at an absolutely terrifying rate. *Best to just get enough altitude to clear most of it.* "Hold on, everyone—this is going to be a little rough."

Then she pointed *Watson*'s nose skyward and shoved the throttle towards maximum.

Three gravities and more shoved her down into her seat; she eased off, remembering that they had a Bemmie passenger and they were not as resilient to acceleration. But even so, *Watson* thundered into the heavens, tearing through the lowering clouds. Lightning flashed, a sharp report even through the armored soundproofing of the shuttle, and she saw a thousand crawling filaments of light spread across the forward port and vanish, but the rescue shuttle ignored the strike. Dark mists streamed by, and suddenly there were faint hisses and then larger rattles as they passed through hail, ice circulating in the updrafts; one of the nuclear jets hiccupped, apparently striking a particularly dense patch, but then roared back to normal.

Without warning, the gray-blackness lightened and then flared brightly, *Watson* now flying free into a deep blue sky with the sun shining down on her. "We are above most of the weather, *Sherlock*," she said, feeling able to, finally, relax a bit. "Setting controls to home and dock. ETA...one hour, eleven minutes from *mark*." The acceleration continued, but no longer at the punishing levels of before. The nuclear jet would take them hypersonic and do most of the work of getting them to orbital speed, with only a moderate rocket burn in about twenty minutes or so.

"Roger that, *Watson*. See you soon. And to all of you from *LS-5* and *LS-88*...looking forward to seeing you."

"As are we, Captain!" Laura Kimei said, and the others burst out laughing.

When that died down, Pearce Greene Haley caught Sue's eye as she turned her chair back around. "Lieutenant Fisher, do you know...I mean to say, how did you *find* us?"

"I'm betting *Outward Initiative*," Sakura said. "She made it back, right?"

Sue nodded. "Yes. She was badly damaged, but *Outward Initiative* did make it back into port. And from that we figured out what happened to the ship."

She outlined the research and their results, gaining some mostly blank stares from the younger children but everything from thoughtful nods to a shake of the head and a "Wouldn't that figure?" from Campbell when he realized that it had been *Outward Initiative*'s superior attention to maintenance that had actually doomed her.

"But that was...so you didn't start a rescue after that?" Hitomi asked finally. "It sounds like you had this big meeting and that was it. That *couldn't* have been it! You sent this rescue ship, right?"

Sue smiled ruefully. "At first, no, Hitomi. We couldn't figure out exactly where in space your lifeboats would have been—even if they were intact, and even if everyone on them survived, and there was a lot of reason to believe that that wasn't the case. And if you *had* survived, it made much more sense that you'd come to Orado, not go to an unexplored system that might not even have a planet to live on."

"She's right, Hitomi," Tavana said. "Space, it is bigger than we can imagine. And what we did...it only makes sense if you know *all* the reasons that we did it. So of course they wouldn't have sent anyone else right then."

"True," agreed Xander. "So what changed your minds?"

"What changed our minds was *LS-42* showing up months later," Sue said, remembering.

"Damnation. They made the trip we couldn't."

"And they almost all died," Sue said. "That told us a lot—the possible ways that the shuttles could have failed, and so on. And then one of them mentioned a star that shouldn't have been there."

"New to you people at Orado too?" Caroline asked. "It wasn't on our charts, but those were Earth charts."

"It turned out it was on our *local* charts, but no one had bothered doing cross-matches to find that there was one extra star in our sky," Sue said.

The rockets ignited, and the sky finished its shift to black, stars now covering the dark velvet of space. "We could see, from Orado, that there *was* a habitable planet, so taking all that together... I thought it was just possible one or both of your shuttles could have ended up there."

"So," said Ayrton's voice—he had obviously been listening, "she convinced Portmaster Ventrella to suggest a survey expedition, with a secondary search-and-rescue function. Thus, *Sherlock*."

Laura and Akira Kimei exchanged glances. "Then we have you to thank for our rescue."

"Well..." Sue shrugged. "A hell of a lot more people had to make the decisions. I may have talked Ventrella into the idea, but he still had to convince the money people, and then there were the shipbuilders...I just get a small part of that credit."

Before they could contest it, she grinned. "To be honest, give *yourselves* all the credit. All we did was show up with a ride more than a year afterwards; *you* people figured out how to rescue yourselves."

That got another laugh from the whole group, including the unmistakable hooting laughter of a Bemmie.

"And believe me, everyone is going to want to hear *your* stories. You'll be in the books right next to *Nebula Storm*, with Madeline Fathom and Helen Sutter and Joe Buckley and all her crew."

The two crews of castaways were momentarily silent. Then Melody just said, "*WOW.*"

And once more laughter filled the cabin of *Watson*, as the clean, bright lines of *Sherlock* grew ahead of them.

Chapter 59

Tavana flopped full-length onto the bunk, luxuriating in the softness, the smoothness, the resilience of an actual, honest-to-goodness *bed*. Not a shuttle acceleration couch, not a sleeping bag, not even a woven bag stuffed with driftseed fluff or the feathery fur from some of Lincoln's animals, but a smooth, luxuriously clean, dry, and firm mattress on a level, even support.

That felt so good that he got up and flopped down again. And a third time, just to be sure it was all real.

"*Mon Dieu*, it *is* real," he whispered to himself.

It was astonishingly hard to believe, to *accept*, that they'd been rescued, that *Sherlock* was, even now, entering Trapdoor Drive for the less-than-two-month journey back to Orado.

He smiled faintly; Both Laura Kimei and the sergeant had apologized for interrupting the survey, even tried—though not *too* hard—to convince them they should continue their work. "After all," Akira Kimei had said, "We can live quite comfortably here."

But Captain Ayrton had—thankfully—insisted they all be returned to civilization. "I appreciate the offer," he'd said, "but rescued civilians are to be returned immediately to the nearest reasonable port. And aside from Sergeant Campbell and Lieutenant Haley, you're all definitely civilians."

He rolled over and looked up at the clean, smooth ceiling, currently colored a relaxing blue and glowing with pure white light. *I want to touch all of this ship just to keep telling myself we're really saved.*

They'd really *accepted* at the end that they were on their own. Whether threatened by disease or stinging giant worms or falling asteroids, they'd all *known* they were alone, that the thirteen of them were the only help and only family and only friends they could ever expect to have.

It was...a little disorienting to find they'd been wrong.

Not that there's anything wrong with it! he thought, hoping the universe didn't take that thought as meaning *put us all back on Lincoln.*

But he did, suddenly, want to see his family right now.

Tavana sat up and went to the door; it opened promptly at his approach, and closed smoothly behind him once he was out into the corridor.

It was ship-night, so the lighting was more subdued. All the castaways had been assigned cabins in one section, so he moved up the hall, listening. In the background, the constant hum of air circulating, and nearly subliminal thumps or murmurs or tap-tap-taps of people working, talking, moving about the other parts of the ship.

He had the door next to his open slightly; the darkness inside was *just* lightened enough for him to see Maddox and Francisco, both dead asleep. The two youngest in each group were roomed together at the moment; all the older people had their own rooms—well, Laura and Akira had one room together, and so did the sergeant and Pearce Haley.

There were low voices audible from ahead, a double cabin they'd been given as a sort of living room. Peeking in, he saw the Kimei family—minus Hitomi and Melody, who were probably sleeping like Maddox and Francisco—sitting around a table, eating what looked like a mountain of chips and a few types of dip.

Laura saw him. "Come in, Tavana."

"Tavana!" Sakura jumped up and gave him a huge hug, then kissed him hard.

He was startled—but not so startled he couldn't kiss back. "Okay, I guess I will come in then, invited so nicely!"

The others laughed as he sat down with Sakura. "Couldn't rest yet?" Akira asked.

"No. I...it is strange, but being here, it still seems like a dream to me, so I needed to see...well, that we were really here."

"We are indeed here. And grateful for it," Akira said. "Maybe we would have found a way to survive even after the impact, but...I am extremely glad we did not have to find out."

"Oh, I am not unhappy with this at all," Tavana said as earnestly as he could. "It's just..."

"I know exactly what you mean, Tav," Caroline said. To one side, Whips gave an assenting wave. "We all knew at best it was going to be years before anyone came here. Instead they show up just at the right time to rescue us? That's *exactly* the kind of dreams we've all had once or twice before, right?" She looked around the table.

Laura nodded. "More than once. A couple of times so real that I woke up thinking I was on a rescue boat." She grimaced. "Those were not good mornings."

"Of course," Tavana said reluctantly, "I suppose it could still be a really realistic dream."

"Yours, yes," Akira said with a smile. "As in that case we would just be figments of your imagination. From my point of view, however, no, it could not, because I mastered lucid dreaming years ago. This is no dream, thank goodness."

Tavana reached out and took a chip, dipping it into an orange-colored salsa. For a few moments he simply savored the taste of a food Lincoln would never have given them.

Finally, he looked at the others again—especially Saki, who smiled and leaned against him for a moment. "So...what is next?"

"That *is* indeed the question," Laura said. "Obviously first we'll be debriefed. *Sherlock* may be heading back, but our year-plus time on Lincoln will certainly give some of their scientists material to work with. Our group also had enough native materials to be interesting for the geologists, biologists, and others to at least start the process of studying. Not to mention Akira's rather meticulous notes on everything we've seen."

Akira grinned. "My career is secure, at any rate. I have enough material to make dozens of papers over the next few years."

"But..." Tavana hesitated, then made himself go on, "after that? I mean, after we are on Orado...what then?"

"I don't suppose we'd thought about it much yet. Why?"

He squeezed Sakura's hand. She looked at him and he saw sudden understanding there. "Oh."

"Because I want to know...where all of my family is going," Tavana said simply.

Tavana didn't have to tell them what it meant for him to say that. They knew what had happened to most of his original family.

He went on, "Our crew—*Emerald Maui*'s crew—I do not know yet either. Maddox and Xander—they will go on to Tantalus, I think. Their mother and father are there. Francisco too, that's where his family is. I don't know what the sergeant or Lieutenant Haley plan to do."

"What do *you* want to do?" Laura asked him gently.

"I...I am not sure," he admitted. "It is not so long ago that I thought I would never have to ask the question! We would live on Lincoln and make our own colony there. That was the future."

"True enough. It *is* enough to throw anyone off," Akira admitted.

"That's for damn sure," came the sergeant's voice. "Mind if we join you?"

Tavana saw it was the sergeant with Lieutenant Haley and Xander. All of them, like Tavana, had the fresh-showered look; the luxury of a real, controllable hot-water shower had probably been the first thing on everyone's mind once they were safe onboard *Sherlock*.

"Not at all, Samuel—Pearce, Xander, please, take a seat."

"Don't mind if we do," Campbell said. "Hey, Whips, how's it feel to be the most valuable player today?"

Embarrassed, happy patterns chased across Whips' surface. "...good. Very good, Sergeant. I hope other people will be so accepting as *Sherlock*'s crew."

"Oh, there'll still be fools who aren't, but don't pay them no mind," Campbell said. He looked back at Tavana. "Tav, I can clarify one thing. Me and the Lieutenant here, we're figuring to be married officially, and I think we'll finish the trip we started on. So all of our crew, anyway, will be going on to Tantalus. Not like they still don't need colonists, and let's face it: after Lincoln, ain't no regular colony going to be much of a problem."

"Can't argue there," Laura said. "And honestly...if the slots are still open, if we can get passage? We gave up everything on Earth to go to Tantalus. There's nothing back on Earth for us, aside from a few friends and relatives we already said good-bye to. I think we should finish our journey too. What do you think, Akira?"

Akira smiled. "I would agree. If we're not going to live out our lives on Lincoln—and I am afraid that will be rather uncomfortable for some few years—let's go where we planned to go anyway."

"I'm certainly less concerned about the colony lifestyle after *this*," Caroline admitted.

"Lieutenant Fisher—Sue—said my family thought I was dead," Whips said quietly. "But they went on anyway. They weren't going to drop the chance we'd been given, to prove ourselves in a real-world challenging setting. So I *have* to go there."

"About that," Akira said slowly. "You have passed, Whips."

Whips eyes blinked, protective membranes sliding back and forth. "What... do you mean?"

"I mean that as one of the scientists most involved with the ongoing study of *Bemmius Novus Sapiens*, it was my particular job to observe your family and be one of the... primary evaluators of how well you functioned in the field, in view of the prior issues of stability in your species," Akira answered.

"Oh."

Tavana could see, by the patterns that were flickering over Whips, that this was not something the Bemmie had ever considered. "I thought you were Whips' friends, not... observers, testers, whatever," he said.

"My *family* are all Whips' friends," Akira said emphatically. "And I am, as well, to him and to his own family. But I am *also* a scientist, and one of those directly charged with the responsibility of observing and justifying the inclusion of his species in our ongoing exploration and colonization of the Galaxy."

He stood and bowed deeply to Whips. "And instead of being sent to a known colony... I got to observe one of you in the most extreme conditions I could have imagined. You passed *every* test, Whips, some that many humans have failed to pass. I had finished writing my evaluation before a full year had passed. You are as stable a person as I have ever been privileged to know—and as fine a young person as any, including my own very fine children."

Whips' patterns resolved themselves. "I... guess I can't get mad at you for doing a job that should have been obvious. I mean, with all the rumors—some very true—about our instability, having a human family living so closely with *Bemmius novus sapiens* would *have* to have had people observing. I should have guessed your family and mine were also an experiment."

Akira nodded. "For what it's worth, I had every confidence in your people from the start. I knew what had caused the old problems, they'd been dealt with, and I was certain that your people now were no more dangerous than ours." He smiled suddenly, a smile with an edge of its own. "Which of course means extremely dangerous indeed...but not to your friends."

Whips flickered a laugh, and Tavana chuckled a bit.

"But you're only one person, Akira," Pearce Haley said seriously. "There has to be some kind of committee or board involved. Won't they have some say?"

"The Colonization Board," Laura said, "is going to take Akira's opinion on Project Triton as policy, or we will *both* ram it down their throats."

Tavana, seeing how the Kimeis looked at Whips and each other, had no doubt they'd do exactly that.

Neither, it seemed, did Campbell. "I rather thought you would. And just for the record, we'll all back you to the hilt. So that's settled."

He turned to Sakura. "Oh, and one more little thing. I had a talk with Captain Ayrton and Pilot Pavla Amberdon, let 'em look at some omni recordings your mom and dad let me copy, and we all agreed, so's we could make this official."

He produced an engraved certificate and handed it to Sakura, who read:

"Having passed a comprehensive and extensive examination of all of her abilities, this certifies that Sakura Kimei is a pilot qualified in air, sublight, and Trapdoor drive for all vessels of less than one thousand tonnes mass."

Tavana grinned at Sakura's stunned expression, and saw tears shimmering almost-shed in her eyes.

"But...I *haven't* passed all my classes! And I *crashed* the only ship I ever flew!"

"Well, true, we've marked in the record that making that cert *final* depends on you completing your training *en route* to Tantalus—we were pretty sure you'd be going there—but Saki, that whole flight of *LS-5* was a thing of beauty, given your handicaps. There are experienced pilots I know that'd have bobbled the transitions you had to make. You all walked away from that one, and if you'd asked anyone beforehand if a half-trained kid could bring that shuttle down like you did? No one would've taken that bet. You showed you have the stuff, Saki. You finish up the work and you're one of us." He offered his hand. "Congratulations, Pilot."

Instead of shaking his hand, Sakura gave the sergeant a huge hug; everyone burst out laughing and clapping, including Tavana. Then, looking embarrassed, Sakura let go and did shake his hand, which got another laugh.

Finally Tavana just looked around and gave another laugh of his own. "So, we stay together?"

"I'll drink to that," Laura said immediately, and raised her cup. Everyone followed suit. "To staying together!"

Tavana drank, feeling the warmth of friends—of *family*—surrounding him.

"Tantalus Tower, this is *LS-11* from *Colony Initiative*, on final orbit to landing. Do we have clearance to proceed?"

"Clearance granted, *LS-11*. Have a smooth flight down. Initiate contact once re-entry blackout ends for final landing instructions."

"Roger that, Tower. *LS-11* out."

Sakura settled back into the acceleration couch and gripped the control stick. Her hand was a little sweaty.

"Relax, Saki," Tavana said from behind her. "This landing, it will be easy!"

"Dammit, Tav, don't jinx her!" the sergeant growled. Then he grinned. "But seriously, Saki, just relax and *fly*. You got all your instruments, all your controls, this ship's in fine condition, and you even got friends downstairs to help. Keep your head, follow the stuff you've learned, and you'll do just fine."

"I'll try, Sergeant. Honestly, I'm more nervous about whether—"

"Don't you worry about that," Campbell said.

"It turns out that Captain Toriyama accepted a post as the representative of the Colonial Initiative Corporation on Tantalus," her father said. "This makes him the Chair of the Colonization Board here on Tantalus. Thus I was able to contact him—as one of the senior members of Project Triton—and you can imagine how overjoyed he was to hear of our survival. He agreed to arrange everything."

"See? Nothing to worry about. It'd be no big deal anyways, just a little loss of dramatics. Now just focus on your job, pilot!" Campbell's grin removed a bit of the edge from his last sentence.

She looked back, seeing everyone in their seats—Hitomi, Francisco, Maddox, Melody, Tavana, Xander, Pearce Haley, her mother and father, and of course the sergeant—and felt a burst of happiness go through her. *We made it. All together, we've made it to Tantalus. We started out afraid and uncertain. And now we have a bigger family than we had.* "All right, everyone—confirm you are strapped in! Like any re-entry, this will be a little bumpy!"

With everyone confirmed ready, she made the adjustments, and slowly *LS-11* began its own journey from space to atmosphere. The omni-linked displays showed the manual piloting paths and she guided *LS-11* down the optimum path. She'd switch off all autoguidance once they were through the atmosphere transition, but she didn't want to take even a tiny chance of turning into a tumbling meteor. And standard pilot practice *was* to rely on the automated guidance, even when doing a manual landing... unless, of course, there *were* no automatics to guide you with. Having done that once, Sakura had no interest in ever doing it again if she could avoid it.

With precise guidance, transition through the atmosphere was much smoother than last time—still a bumpy ride, but no signs of faults in the re-entry shield or any other systems. Finally the fiery stage of the re-entry was complete and her comm systems showed clear. "Tantalus Tower, this is *LS-11*. We have completed re-entry and are now on atmosphere piloting." She slapped the transition trigger and the shuttle configured to the high-mach flight profile. Sakura let the automatic guidance shut down as well. "Please give bearing and beacon for manual landing."

"Are you experiencing problems with the automatics, *LS-11*?"

"Negative, Tantalus Tower. Practice flight for a newly certified pilot and observation by Chief Master Sergeant Samuel Morgan Campbell, certified piloting instructor."

"Understood, *LS-11*. Beacon and bearing for your landing approach are as follows:" The tower read off a string of numbers and Sakura saw the glow of Beacon 101 appear on her screens. "Please land on Strip Five."

"Confirmed, Tantalus Tower. *LS-11* to land on Strip Five following Beacon One-Zero-One."

"That's correct, *LS-11*. Tantalus Tower out."

She brought the ship around in a huge curve, slowly dropping her speed as well as altitude until she could reconfigure for subsonic flight. In the vast, clear distance under a deep, deep blue sky, she could make out a glint from Tantalus Port, the one city on the planet at the moment. "Tantalus Tower, be advised that *LS-11* will be making a slow final approach to a full-vertical landing."

"Understood, *LS-11*. Good luck on your end-conversion!"

Sakura laughed. *That* was someone who'd done this themselves. "Thank you, Tantalus Tower. Good thoughts are appreciated. We have you in visual and are on our final approach."

"Roger that, *LS-11*."

As she saw the clean, sharp lines of Strip Five pass beneath *LS-11*, Sakura flared the ship to near-stall speed and then initiated the conversion, jets swiveling, wings retracting, adjusting her angles and attitude *just* so...

...and *LS-11*, for a moment, hovered in the air, motionless with respect to the ground. With exquisite care, Sakura slowly reduced thrust until the big shuttle settled gradually towards the ground, drifting only the slightest bit in the wind; Sakura compensated, tilting the jets a fraction of a degree, and the shuttle stabilized, lowering itself, ten meters, five, four, now less than a meter...and then a gentle vibration as the wheels touched down.

A cheer went through the cabin and Sakura felt her cheeks flaming happily as she activated the radio once more. "Tantalus Tower, this is *LS-11*. We are down and stable, powering all jets down. You can announce our arrival and location; cargo unloading can commence in a few minutes."

"Affirmative, *LS-11*. Nicely done." Automated chock-wedges sped over the tarmac and inserted themselves beneath the wheels. "Welcome to Tantalus."

Sakura hit the *Full Shutdown* and then unstrapped. "YES!"

"A *very* pretty landing, Saki," Sergeant Campbell said with a grin. "And if you'll open your Omni, I'll send the final code for your permanent cert." A quick flash of transmission. "And there we go. Congratulations, Pilot Sakura Kimei!"

There were a few minutes for celebration, then everyone started grabbing their cases. Her father glanced out the port as they went to lower the ramp. "It seems the captain came through beautifully."

Gathered around *LS-11*, at the minimum distance circle, was a moderate crowd of people, a somewhat strange assortment, with Toriyama himself at the front, plus at least one or two representatives of the local news outlet. *News only travels as fast as ships, after all.*

They all trooped down the ramp.

Suddenly a tall woman near the edge of the crowd gave a shriek and ran forward. She caught up Francisco in a hug and spun about with him in her arms. "*¡Francisco! Francisco, cariño, hijo mío, gracias a Dios, ¡gracias a Dios, estás vivo!*"

Another woman, with a broad Polynesian face that had more than a few familiar features, came forward more slowly, but with the same disbelieving joy. "Tavana? *Tavana!*" she shouted, accompanied by another woman, taller and lighter of skin but, yet, somehow, familiar.

Tavana ran forward to hug his mother and aunt, catching them both in a hug that lifted both from the ground, and now the rest of the people there were talking and the news crews were filming, realizing something extraordinary was happening before their eyes. Xander and Maddox sprinted across the landing strip into the arms of their mother and father, who were crying and laughing in equal measure.

There was an echoing bellow and a pod of Bemmies emerged from the crowd; Whips slid forward, and suddenly Sakura and her whole family were running, helping Whips along, as Tallenal Pod trumpeted their own disbelief, jagged patterns of shock and surprise and joy clashing in brilliant celebration across each and every one of them.

Bemmie arms reached and intertwined and hugged and for a few moments Sakura felt as though a forest of ivy was embracing her and rumbling and cheering with love. Finally they loosened their embrace and all stood, holding hands and tendrils, happily regarding each other—Pageturner, who had grown half a meter since they'd last met, and who was now hugging Melody so close that it looked like he'd never let her go, and big old Numbers— Kryndomerr, Whips' father, one arm entwined with Whips' and another with his lifemate Windharvest, whose pattern showed she was crying with amazement and relief, and Dragline, trying to stretch his arms to cover everyone at once and singing a song so joyful and loud that Sakura didn't know whether to sing along or cover her ears.

But now there were more: Lieutenant Haley and Sergeant Campbell had come, and Francisco, tugging his mother with him, a torrent of Spanish pouring unstoppably from his lips as the rest of his family followed, and Xander and Maddox pulling their parents with them despite an obvious nervousness near the Bemmie family, Captain Toriyama just standing there watching, with a brilliant smile and unabashed tears flowing down his cheeks, and Tavana, trying to introduce his dazed mother and aunt to her and everyone else at once.

Finally, Numbers gave a hoot that broke through the din, and everyone fell silent for an instant. "This...this is a true miracle," he said at last. "By the Vents and the Sky, our family is all reunited, and my soul cannot express my joy, *our* joy. And these about you, my son, my daughters, my human family?"

Whips drew himself up proudly. "They are *more* family, more for Tallenal Pod to hold in love and pride."

The big Bemmie—much longer than Whips and probably three to four times his mass, nearly a ton of massive deliberation— settled and rose in a bow. "It is always a joy to meet new family."

"Family? Tavana...what is it...is he saying?"

Tavana looked at his mother. "He is saying that those of us who returned *are* family. And we are, *Maman*."

"Yes, we are," Sakura said, stepping up next to him, and meeting the eyes of all the newcomers—the other parts of the families who had yet to meet hers.

"But...but *how?*"

Mom laughed, and her laugh carried across the field. "That is going to take a long time to tell," she said.

"A long time," Sakura echoed, and put her arm around Tavana's strong waist. "But now we have time to tell it." She hugged him tight, and with her other arm, reached around to embrace her other best friend. "We have a *lifetime* to tell it, now."